# European
## Phrase Book

**Berlitz Publishing**
New York Munich Singapore

Contacting the Editors
Every effort has been made to provide accurate information in this publication, but changes are inevitable. The publisher cannot be responsible for any resulting loss, inconvenience or injury. We would appreciate it if readers would call our attention to any errors or outdated information. We also welcome your suggestions; if you come across a relevant expression not in our phrase book, please contact us: Berlitz Publishing, 193 Morris Avenue, Springfield, NJ 07081, USA. Email: comments@berlitzbooks.com



First Printing: April 2009
Printed in Singapore

Publishing Director: Sheryl Olinsky Borg
Editor/Project Manager: Eric Zuarino
Cover Design: Claudia Petrilli
Interior Design: Derrick Lim, Juergen Bartz
Production Manager: Elizabeth Gaynor
Cover Photo: © creativ collection/age fotostock
Interior Photos: p. 15 © Quendi Language Services; p. 18 © Corbis Collections/Alamy; p. 31 © Quendi Language Services; p. 36 © 2006 Jupiterimages Corporation; p. 48 © images-of-france/Alamy; p. 53 © Dianne Maire 2006/Used under license from Shutterstock, Inc.; p. 56 © Medio Images/Fotosearch.com; p. 65 © Sean Nel, 2006/Used under license from Shutterstock, Inc.; p. 73 © fStop/Fotosearch.com; p. 75 © Dainis Derics 2007/Shutterstock, Inc.; p. 90 © Rena Schild, 2007/Used under license from Shutterstock, Inc.; p. 96 © 2007 Jupiterimages Corporation; p. 105 © Javier Larrea/Pixtal/AgeFotostock; p. 108 © Creatas/Fotosearch/Jupiterimages Corporation; p. 127 © Iain Davidson Photographic/Alamy; p. 133 © Quendi Language Services; p. 137 © TongRo Image Stock/Alamy; p. 154 © Graca Victoria, 2007/Used under license from Shutterstock, Inc.; p. 157 © 2007 Jupiterimages Corporation; p. 174 © Pilar Echevarria, 2006/Used under license from Shutterstock, Inc.; p. 177 © Miguel Raurich-Iberimage.com; p. 194 © Quendi Language Services; p. 197 © photodisc/2007 Punchstock; p. 217 © Eric Sweet
Inside back cover: © H.W.A.C.

# Contents

# Danish
## Pronunciation

Stress has been indicated in the phonetic transcription with underlining. Bold on vowels indicates a lengthening of the vowel sound.

### Consonants

| Letter | Approximate Pronunciation | Symbol | Example | Pronunciation |
|---|---|---|---|---|
| c | 1. before e, i, y, like s in sit | s | **citron** | s**ee**·<u>tr**oa**n</u> |
| | 2. before a, o, u and a consonant, like k in kite | k | **cafeteria** | k**ah**·feh·<u>t**eh**</u>·ree·a |
| d | 1. at the end of the word after a vowel, or between a vowel and unstressed e or i, like th in this[1] | dh | **med** | medh |
| | 2. otherwise, as in English | d | **dale** | <u>d**a**</u>·ler |
| g | 1. at the beginning of a word or syllable, like g in go | g | **glas** | glas |
| | 2. otherwise, like y in yet[2] | y | **sige** | <u>s**ee**</u>·yer |
| hv | like v in view | v | **hvor** | voar |

[1] The letter **d** is not pronounced in **nd** and **ld** at the end of a word or syllable (**guld** = gooll), or before unstressed **e**, **t** or **s** in the same syllable (**plads** = plass).

[2] The letter **g** occasionally sounds like ch in Scottish loch and can sometimes be mute after **a**, **e**, **o**.

| Letter | Approximate Pronunciation | Symbol | Example | Pronunciation |
|---|---|---|---|---|
| j, hj | like y in yet | y | **ja** | ya |
| k | 1. between vowels, like g in go | g | **ikke** | ig·ger |
| | 2. otherwise like k in kite | k | **kaffe** | kah·fer |
| ng | like ng in sing | ng | **ingen** | ing·ern |
| p | 1. between vowels, like b in bit | b | **stoppe** | stoh·ber |
| | 2. otherwise like p in pill | p | **pude** | poo·dher |
| r | at the beginning of a word, pronounced in the back of the throat, but otherwise often omitted | r | **rose** | roa·ser |
| s | like s in see | s | **skål** | skowl |
| sj | usually like sh in sheet | sh | **sjælden** | sheh·lern |
| t | 1. between vowels, like d in do | d | **lytte** | lew·der |
| | 2. otherwise like t in to[3] | t | **torsk** | toarsk |

Letters b, f, h, l, m, n, v are generally pronounced as in English.

[3] In nouns that end with an **e**, an **r** is added to create the plural. In verbs that end with an **e**, an **r** at the end indicates the first person form. This **er** sound, in both cases, sounds like **ah**.

## Vowels

| Letter | Approximate Pronunciation | Symbol | Example | Pronunciation |
|---|---|---|---|---|
| a | 1. when long, like a in father | ah | **klare** | kl**ah**·rah |
| | 2. when short, like a in cat | a | **hat** | hat |
| e | 1. when long, like er in fern | er | **svare** | sv**ah**·rer |
| | 2. when short, like e in met | eh | **let** | leht |
| i | 1. when long, like ee in bee | ee | **ile** | **ee**·ler |
| | 2. when short, like i in pin | i | **drikke** | drig·ger |
| o | 1. when long, like oa in boat | oa | **sol** | soal |
| | 2. when short, like o in lot | oh | **godt** | goht |
| u | 1. when long, like oo in pool | oo | **frue** | fr**oo**·er |
| | 2. when short, like oa in boat | oa | **luft** | loaft |
| y | like ew in new | ew | **nyde** | n**ew**·dher |
| æ | 1. when long, like ay in day | ay | **sæbe** | s**ay**·ber |
| | 2. when short, like e in get | eh | **ægte** | ehg·ter |
| ø | like ur in fur | ur | **frøken** | fr**ur**·kern |
| å | 1. when long, like ow in tow | ow | **åben** | **ow**·bern |
| | 2. when short, like aw in saw | aw | **sådan** | saw·dan |

i

A vowel is generally long in stressed syllables when it's the final letter or followed by only one consonant. If followed by two or more consonants, or in unstressed syllables, the vowel is generally short.

In or after some vowels, a short puff of air (glottal stop) is added following the sound. The glottal stop significantly changes the meaning of certain words, e.g., **tænder** with a glottal stop means "teeth" whereas **tænder** without a glottal stop means "to turn on". As that foreigners will be understood without using the glottal stop, this sound has not been included in the phonetics.

## Sound Combinations

| Letter | Approximate Pronunciation | Symbol | Example | Pronunciation |
|---|---|---|---|---|
| av, af | like ow in now | ow | **hav** | how |
| ej, eg | like ie in lie | ie | **nej** | nie |
| ev | like e in get plus oo sound | eu | **levned** | leu•nerdh |
| ov | like ow in show | ow | **sjov** | show |
| øj | ike oi in oil | oi | **øje** | oi•er |
| øv | like o in so | oh | **søvnig** | soh•nee |

# *Basic Expressions*

Hello! **Hej!** hie

Goodbye. **Farvel.** fah•vehl

Yes. **Ja.** ya

No. **Nej.** nie

OK. **Okay.** ow•kay

Excuse me! (to get attention, to get past) **Undskyld!** ohn•skewl

Please. **Vær så venlig.** vehr sow vehn•lee

| | |
|---|---|
| Thank you. | **Tak.** tahk |
| You're welcome. | **Åh, jeg be'r.** ow yie behr |
| Where is the restroom [toilet]? | **Hvor er toilettet?** voar ehr toa•ee•leh•derdh |

## *Arrival and Departure*

| | |
|---|---|
| I'm here on *vacation [holiday]/business*. | **Jeg er her på *ferie/forretningsrejse*.** yie ehr hehr paw *fehr•yer/foh•reht•nings•rie•ser* |
| I'm going to… | **Jeg skal til…** yie skal til… |
| I'm staying at the…Hotel. | **Jeg bor på Hotel…** yie boar paw hoa•tehl… |

### Passport Control and Customs

| | |
|---|---|
| I'm just passing through. | **Jeg er her kun på gennemrejse.** yie ehr hehr koon paw geh•nehm•rie•ser |
| I would like to declare… | **Jeg vil gerne fortolde…** yie vil gehr•ner for•toh•ler… |
| I have nothing to declare. | **Jeg har ikke noget at fortolde.** yie hah ig•ger noa•erdh ad foh•toh•ler |

## *Money and Banking*

| | |
|---|---|
| Where's…? | **Hvor er…?** voar ehr… |
| – the ATM | **– pengeautomaten** pehng•er•ow•toa•ma•dern |
| – the bank | **– banken** bahnk•ern |
| – the currency exchange office | **– vekselkontor** vehk•serl•kohn•toar |
| What time does the bank *open/close*? | **Hvornår *åbner/lukker* banken?** voar•naw *owb•nah/loa•gah* bahnk•ern |
| I'd like to change *dollars/pounds* into kroner. | **Jeg vil gerne veksle nogle *dollars/pund* til kroner.** yie vil gehr•ner vehks•ler noa•ler *doh•lahs/poon* til kroa•ner |
| I want to cash a traveler's check [cheque]. | **Jeg vil gerne indløse en rejsecheck.** yie vil gehr•ner in•lur•ser ehn rie•ser•shehk |

## *Transportation*

| | |
|---|---|
| How do I get to town? | **Hvordan kommer jeg ind til byen?** voar•dan kohm•ah yie in til bew•ern |
| Where's…? | **Hvor er…?** voar ehr… |
| – the airport | **– lufthavnen** loaft•how•nern |
| – the train [railway] station | **– togstationen** tow•sta•shoa•nern |
| – the bus station | **– busstationen** boos•sta•shoa•nern |
| – the subway [underground] station | **– metrostationen** meh•troa•sta•shoa•nern |
| How far is it? | **Hvor langt er der?** voar lahngt ehr dehr |
| Where can I buy tickets? | **Hvor køber man billetter?** voar kur•ber man bee•leh•dah |
| A *one-way [single]/ round-trip [return]* ticket. | **En *enkeltbillet/returbillet.*** ehn *ehn•kerld•bee•lehd/reh•toor•bee•lehd* |
| How much? | **Hvor meget koster det?** voar mie•erdh kohs•dah deh |
| Are there any discounts? | **Er der nogen rabatter?** ehr der noa•ern rah•ba•dah |
| Which…? | **Hvilken…?** vil•kern… |
| – gate | **– gate** gayd |
| – line | **– tog** tow |
| Where can I get a taxi? | **Hvor kan jeg få en taxa?** voar kan yie fow ehn tahk•sa |
| Take me to this address. | **Kør mig til denne adresse.** kur mie til deh•ner a•drah•ser |
| Where can I rent [hire] a car? | **Hvor kan jeg leje en bil?** voar kan yie lie•er ehn beel |
| Can I have a map? | **Har du et vejkort?** har doo eht vie•kawd |

## Asking Directions

| | |
|---|---|
| How far is it to...? | **Hvor langt er der til...?** voar lahngt ehr dehr til... |
| Where's...? | **Hvor er...?** voar ehr... |
| – ...Street | **– ...gade** ...ga·dher |
| – this address | **– denne adresse** deh·ner ah·drah·ser |
| Can you show me on the map? | **Kan du vise mig det på kortet?** kan doo vee·ser mie deh paw kaw·derdh |
| I'm lost. | **Jeg er faret vild.** yie ehr fah·erdh veel |

### You May Hear...

| | |
|---|---|
| **ligeud** lee·er·oodh | straight ahead |
| **til venstre** til vehn·sdrah | on the left |
| **til højre** til hoi·ah | on the right |
| ***på/rundt om*** **hjørnet** *paw/roundt ohm* yur·nerdh | *on/around* the corner |
| **ved siden af...** vehdh see·dhern a... | next to... |
| **efter...** ehf·dah... | after... |
| **nord/syd** noar/sewdh | north/south |
| **øst/vest** ursd/vehsd | east/west |

## *Accommodations*

| | |
|---|---|
| Can you recommend a hotel? | **Kan du anbefale et hotel?** kan doo an·beh·fa·ler eht hoa·tehl |
| I have a reservation. | **Jeg har bestilt værelse.** yie har beh·stild vehrl·ser |
| My name is... | **Mit navn er...** meet nown ehr... |
| When's check-out? | **Hvornår skal vi tjekke ud?** voar·naw skal vee tjeh·ker oodh |

| | |
|---|---|
| Can I leave this in the safe? | **Må jeg lade dette være i boksen?** mow yie la deh•ter **vay**•er i bohk•sern |
| Can I leave my bags? | **Må jeg lade mine tasker være her?** mow yie la m**ee**•ner tas•gah **vay**•er hehr |
| Can I have *the bill/ a receipt*? | **Kan jeg få *regningen/en kvittering*?** kan yie fow *rie•ning•ern/ehn kvee•**teh**•ring* |

# *Internet and Communications*

| | |
|---|---|
| Where's an internet cafe? | **Hvor ligger der en internetcafé?** voar li•gah dehr ehn in•tah•neht•ca•**feh** |
| Can I *access the internet here/check e-mail*? | **Kan jeg gå på *internettet herfra/tjekke min e-mail*?** kan yie gow paw *in•tah•neh•derdh hehr•frah/tjay•ker meen **ee**•mail* |
| Can I have your phone number? | **Kan jeg få dit telefonnummer?** kan yie fow deet teh•ler•**foa**n•noa•mer |
| Here's my *number/ e-mail address*. | **Her er *mit telefonnumer/min e-mail-adresse*.** hehr ehr *meet teh•ler•**foa**n•noa•mer/ meen **ee**•mail•a•drah•ser* |
| Call me. | **Ring til mig.** ring til mie |
| E-mail me. | **Send mig en e-mail.** sehn mie ehn **ee**•mail |
| Hello. This is... | **Hallo. Det er...** ha•loa deh ehr... |
| I'd like to speak to... | **Jeg vil gerne tale med...** yie vil gehr•ner **ta**•ler medh... |
| Can you repeat that? | **Kan du gentage det?** kan doo gehn•ta deh |
| I'll call back later. | **Jeg ringer tilbage senere.** yie ring•ah til•**ba**•yer **seh**•nah |
| Bye. | **Farvel.** fah•vehl |
| Where's the post office? | **Hvor ligger posthuset?** voar li•gah pohsd•h**oo**•serdh |

# Eating Out

| | |
|---|---|
| Can you recommend a good *restaurant/ bar*? | **Kan du anbefale en god *restaurant/ bar*?** kan doo an•beh•**fa**•ler ehn goadh *reh•stoa•rang/b***ah** |
| Is there *a traditional Danish/ an inexpensive* restaurant nearby? | **Ligger der en *typisk dansk/ikke så dyr* restaurant i nærheden?** li•gah dah ehn *tew•peesk dansk/ig•ger saw dewr* reh•stoa•rang ee nehr•h**eh**•dhern |
| A table for…, please. | **Et bord til…tak.** eht boar til…tahk |
| I'd like a menu, please. | **Jeg vil gerne bede om et menukort, tak.** yie vil gehr•ner beh ohm eht meh•new•kawd tahk |
| What do you recommend? | **Hvad kan du anbefale?** vadh kan doo an•beh•f**a**•ler |
| I'd like… | **Jeg vil gerne have…** yie vil gehr•ner ha… |
| Some more, please. | **Jeg vil gerne have lidt mere, tak.** yie vil gehr•ner ha lit m**eh**•ah tahk |
| Enjoy your meal. | **Velbekomme.** vehl•beh•koh•mer |
| Can I have the check [bill]? | **Kan jeg få regningen?** kan yie fow rie•ning•ern |
| Is service included? | **Er drikkepenge inkluderet?** ehr drig•ger•pehng•er in•kloo•d**eh**•rerdh |
| Can I have a receipt? | **Kan jeg få en kvittering?** kan yie fow ehn kvee•t**eh**•ring |

## Breakfast

| | |
|---|---|
| **omelet** oa•mer•leht | omelet |
| **røræg** rur•ayg | scrambled eggs |
| **smør** smur | butter |
| **syltetøj** sewl•der•toi | jam |
| **yoghurt** yoo•goord | yogurt |

## Appetizers [Starters]

| | |
|---|---|
| **kaviar** ka·vee·**ah** | caviar |
| **(marineret/røget) makrel** (mah·ree·**neh**·rahdh/roi·erdh) ma·krehl | (marinated/smoked) mackerel |
| **rollmops** rohl·mops | pickled herring [rollmops] |
| ***røget/graved* laks** *roi·erdh/grah·verdh* lahks | *smoked/cured* salmon |
| **salat** sa·lat | salad |

## Soup

| | |
|---|---|
| **aspargessuppe** a·spahs·soa·per | asparagus soup |
| **champignonsuppe** sham·pin·yong·soa·per | mushroom soup |
| **gule ærter** goo·ler **eh**r·dah | split-pea soup with salt pork |
| **hønsekødsuppe** hurn·ser·kurdhs·soa·per | chicken and vegetable soup |

## Fish and Seafood

| | |
|---|---|
| **hummer** hoa·mah | lobster |
| **laks** lahks | salmon |
| **rejer** rie·ah | shrimp [prawns] |
| **rødspætte** rurdh·spay·der | plaice |
| **sild** seel | herring [whitebait] |

## Meat and Poultry

| | |
|---|---|
| **and** an | duck |
| **forloren skildpadde** foh·loarn skil·pa·dher | "mock turtle": a very traditional Danish dish consisting of meat from a calf's head with meatballs and fish balls |
| **hakkebøf** hah·ker·burf | ground beef patty |

**kalvekød** kal•ver•kurdh — veal
**kylling** kew•ling — chicken
**lam** lahm — lamb
**medisterpølse** meh•dees•dah•purl•ser — spiced pork sausage
**oksekød** ohk•ser•kurdh — beef
**svinekød** svee•ner•kurdh — pork

| | |
|---|---|
| rare | **letstegt** leht•stehgt |
| medium | **medium** meh•dee•oam |
| well-done | **gennemstegt** geh•nerm•stehgt |

## Danish Sandwiches: Smørrebrød

**brød** brurdh — bread
**bøftartar** burf•tah•tah — beef tartare
**franskbrød** frahnsk•brurdh — white bread
**fuldkornsbrød** fool•koarns•brurdh — whole-grain bread
**leverpaté** leh•wah•pa•teh — liver paté

## Vegetables

**agurk** a•goork — cucumber
**løg** loi — onions
**kartofler** ka•tohf•lah — potatoes
**tomater** toa•ma•dah — tomatoes
**ærter** ehr•dah — peas

## Fruit

**appelsin** ah•berl•seen — orange
**banan** ba•nan — banana
**blommer** bloh•mah — plums
**citron** see•troan — lemon
**jordbær** yoar•behr — strawberries

| | |
|---|---|
| **rabarber** rah·bah·bah | rhubarb |
| **æble** ay·bler | apple |

## Dessert

| | |
|---|---|
| **fromage** froa·ma·sher | mousse |
| **is** ees | ice cream |
| **pandekager** pa·ner·ka·yah | thin pancakes |
| **rødgrød med fløde** rurdh·grurdh mehdh flur·dher | fruit jelly served with cream |
| **æblekage med rasp og flødeskum** ay·ble·ka·yer mehdh rahsp ow flur·dher·skoam | layers of stewed apple and cookie crumbs topped with whipped cream |

# *Drinks*

| | |
|---|---|
| May I see the *wine list/drink menu*? | **Må jeg se *vinlisten/listen med drinks*?** mow yie seh *veen·lis·tern/lis·tern mehdh drinks* |
| I'd like a *bottle/glass* of *red/white* wine. | **Jeg vil gerne bede om en *flaske/et glas rødvin/hvidvin.*** yie vil gehr·ner beh ohm *ehn flas·ger/eht glas rurdh·veen/veedh·veen* |
| Another *bottle/glass*, please. | ***En flaske/Et glas* mere, tak.** *ehn flas·ger/ eht glas* meh·ah tahk |
| I'd like a local beer. | **Jeg vil gerne bede om en lokal øl.** yie vil gehr·ner beh ohm ehn loa·kal url |

| | |
|---|---|
| Cheers! | **Skål!** skowl |
| A *coffee/tea*, please. | **En kop *kaffe/te*, tak.** ehn kohp *kah·fer/teh* tahk |
| With milk. | **Med mælk.** mehdh mehlk |
| With sugar. | **Med sukker.** mehdh soa·gah |
| With artificial sweetener. | **Med sødemiddel.** mehdh sur·dher·mee·dherl |
| ...please. | **...tak.** ...tahk |
| – Juice | **– Juice** djoos |
| – Soda | **– Sodavand** soa·da·van |
| – *Sparkling/Still* water | **– Danskvand/Kildevand** dansk·van/kee·ler·van |

## Aperitifs, Cocktails and Liqueurs

| | |
|---|---|
| **akvavit** ah·kva·veet | aquavit |
| **cognac** kon·yahk | brandy |
| **snaps** snahps | schnapps |
| **likør** lee·kur | liquer |
| **whisky** wis·keei | whisky |

# *Talking*

| | |
|---|---|
| Hello! | **Hej!** hie |
| Good morning. | **God morgen.** goadh·mohn |
| Good afternoon. | **God eftermiddag.** goadh·ef·tah·mi·da |
| Good evening. | **God aften.** goadh·ahf·tern |
| How are you? | **Hvordan har du det?** voar·dan har doo deh |
| Fine, thanks. | **Godt, tak.** goht tahk |
| Excuse me! | **Undskyld!** ohn·skewl |
| What's your name? | **Hvad hedder du?** vadh heh·dhah doo |
| My name is... | **Mit navn er...** meet nown ehr... |
| Nice to meet you. | **Det glæder mig at træffe dig.** deh glay·dhah mie ad treh·fer die |

| | |
|---|---|
| Where are you from? | **Hvor kommer du fra?** voar koh•mah doo frah |
| I'm from *the U.S./ the U.K.* | **Jeg kommer fra *USA/England.*** yie koh•mah frah *oo•ehs•a/ehng•lan* |
| Goodbye. | **Farvel.** fah•vehl |
| See you later. | **På gensyn.** paw gehn•sewn |

**De** (the formal form of you) is generally no longer used to address strangers, but is restricted to formal letters, addressing the elderly or addressing members of the royal family. As a general rule, **du** can be used in all situations without offending anyone.

## Communication Difficulties

| | |
|---|---|
| Do you speak English? | **Kan du tale engelsk?** kan doo ta•ler ehng•erlsk |
| I don't speak (much) Danish. | **Jeg kan ikke tale (ret meget) dansk.** yie kan ig•ger ta•ler (reht mie•erdh) dansk |
| Can you speak more slowly? | **Kan du tale lidt langsommere?** kan doo ta•ler lit lang•sohm•ah |
| I understand. | **Jeg forstår det godt.** yie foh•staw deh goht |
| I don't understand. | **Jeg forstår det ikke.** yie foh•staw deh ig•ger |

# *Sightseeing*

| | |
|---|---|
| Where's the tourist information office? | **Hvor ligger turistinformationen?** voar li•gah too•reest•in•foh•ma•shoa•nern |
| Do you offer tours in English? | **Tilbyder I ture på engelsk?** til•bew•dhah ee too•ah paw ehng•erlsk |
| Can I have a *map/ guide*? | **Må jeg få *et kort/en guidebog*?** mow yie fow *eht kawd/ehn guide•bow* |

## Sights

| | |
|---|---|
| Where is...? | **Hvor er...?** voar ehr... |
| – the castle | **– slottet** sloh•derdh |
| – the cathedral | **– domkirken** dohm•keer•gem |

| | |
|---|---|
| – the downtown area | **– den indre by** dehn in•drah bew |
| – the museum | **– museet** moo•say•erdh |
| – the shopping area | **– indkøbscentret** in•kurbs•sehn•tahdh |

## *Shopping*

| | |
|---|---|
| Where is the *market/ mall [shopping centre]*? | **Hvor ligger *markedet/butikscentret*?** voar li•gah *mah•ker•dherd/boo•teeks•sehn•tahdh* |
| I'm just looking. | **Jeg ser mig bare omkring.** yie sehr mie b**ah** ohm•kring |
| Can you help me? | **Kan du hjælpe mig?** kan doo yehl•per mie |
| I'm being helped. | **Jeg får hjælp.** yie faw yehlp |
| How much? | **Hvor meget koster det?** voar mie•erdh kohs•dah deh |
| That's all, thanks. | **Det var det hele, tak.** deh vah deh **heh**•ler tahk |
| Where do I pay? | **Hvor kan jeg betale?** voar kan yie beh•**ta**•ler |

| | |
|---|---|
| I'll pay *in cash/by credit card.* | **Jeg vil gerne betale *kontant/med kreditkort.*** yie vil gehr·ner beh·ta·ler *kohn·tant/mehdh kreh·deet·kawd* |
| Can I have a receipt? | **Kan jeg få en kvittering?** kan yie fow ehn kvee·teh·ring |

## Stores

| | |
|---|---|
| Where is...? | **Hvor er...?** voar ehr... |
| – the bakery | – **bageriet** ba·yah·ree·erdh |
| – the bookstore | – **boghandleren** bow·han·lahn |
| – the department store | – **stormagasinet** stoar·mah·ga·see·nerdh |
| – the pharmacy [chemist] | – **apoteket** ah·poh·teh·kerdh |
| – the supermarket | – **supermarkedet** soo·pah·mah·kerdh |

## Clothing

| | |
|---|---|
| I'd like... | **Jeg vil gerne have...** yie vil gehr·ner ha... |
| Can I try this on? | **Må jeg prøve det?** mow yie prur·ver deh |
| It doesn't fit. | **Den passer ikke.** dehn pa·sah ig·ger |
| Do you have this in a *bigger/smaller* size? | **Har du den i en *større/mindre* størrelse?** hah doo dehn ee ehn *stur·ah/min·drah* stur·erlser |

### Color

| | |
|---|---|
| I'd like something... | **Jeg vil gerne have noget...** yie vil gehr·ner ha noa·erdh... |
| – black | – **sort** soart |
| – blue | – **blåt** blawht |
| – brown | – **brunt** broonht |
| – red | – **rødt** rurdht |
| – white | – **hvidt** veedht |

| | |
|---|---|
| – yellow | **– gult** goolt |
| – green | **– grønt** grurnht |
| – orange | **– orange** oa·rang·sher |

## Sports and Leisure

| | |
|---|---|
| Where's…? | **Hvor er…?** voar ehr… |
| – the beach | **– stranden** strah·nern |
| – the park | **– parken** pah·gern |
| – the pool | **– svømmebassinet** svur·mer·ba·sehng·erdh |
| Can I rent [hire] golf clubs? | **Kan jeg leje golfkøller?** kan yie lie·er gohlf·kur·lah |

## Culture and Nightlife

| | |
|---|---|
| Do you have a program of events? | **Har du et program over arrangementerne?** hah doo eht proa·grahm ow·ah ah·rahng·sheh·mang·ah·ner |
| Where's…? | **Hvor er…?** voar ehr… |
| – the downtown area | **– den indre by** dehn in·drah bew |
| – the bar | **– baren** bah·ern |
| – the dance club | **– diskoteket** dees·koa·teh·kerdh |

## Business Travel

| | |
|---|---|
| I'm here on business. | **Jeg er her på forretningsrejse.** yie ehr hehr paw foh·reht·nings·rie·ser |
| Here's my business card. | **Her er mit visitkort.** hehr ehr meet vee·seet·kawd |
| Can I have your card? | **Må jeg få dit visitkort?** mow yie fow deet vee·seet·kawd |
| I have a meeting with… | **Jeg har et møde med…** yie hah eht mur·dher mehdh… |
| Where's…? | **Hvor er…?** voar ehr… |

| | |
|---|---|
| – the business center | – **businesscentret** bis·nis·sehn·tahdh |
| – the convention hall | – **konferencesalen** kohn·fer·rahng·ser·sa·lern |
| – the meeting room | – **mødelokalet** mur·dher·loa·ka·lerdh |

## Travel with Children

| | |
|---|---|
| Is there a discount for kids? | **Er det billigere for børn?** ehr deh bee·lee·ah foh burn |
| Can you recommend a babysitter? | **Kan du anbefale en babysitter?** kan doo an·beh·fa·ler ehn bay·bee·si·dah? |
| Can we have a *child's seat/highchair*? | **Må vi få *et barnesæde/en høj stol*?** mow vee fow *eht bah·ner·say·dher/ehn hoi stoal* |
| Where can I change the baby? | **Hvor kan jeg skifte babyen?** voar kan yie skeef·der bay·bee·ern |

## For the Disabled

| | |
|---|---|
| Is there…? | **Er der…?** ehr dehr… |
| – access for the disabled | – **adgang for handicappede** adh·gahng for han·dee·kahp·per·dher |
| – a wheelchair ramp | – **en rampe til kørestole** ehn rahm·ber til kur·ah·stoa·ler |
| – a handicapped- [disabled-] accessible toilet | – **et handicaptoilet** eht han·dee·kahp·toa·ee·lehd |
| I need… | **Jeg har brug for…** yie hah broo foh… |
| – assistance | – **hjælp** yehlp |
| – an elevator [lift] | – **en elevator** ehn eh·ler·va·toh |

## Emergencies

| | |
|---|---|
| Help! | **Hjælp!** yehlp |
| Go away! | **Gå væk!** gow vehk |
| Stop thief! | **Stop tyven!** stohp tew·vern |
| Get a doctor! | **Tilkald læge!** til·kal lay·er |

| | |
|---|---|
| Fire! | **Det brænder!** deh brahn•nah |
| I'm lost. | **Jeg er faret vild** yie ehr fah•erdh veel |

## Health

| | |
|---|---|
| Can you help me? | **Kan du hjælpe mig?** kan doo yehl•per mie |
| Call the police! | **Ring til politiet!** ring til poa•lee•tee•erdh |
| I'm sick [ill]. | **Jeg er syg.** yie ehr sew |
| I need an English-speaking doctor. | **Jeg har brug for en læge, der taler engelsk.** yie hah broo foh ehn lay•er dehr ta•lah ehng•erlsk |
| It hurts here. | **Det gør ondt her.** deh gur ohnt hehr |

# Reference

## Numbers

0 **nul** noal
1 **en** ehn
2 **to** toa
3 **tre** treh
4 **fire** fee•ah
5 **fem** fehm
6 **seks** sehks
7 **syv** sew
8 **otte** oa•der
9 **ni** nee
10 **ti** tee
11 **elleve** ehl•ver
12 **tolv** toal
13 **tretten** treh•dern
14 **fjorten** fyoar•dern
15 **femten** fehm•dern
16 **seksten** sie•stern
17 **sytten** sur•dern
18 **atten** a•dern
19 **nitten** ni•dern
20 **tyve** tew•ver
21 **enogtyve** ehn•oh•tew•ver
22 **tooggyve** toa•oh•tew•ver
30 **tredive** trehdh•ver
31 **enogtredive** ehn•oh•trehdh•ver
40 **fyrre** fur•er
50 **halvtreds** hal•trehs
60 **tres** trehs
70 **halvfjerds** hal•fyehrs
80 **firs** feers
90 **halvfems** hal•fehms
100 **hundrede** hoon•rah•dher
101 **hundrede og et** hoon•rah•dher ow eht
200 **to hundrede** toa hoon•rah•dher
500 **fem hundrede** fehm hoon•rah•dher
1000 **tusind** too•sin
10,000 **ti tusind** tee too•sin
1,000,000 **en million** ehn meel•yoan

## Time

| | |
|---|---|
| What time is it? | **Hvad er klokken?** vadh ehr kloh·gern |
| From nine o'clock to 5 o'clock. | **Fra klokken ni til sytten.** frah kloh·gern nee til surd·den |
| 5:30 *a.m./p.m.* | **Halv seks om *morgenen/aftenen*.** hal sehks ohm *m**oh**·nern/af·tern* |

## Days

| | |
|---|---|
| Monday | **mandag** man·da |
| Tuesday | **tirsdag** teers·da |
| Wednesday | **onsdag** oans·da |
| Thursday | **torsdag** t**oh**s·da |
| Friday | **fredag** freh·da |
| Saturday | **lørdag** lur·da |
| Sunday | **søndag** surn·da |

## Dates

| | |
|---|---|
| yesterday | **i går** ee g**aw** |
| today | **i dag** ee da |
| tomorrow | **i morgen** ee m**oh**n |

## Months

| | | | |
|---|---|---|---|
| January | **januar** ya·noo·ah | July | **juli** yoo·lee |
| February | **februar** feh·broo·ah | August | **august** ow·goast |
| March | **marts** m**ah**ts | September | **september** sehp·tehm·bah |
| April | **april** a·pr**ee**l | October | **oktober** ohk·**toa**·bah |
| May | **maj** mie | November | **november** noa·vehm·bah |
| June | **juni** yoo·nee | December | **december** deh·sehm·bah |

Danish

# Dutch

## Pronunciation

Stress has been indicated in the phonetic transcription with underlining.

### Consonants

| Letter | Approximate Pronunciation | Symbol | Example | Pronunciation |
|---|---|---|---|---|
| ch | ch as in loch | kh | **nacht** | nahkht |
| d | 1. as in English | d | **dag** | dahkh |
| | 2. t as in cat if at the end of a word | t | **bed** | beht |
| g | ch as in loch | kh | **groot** | khroat |
| j | y as in yes | y | **ja** | yaa |
| r | r as in ran, but rolled | r | **rijst** | riest |
| s | always hard as in pass | s | **stop** | stohp |
| sch | s followed by ch as in loch | skh | **schrijven** | skhrie·fuhn |
| v | f as in fan | f | **vader** | faa·duhr |
| w | v as in van | v | **water** | vaa·tuhr |

Letters b, c, f, h, k, l, m, n, p, q, t, x, y, z are generally pronounced as in English.

### Vowels

| Letter | Approximate Pronunciation | Symbol | Example | Pronunciation |
|---|---|---|---|---|
| a | a as in father | ah | **nacht** | nahkht |
| aa | aa as in aardvark | aa | **maar** | maar |

| Letter | Approximate Pronunciation | Symbol | Example | Pronunciation |
|---|---|---|---|---|
| e | 1. e as in red | eh | **bed** | beht |
| | 2. u as in up | uh | **meneer** | muh•nayr |
| ë | u as in up | uh | **drieën** | dree•yuhn |
| ee | ay as in hay | ay | **nee** | nay |
| i | 1. i as in bit | ih | **kind** | kihnt |
| | 2. ee as in seen | ee | **mini** | mee•nee |
| o | o as in not | oh | **pot** | poht |
| oo | oa as in boat | oa | **roos** | roas |
| u | 1. u as in up | uh | **bus** | buhs |
| | 2. ew as in new | ew | **nu** | new |
| uu | ew as in new | ew | **duur** | dewr |

## Vowel Combinations

| Letter | Approximate Pronunciation | Symbol | Example | Pronunciation |
|---|---|---|---|---|
| ie | ee as in seen | ee | **zien** | zeen |
| ei[1] | ie as in tie | ie | **klein** | klien |
| ij[2] | 1. ie as in tie | ie | **wij** | wie |
| | 2. u as in up | uh | **lelijk** | lay•luhk |
| oe | oo as in too | oo | **hoeveel** | hoo•fayl |
| ou, au | ow in now | ow | **koud** | kowt |
| | | | **auto** | ow•toa |
| eu | u as in murky | u | **deur** | dur |
| ui | aw as in awe | aw | **huis** | haws |

[1] Called **korte ei** (short i).
[2] Called **lange ij** (long i).

*i* Dutch has many vowel sounds, and some may be unfamiliar to your ear. The best approximation is provided above, but try to listen to Dutch speakers to begin to develop accuracy in pronunciation.

## Basic Expressions

| | |
|---|---|
| Hello./Hi! | **Dag./Hallo!** dakh/hah·loa |
| Goodbye. | **Dag.** dakh |
| Yes. | **Ja.** yaa |
| No. | **Nee.** nay |
| Excuse me! (to get attention) | **Meneer ♂/Mevrouw ♀!** muh·nayr ♂/muh·frow ♀ |
| Excuse me. (to get past) | **Pardon.** pahr·dohn |
| Please. | **Alstublieft.** ahls·tew·bleeft |
| Thank you. | **Dank u wel.** dahngk ew vehl |
| You're welcome. | **Geen dank.** khayn dahngk |
| Where is the restroom [toilet]? | **Waar is het toilet?** vaar ihs heht twaa·leht |

## Arrival and Departure

| | |
|---|---|
| I'm here on *vacation [holiday]/business*. | **Ik ben hier *met vakantie/voor zaken*.** ihk behn heer *meht faa·kahn·see/foar zaa·kuhn* |
| I'm going to… | **Ik ga naar…** ihk khaa naar… |
| I'm staying at the… Hotel. | **Ik logeer in Hotel…** ihk loa·zhayr ihn hoa·tehl… |

### Passport Control and Customs

| | |
|---|---|
| I'm just passing through. | **Ik ben op doorreis.** ihk behn ohp doar·ries |
| I'd like to declare… | **Ik wil graag…aangeven.** ihk vihl khraakh… aan·khay·fuhn |
| I have nothing to declare. | **Ik heb niets aan te geven.** ihk hehp neets aan tuh khay·fuhn |

## Money and Banking

| | |
|---|---|
| Where's...? | **Waar is...?** vaar ihs... |
| – the ATM | **– de geldautomaat** duh khehlt•ow•toa•maat |
| – the bank | **– de bank** duh bahngk |
| – the currency exchange office | **– het geldwisselkantoor** heht khehlt•vihs•suhl•kahn•toar |
| What time does the bank *open/close*? | **Hoe laat gaat de bank *open/dicht*?** hoo laat khaat duh bahngk *oa•puhn/dihkht* |
| I'd like to change some *dollars/pounds* into euros. | **Ik wil graag wat *dollars/ponden* in euro's omwisselen.** ihk vihl khraakh vaht *dohl•lahrs/pohn•duhn* ihn u•roas ohm•vihs•suh•luhn |
| I want to cash some traveler's checks [cheques]. | **Ik wil wat reischeques verzilveren.** ihk vihl vaht ries•shehks fuhr•zihl•fuhr•uhn |

## Transportation

| | |
|---|---|
| How do I get to town? | **Hoe kom ik in de stad?** hoo kohm ihk ihn duh staht |
| Where's...? | **Waar is...?** vaar ihs... |
| – the airport | **– het vliegveld** heht fleekh•fehlt |
| – the train [railway] station | **– het station** heht staa•shohn |
| – the bus station | **– het busstation** heht buhs•staa•shohn |
| – the subway [underground] station | **– het metrostation** heht may•troa•staa•shohn |
| How far is it? | **Hoe ver is het?** hoo fehr ihs heht |
| Where can I buy tickets? | **Waar kan ik kaartjes kopen?** vaar kahn ihk kaart•yuhs koa•puhn |
| A *one-way [single]/ round-trip [return]* ticket. | **Enkeltje/Retourtje.** ehng•kuhl•tyuh/ ruh•toor•tyuh |

| | |
|---|---|
| How much? | **Hoeveel kost het?** hoo•fayl kohst heht |
| Are there any discounts? | **Kan ik korting krijgen?** kahn ihk kohr•tihng krie•khuhn |
| Which *gate/line*? | **Welke *gate/lijn*?** vehl•kuh *gayt/lien* |
| Which platform? | **Welk spoor?** vehlk spoar |
| Where can I get a taxi? | **Waar kan ik een taxi krijgen?** vaar kahn ihk uhn tahk•see krie•khuhn |
| Could you take me to this address? | **Kunt u me naar dit adres brengen?** kuhnt ew muh naar diht ah•drehs brehng•uhn |
| Where can I rent a car? | **Waar kan ik een auto huren?** vaar kahn ihk uhn ow•toa hew•ruhn |
| Can I have a map? | **Heeft u een kaart voor mij?** hayft ew uhn kaart foar mie |

## Asking Directions

| | |
|---|---|
| How far is it to... from here? | **Hoe ver is het hiervandaan naar...?** hoo fehr ihs heht heer•fahn•daan naar... |
| Where's...? | **Waar vind ik...?** vaar fihnt ihk... |
| – ...Street | **– de...straat** duh...straat |
| – this address | **– dit adres** diht ah•drehs |
| Can you show me on the map? | **Kunt u dat op de kaart laten zien?** kuhnt ew daht ohp duh kaart laa•tuhn zeen |

### You May Hear...

| | |
|---|---|
| **rechtdoor** rehkht•doar | straight ahead |
| **links** lihnks | left |
| **rechts** rehkhts | right |
| ***op/om* de hoek** *ohp/ohm* duh hook | *on/around* the corner |
| **naast** naast | next to |

| | |
|---|---|
| **na** naa | after |
| **ten noorden/ten zuiden** tehn noar·duhn/tehn zaw·duhn | north/south |
| **ten oosten/ten westen** tehn oas·tuhn/tehn vehs·tuhn | east/west |

## Accommodations

| | |
|---|---|
| Can you recommend a hotel? | **Kunt u een hotel aanbevelen?** kuhnt ew uhn hoa·tehl aan·buh·fay·luhn |
| I have a reservation. | **Ik heb een reservering.** ihk hehp uhn ray·zuhr·vay·rihng |
| My name is... | **Mijn naam is...** mien naam ihs... |
| When's check-out? | **Hoe laat moeten we uitchecken?** hoo laat moo·tuhn vie awt·check·uhn |
| Can I leave this in the safe? | **Mag ik dit in de kluis bewaren?** mahkh ihk diht ihn duh klaws buh·waa·ruhn |
| Can we leave our bags? | **Mogen we onze bagage hier laten staan?** moa·khuhn wie ohn·zuh baa·khaa·zhuh heer laa·tuhn staan |
| Can I have *the bill/ a receipt*? | **Mag ik *de rekening/een kwitantie*?** mahkh ihk *duh ray·kuh·nihng/uhn kvee·tahnt·see* |

## Internet and Communications

| | |
|---|---|
| Where's an internet cafe? | **Waar vind ik een internetcafé?** vaar fihnt ihk uhn ihn·tuhr·neht·kaa·fay |
| Can I *access the internet/check e-mail* here? | **Kan ik hier *internetten/mijn e-mail checken*?** kahn ihk heer *ihn·tuhr·neh·tuhn/ mien ee·mayl tsheh·kuhn* |
| Can I have your phone number? | **Mag ik uw telefoonnummer?** mahkh ihk ew tay·luh·foan·nuh·muhr |
| Here's my *number/ e-mail address*. | **Hier is mijn *telefoonnummer/ e-mailadres.*** heer ihs mien *tay·luh·foan·nuh·muhr/ee·mayl·aa·drehs* |

| | |
|---|---|
| Call me. | **Bel me.** behl muh |
| E-mail me. | **Stuur me een e-mail.** stewr muh uhn ee•mayl |
| Hello. This is… | **Dag. U spreekt met…** dahkh ew spraykt meht… |
| I'd like to speak to… | **Ik wil graag met…spreken.** ihk vihl khraakh meht…spray•kuhn |
| Can you repeat that? | **Kunt u dat herhalen?** kuhnt ew daht hehr•haa•luhn |
| I'll call back later. | **Ik bel straks wel even terug.** ihk behl strahks vehl ay•fuhn truhkh |
| Bye. | **Dag.** dahkh |
| Where's the post office? | **Waar is het postkantoor?** vaar ihs heht pohst•kahn•toar |

## Eating Out

| | |
|---|---|
| Can you recommend a *good restaurant/ bar*? | **Kunt u een *goed restaurant/goede bar* aanbevelen?** kuhnt ew uhn *khoot rehs•toa•rahnt/khoo•duh bahr* aan•buh•fay•luhn |
| Is there *a traditional Dutch/an inexpensive* restaurant near here? | **Is er een *traditioneel Nederlands/ goedkoop* restaurant in de buurt?** ihs ehr uhn *traa•dee•shoa•nayl nay•duhr•lahnds/ khoot•koap* rehs•toa•rahnt ihn duh bewrt |
| A table for…, please. | **Een tafel voor…, alstublieft.** uhn taa•fuhl foar…ahls•tew•bleeft |
| Can I have a menu, please? | **Mag ik een menukaart, alstublieft?** mahkh ihk uhn muh•new•kaart ahls•tew•bleeft |
| What do you recommend? | **Wat kunt u aanbevelen?** vaht kuhnt ew aan•buh•fay•luhn |
| I'd like… | **Ik wil graag…** ihk vihl khraakh… |
| Some more…, please. | **Nog wat…, alstublieft.** nohkh vaht… ahls•tew•bleeft |
| Enjoy your meal. | **Eet smakelijk.** ayt smaa•kuh•luhk |

Can I have the check [bill]? **Mag ik de rekening?** mahkh ihk duh ray•kuh•nihng

Is service included? **Is de bediening inbegrepen?** ihs duh buh•dee•nihng ihn•buh•khray•puhn

Can I have a receipt, please? **Mag ik een kwitantie, alstublieft?** mahkh ihk uhn kvee•tahnt•see ahls•tew•bleeft

## Breakfast

**boter** boa•tuhr butter

**brood** broat bread

**broodje** broat•yuh roll

**ei** ie egg

**honing** hoa•nihng honey

**jam** zhehm jam

## Appetizers [Starters]

**gerookte paling** khuh•roak•tuh paa•lihng smoked eel

**huzarensalade** hew•zaa•ruhn•saa•laa•duh potato, vegetables and meat with mayonnaise

**nieuwe haring** neeew•vuh haa•rihng freshly caught, salt-cured herring

**pasteitje** pahs•tie•tyuh pastry filled with meat or fish

## Soup

| | |
|---|---|
| **erwtensoep** ehr·tuhn·soop | famous thick Dutch pea soup with pig's knuckle, smoked sausage and bacon |
| **groentesoep (met balletjes)** khroon·tuh·soop (meht bah·luh·tyuhs) | vegetable soup (with meatballs) |
| **kippensoep** kih·puhn·soop | chicken soup |
| **tomatensoep** toa·maa·tuhn·soop | tomato soup |
| **uiensoep** aw·yuhn·soop | onion soup |

## Fish and Seafood

| | |
|---|---|
| **haring** haa·rihng | herring [whitebait] |
| **kabeljauw** kaa·buhl·yow | cod |
| **mossel** moh·suhl | mussel |
| **tonijn** toa·nien | tuna |
| **zalm** zahlm | salmon |

## Meat and Poultry

| | |
|---|---|
| **biefstuk** beef·stuhk | steak |
| **eend** aynt | duck |
| **kalfsvlees** kahlfs·flays | veal |
| **kip** kihp | chicken |
| **lamsvlees** lahms·flays | lamb |
| **rundvlees** ruhnt·flays | beef |
| **spek** spehk | bacon |
| **varkensvlees** fahr·kuhns·flays | pork |
| **wienerschnitzel** vee·nuhr shniht·suhl | breaded veal chops |
| **worst** vohrst | sausage |

| | |
|---|---|
| rare | **kort gebakken** kohrt khuh·bah·kuhn |
| medium | **medium** may·dee·yuhm |
| well-done | **goed doorbakken** khoot doar·bah·kuhn |

## Vegetables

| | |
|---|---|
| **aardappel** aar·dah·puhl | potato |
| **bloemkool** bloom·koal | cauliflower |
| **komkommer** kohm·kohm·muhr | cucumber |
| **paprika (rode/groene)** paa·pree·kaa (roa·duh/khroo·nuh) | (red/green) pepper |
| **sla** slaa | lettuce |
| **sperziebonen** spehr·see·boa·nuhn | green beans |
| **wortel** vohr·tuhl | carrot |

## Fruit

| | |
|---|---|
| **aardbei** aart·bie | strawberry |
| **appel** ah·puhl | apple |
| **banaan** baa·naan | banana |
| **druif** drawf | grape |
| **kers** kehrs | cherry |
| **perzik** pehr·zihk | peach |
| **sinaasappel** see·naas·ah·puhl | orange |

## Dessert

| | |
|---|---|
| **appeltaart** ah·puhl·taart | Dutch apple tart |
| **kwarktaart** kvahrk·taart | light cheesecake |
| **pannenkoek** pah·nuhn·kook | thin pancake |
| **vla** flaa | custard |

# *Drinks*

| | |
|---|---|
| May I see the *wine list/drink menu*? | **Mag ik de *wijnkaart/drankkaart* zien?** mahkh ihk duh *vien·kaart/drahnk·kaart* zeen |
| I'd like a *bottle/glass* of *red/white* wine. | **Ik wil graag een *fles/glas rode/witte* wijn.** ihk vihl khraakh uhn *flehs/khlahs roa·duh/vih·tuh* vien |
| Another *bottle/glass*, please. | **Nog een *fles/glas*, alstublieft.** nohkh uhn *flehs/khlahs* ahls·tew·bleeft |

| | |
|---|---|
| I'd like a local beer. | **Ik wil graag een lokaal biertje.** ihk vihl khraakh uhn loa•kaal beer•tyuh |
| Cheers! | **Proost!** proast |
| A *coffee/tea*, please. | **Een *koffie/thee*, alstublieft.** uhn *koh•fee/tay* ahls•tew•bleeft |
| *With/Without* milk. | ***Met/Zonder* melk.** *meht/zohn•duhr* mehlk |
| With sugar. | **Met suiker.** meht zaw•kuhr |
| With artificial sweetener. | **Met zoetjes.** meht zoo•tyuhs |
| ..., please. | **..., alstublieft.** ...ahls•tew•bleeft |
| – Juice | **– Een vruchtensap** uhn fruhkh•tuhn•sahp |
| – Soda | **– Een frisdrank** uhn frihs•drahngk |
| – (*Sparkling/Still*) Water | **– *(Koolzuurhoudend/Koolzuurvrij)* Water** (*koal•zewr•how•duhnt/koal•zewr•frie*) vaa•tuhr |

## Aperitifs, Cocktails and Liqueurs

| | |
|---|---|
| **advocaat** aht•foa•kaat | famous Dutch egg liqueur |
| **cognac** kohn•yahk | brandy |
| **gin-tonic** zhihn•toh•nihk | gin and tonic |
| **jenever** yuh•nay•vuhr | Dutch gin |
| **wodka** vohd•kaa | vodka |

# *Talking*

| | |
|---|---|
| Hello./Hi! | **Dag./Hallo!** dakh/hah•loa |
| Good morning. | **Goedemorgen.** khoo•duh•mohr•khuhn |
| Good afternoon. | **Goedemiddag.** khoo•duh•mih•dahkh |
| Good evening. | **Goedenavond.** khoo•duh•naa•fohnt |
| How are you? | **Hoe gaat het met u?** hoo khaat heht meht ew |
| Fine, thanks. | **Prima, dank u.** pree•maa dangk ew |
| Excuse me! (to a man/woman) | **Meneer♂/Mevrouw♀!** muh•nayr♂/ muh•frow♀ |

| | |
|---|---|
| What's your name? | **Hoe heet u?** hoo hayt ew |
| My name is… | **Mijn naam is…** mien naam ihs… |
| Nice to meet you. | **Aangenaam.** aan•khuh•naam |
| Where are you from? | **Waar komt u vandaan?** vaar kohmt ew fahn•daan |
| I'm from *the U.S./U.K.* | **Ik kom uit *de Verenigde Staten/Groot-Brittannië*.** ihk kohm awt duh *fuhr•ay•nihkh•duh staa•tuhn/khroat•brih•tah•nee•yuh* |
| Goodbye. | **Dag.** dakh |
| See you later. | **Tot ziens.** toht zeens |

When addressing people you don't know, use **u** (formal you) or **meneer** (sir) and **mevrouw** (ma'am or madam), particularly with strangers and older people. It is impolite to address someone with the familiar **jij** and **je** (**jullie**, in the plural) until invited to do so.

## Communication Difficulties

| | |
|---|---|
| Do you speak English? | **Spreekt u Engels?** spraykt ew ehng•uhls |
| I don't speak much Dutch. | **Ik spreek maar weinig Nederlands.** ihk sprayk maar vie•nihkh nay•duhr•lahnts |
| Can you speak more slowly? | **Kunt u iets langzamer spreken?** kuhnt ew eets lahng•zaa•muhr spray•kuhn |
| I (don't) understand. | **Ik begrijp het (niet).** ihk buh•khrayp heht (neet) |

# *Sightseeing*

| | |
|---|---|
| Where's the tourist information office? | **Waar is het VVV-kantoor?** vaar ihs heht vay•vay•vay•kahn•toar |
| Do you have tours in English? | **Verzorgt u excursies in het Engels?** fuhr•zohrkht ew ehks•kuhr•sees ihn heht ehng•uhls |
| Can I have a *map/guide* please? | **Mag ik een *kaart/gids*, alstublieft?** mahkh ihk uhn *kaart/khihts* ahls•tew•bleeft |

## Sights

| | |
|---|---|
| Where *is*? | **Waar *is*?** vaar *ihs* |
| – the castle | **– het kasteel** heht kahs·tayl |
| – the downtown area | **– het stadscentrum** heht staht·sehn·truhm |
| – the museum | **– het museum** heht mew·zay·uhm |
| – the shopping area | **– de winkels** duh vihn·kuhls |

## *Shopping*

| | |
|---|---|
| Where is the *market/ mall [shopping centre]*? | **Waar is *de markt/het winkelcentrum*?** vaar ihs *duh mahrkt/heht vihn·kuhl·sehn·truhm* |
| I'm just looking. | **Ik kijk alleen.** ihk kiek ah·layn |
| Can you help me? | **Kunt u me helpen?** kuhnt ew muh hehl·puhn |
| I'm being helped. | **Ik word al geholpen.** ihk vohrt ahl khuh·hohl·puhn |
| How much? | **Hoeveel kost het?** hoo·fayl kohst heht |
| That one. | **Die daar.** dee daar |
| That's all, thanks. | **Meer niet, dank u.** mayr neet dangk ew |
| Where do I pay? | **Waar moet ik betalen?** vaar moot ihk buh·taa·luhn |
| I'll pay *in cash/by credit card.* | **Ik wil graag *contant/met een creditcard* betalen.** ihk vihl *khraakh kohn·tahnt/meht uhn kreh·diht·kaart* buh·taa·luhn |

| | |
|---|---|
| A receipt, please. | **Een kwitantie, alstublieft.** uhn kvee•tahn•see ahls•tew•bleeft |

## Stores

| | |
|---|---|
| Where is...? | **Waar is...?** vaar ihs... |
| – the bakery | **– de bakker** duh bah•kuhr |
| – the bookstore | **– de boekwinkel** duh book•vihn•kuhl |
| – the department store | **– het warenhuis** heht vaa•ruhn•haws |
| – the pharmacy [chemist] | **– de apotheek** duh ah•poa•tayk |
| – the supermarket | **– de supermarkt** duh sew•puhr•mahrkt |

## Clothing

| | |
|---|---|
| I'd like... | **Ik wil graag...** ihk vihl khraakh... |
| Can I try this on? | **Mag ik dit passen?** mahkh ihk diht pah•suhn |
| It doesn't fit. | **Het past niet.** heht pahst neet |
| Do you have this in a *bigger/smaller* size? | **Heeft u dit in een *grotere/kleinere* maat?** hayft ew diht ihn *uhn khroa•tuh•ruh/ klie•nuh•ruh* maat |

### Color

| | |
|---|---|
| I'd like something in... | **Ik wil graag iets...** ihk vihl khraakh eets... |
| – black | **– zwarts** zvahrts |
| – blue | **– blauws** blows |
| – brown | **– bruins** brawns |
| – green | **– groens** khroons |
| – orange | **– oranjes** oa•rahn•yuhs |
| – red | **– roods** roats |
| – white | **– wits** vihts |
| – yellow | **– geels** khayls |

## Sports and Leisure

| | |
|---|---|
| Where's…? | **Waar is…?** vaar ihs… |
| – the beach | **– het strand** heht strahnt |
| – the park | **– het park** heht pahrk |
| – the pool | **– het zwembad** heht zvehm•baht |
| Can I rent [hire] golf clubs? | **Kan ik golfclubs huren?** kahn ihk gohlf•kluhps hew•ruhn |

## Culture and Nightlife

| | |
|---|---|
| Do you have a program of events? | **Heeft u een evenementenprogramma?** hayft ew uhn ay•fuh•nuh•mehn•tuhn•proa•khrah•maa |
| Where's…? | **Waar is…?** vaar ihs… |
| – the downtown area | **– het stadscentrum** heht staht•sehn•truhm |
| – the bar | **– de bar** duh bahr |
| – the dance club | **– de discotheek** duh dihs•koa•tayk |

## Business Travel

| | |
|---|---|
| I'm here on business. | **Ik ben hier voor zaken.** ihk behn heer foar zaa•kuhn |
| Here's my business card. | **Hier is mijn visitekaartje.** heer ihs mien fee•zee•tuh•kaart•yuh |
| Can I have your card? | **Mag ik uw visitekaartje?** mahkh ihk ew fee•zee•tuh•kaart•yuh |
| I have a meeting with… | **Ik heb een afspraak met…** ihk hehp uhn ahf•spraak meht… |
| Where's…? | **Waar is…?** vaar ihs… |
| – the business center | **– het bedrijvencomplex** heht buh•drie•fuhn•kohm•plehks |
| – the convention hall | **– het congresgebouw** heht kohn•khrehs•khuh•bow |
| – the meeting room | **– de vergaderruimte** duh fuhr•khaa•duhr•rawm•tuh |

## Travel with Children

| | |
|---|---|
| Is there a discount for children? | **Is er korting voor kinderen?** ihs ehr kohr•tihng foar kihn•duh•ruhn |
| Can you recommend a babysitter? | **Kunt u een oppas aanbevelen?** kuhnt ew uhn ohp•pahs aan•buh•fay•luhn |
| Can I have a highchair? | **Mogen we een kinderstoel?** moa•khuhn vuh uhn kihn•duhr•stool |
| Where can I change the baby? | **Waar kan ik de baby verschonen?** vaar kahn ihk duh bay•bee fuhr•skhoa•nuhn |

## For the Disabled

| | |
|---|---|
| Is there access for the disabled? | **Is het toegankelijk voor gehandicapten?** is heht too•khahng•kuh•luhk foar khuh•hehn•dee•kehp•tuhn |
| Is there a wheelchair ramp? | **Is er een rolstoeloprit?** uhn rohl•stool•ohp•riht |
| Is there a handicapped-[disabled-] accessible toilet? | **Is er een toilet dat toegankelijk is voor gehandicapten?** uhn tvaa•leht daht too•khahng•kuh•luhk ihs foar khuh•hehn•dee•kehp•tuhn |
| I need… | **Ik heb…nodig.** ihk hehp…noa•dihkh |
| – assistance | **– hulp** huhlp |
| – an elevator [lift] | **– een lift** uhn lihft |

## Emergencies

| | |
|---|---|
| Help! | **Help!** hehlp |
| Go away! | **Ga weg!** khaa vehkh |
| Stop thief! | **Houd de dief!** howt duh deef |
| Get a doctor! | **Haal een dokter!** haal uhn dohk•tuhr |
| Fire! | **Brand!** brahnt |
| I'm lost. | **Ik ben verdwaald.** ihk behn fuhr•dvaalt |
| Can you help me? | **Kunt u me helpen?** kuhnt ew muh hehl•puhn |
| Call the police! | **Bel de politie!** bel duh poa•leet•see |

# Health

| | |
|---|---|
| I'm sick [ill]. | **Ik ben ziek.** ihk behn zeek |
| I need an English-speaking doctor. | **Ik zoek een dokter die Engels spreekt.** ihk zook uhn dohk•tuhr dee ehng•uhls spraykt |
| It hurts here. | **Het doet hier pijn.** heht doot heer pien |

# Reference

## Numbers

| | | | |
|---|---|---|---|
| 0 | **nul** nuhl | 19 | **negentien** nay•khuhn•teen |
| 1 | **één** ayn | 20 | **twintig** tvihn•tuhkh |
| 2 | **twee** tvay | 21 | **eenentwintig** ayn•uhn•tvihn•tuhkh |
| 3 | **drie** dree | 22 | **tweeëntwintig** tvay•uhn•tvihn•tuhkh |
| 4 | **vier** feer | 30 | **dertig** dehr•tihkh |
| 5 | **vijf** fief | 31 | **eenendertig** ayn•uhn•dehr•tihkh |
| 6 | **zes** zehs | 40 | **veertig** fayr•tihkh |
| 7 | **zeven** zay•fuhn | 50 | **vijftig** fief•tihkh |
| 8 | **acht** ahkht | 60 | **zestig** zehs•tihkh |
| 9 | **negen** nay•khuhn | 70 | **zeventig** zay•fuhn•tihkh |
| 10 | **tien** teen | 80 | **tachtig** tahkh•tikh |
| 11 | **elf** ehlf | 90 | **negentig** nay•khuhn•tihkh |
| 12 | **twaalf** tvaalf | 100 | **honderd** hohn•duhrt |
| 13 | **dertien** dehr•teen | 101 | **honderdéén** hohn•duhrt•ayn |
| 14 | **veertien** fayr•teen | 200 | **tweehonderd** tvay•hohn•duhrt |
| 15 | **vijftien** fief•teen | 500 | **vijfhonderd** fief•hohn•duhrt |
| 16 | **zestien** zehs•teen | 1,000 | **duizend** daw•zuhnt |
| 17 | **zeventien** zay•fuhn•teen | 10,000 | **tienduizend** teen•daw•zuhnt |
| 18 | **achttien** ahkh•teen | 1,000,000 | **één miljoen** uhn mihl•yoon |

## Time

| | |
|---|---|
| What time is it? | **Hoe laat is het?** hoo laat ihs heht |
| From nine o'clock to 5 o'clock. | **Van negen tot vijf.** fahn nay•khuhn toht fief |
| 5:30 a.m./p.m. | **Half zes 's morgens/Half zes 's avonds.** hahlf zehs smohr•khuhns/hahlf zehs saa•fohnts |

## Days

| | |
|---|---|
| Monday | **maandag** maan•dahkh |
| Tuesday | **dinsdag** dihns•dahkh |
| Wednesday | **woensdag** voons•dahkh |
| Thursday | **donderdag** dohn•duhr•dahkh |
| Friday | **vrijdag** frie•dahkh |
| Saturday | **zaterdag** zaa•tuhr•dahkh |
| Sunday | **zondag** zohn•dahkh |

## Dates

| | |
|---|---|
| yesterday | **gisteren** khihs•tuh•ruhn |
| today | **vandaag** fahn•daakh |
| tomorrow | **morgen** mohr•khuhn |

## Months

| | | | |
|---|---|---|---|
| January | **januari** yah•new•aa•ree | July | **juli** yew•lee |
| February | **februari** fay•brew•aa•ree | August | **augustus** ow•khuhs•tuhs |
| March | **maart** maart | September | **september** sehp•tehm•buhr |
| April | **april** ah•prihl | October | **oktober** ohk•toa•buhr |
| May | **mei** mie | November | **november** noa•fehm•buhr |
| June | **juni** yew•nee | December | **december** day•sehm•buhr |

# French

## Pronunciation

In French, all syllables are pronounced the same, with no extra stress on any particular syllable. The French language contains nasal vowels, which are indicated in the pronunciation by a vowel symbol followed by an N. This N should not be pronounced strongly, but it is there to show the nasal quality of the previous vowel. A nasal vowel is pronounced simultaneously through the mouth and the nose.

In French, the final consonants of words are not always pronounced. When a word ending in a consonant is followed with a word beginning with a vowel, the two words are often run together. The consonant is therefore pronounced as if it begins the following word.

| Example | Pronunciation |
|---|---|
| **comment** | koh•mawN |
| **Comment allez-vous?** | koh•mawN tah•lay-voo |

### Consonants

| Letter | Approximate Pronunciation | Symbol | Example | Pronunciation |
|---|---|---|---|---|
| cc | 1. before e, i, like cc in accident | ks | **accessible** | ahk•seh•see•bluh |
| | 2. elsewhere, like cc in accommodate | k | **d'accord** | dah•kohr |
| ch | like sh in shut | sh | **chercher** | shehr•shay |
| ç | like s in sit | s | **ça** | sah |
| g | 1. before e, i, y, like s in pleasure | zh | **manger** | mawN•zhay |
| | 2. before a, o, u, like g in go | g | **garçon** | gahr•sohN |
| h | always silent | | **homme** | ohm |

| Letter | Approximate Pronunciation | Symbol | Example | Pronunciation |
|---|---|---|---|---|
| j | like s in pleasure | zh | **jamais** | zhah•may |
| qu | like k in kill | k | **qui** | kee |
| r | rolled in the back of the mouth, like gargling | r | **rouge** | roozh |
| w | usually like v in voice | v | **wagon** | vah•gohN |

B, c, d, f, k, l, m, n, p, s, t, v, x and z are pronounced as in English.

## Vowels

| Letter | Approximate Pronunciation | Symbol | Example | Pronunciation |
|---|---|---|---|---|
| a, à, â | between the a in hat and the a in father | ah | **mari** | mah•ree |
| e | sometimes like a in about | uh | **je** | zhuh |
| è, ê, e | like e in get | eh | **même** | mehm |
| é, ez | like a in late | ay | **été** | ay•tay |
| i | like ee in meet | ee | **il** | eel |
| o, ô | generally like o in roll | oh | **donner** | doh•nay |
| u | like ew in dew | ew | **une** | ewn |

### Sounds spelled with two or more letters

| Letter | Approximate Pronunciation | Symbol | Example | Pronunciation |
|---|---|---|---|---|
| ai, ay, aient, ais, ait, aî, ei | like a in late | ay | **j'ai**<br>**vais** | zhay<br>vay |

| Letter | Approximate Pronunciation | Symbol | Example | Pronunciation |
|---|---|---|---|---|
| ai, ay, aient, ais, ait, aî, ei | like e in get | eh | **chaîne** **peine** | shehn pehn |
| (e)au | similar to o | oh | **chaud** | shoh |
| eu, eû, œu | like u in fur but short like a puff of air | uh | **euro** | uh•roh |
| euil, euille | like uh + y | uhy | **feuille** | fuhy |
| ail, aille | like ie in tie | ie | **taille** | tie |
| ille | 1. like yu in yucca | eeyuh | **famille** | fah•meeyuh |
| | 2. like eel | eel | **ville** | veel |
| oi, oy | like w followed by the a in hat | wah | **moi** | mwah |
| ou, oû | like o in move or oo in hoot | oo | **nouveau** | noo•voh |
| ui | approximately like wee in between | wee | **traduire** | trah•dweer |

## *Basic Expressions*

| | |
|---|---|
| Hello. | **Bonjour.** bohN•zhoor |
| Goodbye. | **Au revoir.** oh ruh•vwahr |
| Yes. | **Oui.** wee |
| No. | **Non.** nohN |
| OK. | **D'accord.** dah•kohr |
| Excuse me! (to get attention) | **Excusez-moi!** ehk•skew•zay•mwah |

Excuse me. (to get past) — **Pardon.** pahr•dohN

I'm sorry. — **Je suis désolé♂/désolée♀.** zhuh swee day•zoh•lay

Please. — **S'il vous plaît.** seel voo play

Thank you. — **Merci.** mehr•see

You're welcome. — **De rien.** duh reeyehN

Where's the restroom [toilet]? — **Où sont les toilettes?** oo sohN lay twah•leht

# Arrival and Departure

I'm on *vacation [holiday]/business*. — **Je suis en *vacances/voyage d'affaires*.** zhuh swee zawN *vah•kawNs/vwah•yahzh dah•fehr*

I'm going to… — **Je vais *à/aux*…** zhuh vay *ah/oh*…

I'm staying at the…Hotel. — **Je reste à l'hôtel…** zhuh rehst ah loh•tehl…

## Passport Control and Customs

I'm just passing through. — **Je suis juste en transit.** zhuh swee zhews tawN trawN•zeet

I'd like to declare… — **Je voudrais déclarer…** zhuh voo•dray day•klah•ray…

I have nothing to declare. — **Je n'ai rien à déclarer.** zhuh nay reeyehN nah day•klah•ray

# Money and Banking

Where's…? — **Où est…?** oo ay…

– the ATM — **– le distributeur automatique de billets** luh dee•stree•bew•tuhr oh•toh•mah•teek duh bee•yay

– the bank — **– la banque** lah bawNk

– the currency exchange office — **– le bureau de change** luh bew•roh duh shawNzh

| | |
|---|---|
| When does the bank *open/close*? | **Quand est-ce que la banque *ouvre/ferme*?** kawN tehs kuh lah bawNk *oo•vruh/fehrm* |
| I'd like to change *dollars/pounds* into euros. | **Je voudrais échanger des *dollars/livres sterling* en euros.** zhuh voo•dray ay•shawN•zhay day *doh•lahr/lee•vruh stayr•leeng* awN nuh•roh |
| I'd like to cash traveler's checks [cheques]. | **Je voudrais encaisser des chèques de voyages.** zhuh voo•dray awN•kay•say day shehk duh vwah•yahzh |

## *Transportation*

| | |
|---|---|
| How do I get to town? | **Comment vais-je en ville?** koh•mawN vay•zhuh awN veel |
| Where's...? | **Où est...?** oo ay... |
| – the airport | **– l'aéroport** lah•ay•roh•pohr |
| – the train [railway] station | **– la gare** lah gahr |
| – the bus station | **– la gare routière** lah gahr roo•tee•yehr |
| – the subway [underground] station | **– le métro** luh may•troh |
| Is it far from here? | **C'est loin d'ici?** say lwehN dee•see |
| Where do I buy a ticket? | **Où puis-je acheter un billet?** oo pwee•zhuh ah•shtay uhN bee•yay |
| A *one-way/ round-trip* [return] ticket to... | **Un billet *aller simple/aller-retour*...** uhN bee•yay *ah•lay sehN•pluh/ah•lay•ruh•toor*... |
| How much? | **Combien ça coûte?** kohN•beeyehN sah koot |
| Which *gate/line*? | **Quelle *porte/ligne*?** kehl *pohrt/lee•nyuh* |
| Which platform? | **Quel quai?** kehl kay |
| Where can I get a taxi? | **Où puis-je prendre un taxi?** oo pwee•zhuh prawN•druh uhN tahk•see |
| Take me to this address. | **Conduisez-moi à cette adresse.** kohN•dwee•zay•mwah ah seh tah•drehs |
| Can I have a map? | **Puis-je avoir une carte?** pwee•zhuh ah•vwahr ewn kahrt |

## Asking Directions

| | |
|---|---|
| How far is it to...? | **À quelle distance se trouve...?** ah kehl dees•tawNs suh troov... |
| Where's...? | **Où est...?** oo ay... |
| – ...Street | **– la rue...** lah rew... |
| Can you show me on the map? | **Pouvez-vous me montrer sur la carte?** poo•vay•voo muh mohN•tray sewr lah kahrt |
| I'm lost. | **Je suis perdu♂/perdue♀.** zhuh swee pehr•dew |

### You May Hear...

| | |
|---|---|
| **tout droit** too drwah | straight ahead |
| **à gauche** ah gohsh | left |
| **à droite** ah drwaht | right |
| **au coin** oh kwehN | *around* the corner |
| **près de** pray duh | next to |
| **après** ah•pray | after |
| **nord/sud** nohr/sewd | north/south |
| **est/ouest** ehst/oowehst | east/west |

## *Accommodations*

| | |
|---|---|
| I made a reservation. | **J'ai fait une réservation.** zhay fay ewn ray•zehr•vah•seeyohN |
| My name is... | **Mon nom est...** mohN nohN may... |
| When's check-out? | **Quand dois-je quitter la chambre?** kawN dwah•zhuh kee•tay lah shawN•bruh |
| Can I leave this in the safe? | **Puis-je laisser ceci dans le coffre?** pwee•zhuh lay•say suh•see dawN luh koh•fruh |
| Can I leave my bags? | **Puis-je laisser mes bagages?** pwee•zhuh lay•say meh bah•gahzh |
| Can I have *my bill/ a receipt*? | **Puis-je avoir *ma facture/un reçu*?** pwee•zhuh ah•vwahr *mah fahk•tewr/uhN ruh•sew* |

## *Internet and Communications*

| | |
|---|---|
| Where's an internet cafe? | **Où y-a-t-il un cyber café?** oo yah•teel uhN see•behr kah•fay |
| Can I *access the internet/check my e-mail*? | **Puis-je *me connecter à Internet/ consulter mes mails*?** pwee•zhuh *muh koh•nehk•tay ah ehN•tehr•neht/kohN•sewl•tay may mehyl* |
| Can I have your phone number? | **Puis-je avoir votre numéro de téléphone?** pwee•zhuh ah•vwahr voh•truh new•meh•roh duh tay•lay•fohn |
| Here's my *number/e-mail.* | **Voici mon *numéro/mail.*** vwah•see mohN *new•meh•roh/mehyl* |
| Call me. | **Appelle-moi.** ah•pehl•mwah |
| E-mail me. | **Envoie-moi un mail.** awN•vwah•mwah uhN mehyl |
| Hello. This is… | **Bonjour. C'est…** bohN•zhoor say… |
| Can I speak to…? | **Puis-je parler à…?** pwee•zhuh pahr•lay ah… |
| Can you repeat that? | **Pouvez-vous répéter cela?** poo•vay•voo ray•pay•tay suh•lah |
| I'll call back later. | **Je rappellerai plus tard.** zhuh rah•peh•luh•ray plew tahr |

| | |
|---|---|
| Bye. | **Au revoir.** oh ruh•vwahr |
| Where's the post office? | **Où est la poste?** oo ay lah pohst |

# Eating Out

| | |
|---|---|
| Can you recommend a good *restaurant/ bar*? | **Pouvez-vous me conseiller un bon *restaurant/bar*?** poo•vay-voo muh kohN•say•yay uhN bohN *reh•stoh•rawN/bahr* |
| Is there a *traditional French/inexpensive* restaurant nearby? | **Y-a-t-il un restaurant *traditionnel français/ bon marché* près d'ici?** yah•teel uhN reh•stoh•rawN *trah•dee•seeyohN•nehl frawN•say/bohN mahr•shay* pray dee•see |
| A table for…, please. | **Une table pour…, s'il vous plaît.** ewn tah•bluh poor…seel voo play |
| The menu, please. | **La carte, s'il vous plaît.** lah kahrt seel voo play |
| What do you recommend? | **Que recommandez-vous?** kuh reh•koh•mawN•day-voo |
| I'd like… | **Je voudrais…** zhuh voo•dray… |
| Some more…, please. | **Un peu plus de…, s'il vous plaît.** uhN puh plew duh…seel voo play |
| Enjoy your meal! | **Bon appétit!** bohN nah•peh•tee |
| The check [bill], please. | **L'addition, s'il vous plaît.** lah•dee•seeyohN seel voo play |
| Is service included? | **Est-ce que le service est compris?** ehs kuh luh sehr•vees ay kohN•pree |
| Can I *pay by credit card/have a receipt*? | **Puis-je *payer par carte de crédit/avoir un reçu*?** pwee•zhuh *pay•yay pahr kahrt duh kray•dee/ah•vwahr uhN ruh•sew* |

## Breakfast

| | |
|---|---|
| **le beurre** luh buhr | butter |
| **les céréales *chaudes/froides*** lay say•ray•ahl *shohd/frwahd* | *cold/hot* cereal |

| | |
|---|---|
| **le croissant** luh krwah•sawN | croissant |
| **la confiture** lah kohN•fee•tewr | jam/jelly |
| **le yaourt** luh yah•oort | yogurt |
| **l'œuf** luhf | egg |
| **le pain** luh pehN | bread |

## Appetizers [Starters]

| | |
|---|---|
| **la bouchée à la reine** lah boo•shay ah lah rehn | pastry shell filled with creamed sweetbreads and mushrooms |
| **les crudités variées** lay krew•dee•tay vah•reeyay | assorted vegetables in a vinaigrette dressing |
| **le pâté de foie** luh pah•tay duh fwah | liver pâté |
| **la quiche lorraine** lah keesh loh•rayn | open-faced egg and cheese tart filled with bacon |

## Soup

| | |
|---|---|
| **la bisque** lah beesk | seafood stew |
| **la bouillabaisse** lah boo•yah•behs | seafood soup, a specialty of Marseilles |
| **la soupe aux légumes** lah soop oh lay•gewm | vegetable soup |
| **la soupe à l'oignon** lah soop ah loh•nyohN | French onion soup |
| **le velouté** luh vuh•loo•tay | cream soup |

## Fish and Seafood

| | |
|---|---|
| **les coquilles Saint-Jacques** lay koh•keeyuh sehN•zhahk | breaded scallops sautéed in lemon juice and herbs (usually served as a scallop and mushroom casserole in a scallop shell) |
| **les moules marinières** lay mool mah•ree•neeyehr | mussels in white wine sauce |

| | |
|---|---|
| **le plateau de fruits de mer** luh plah•toh duh frwee duh mehr | assorted seafood platter |
| **le saumon à l'oseille** luh soh•mohN ah loh•zehy | salmon with sorrel sauce |
| **la truite meunière** lah trweet muh•neeyehr | seasoned, breaded trout, pan-fried in butter |

## Meat and Poultry

| | |
|---|---|
| **l'agneau** lah•nyoh | lamb |
| **le bœuf** luh buhf | beef |
| **le canard** luh kah•nahr | duck |
| **le cassoulet toulousain** luh kah•soo•lay too•loo•zehN | casserole of white beans, mutton or salt pork, sausage and preserved goose |
| **le coq au vin** luh koh koh vehN | chicken in red wine sauce |
| **le porc** luh pohr | pork |
| **le poulet** luh poo•lay | chicken |
| **le tournedos** luh toor•nuh•doh | small filet of beef |
| **le veau** luh voh | veal |

| | |
|---|---|
| rare | **saignant** say•nyawN |
| medium | **à point** ah pwehN |
| well-done | **bien cuit** beeyehN kwee |

## Vegetables and Staples

| | |
|---|---|
| **les asperges** lay zah•spehrzh | asparagus |
| **le chou-fleur au gratin** luh shoo•fluhr oh grah•tehN | baked cauliflower, covered in cheese |
| **les haricots verts** lay ah•ree•koh vehr | green beans |
| **le maïs** luh mah•ees | corn |
| **les pâtes** lay paht | pasta |

| | |
|---|---|
| **le riz** luh ree | rice |
| **la tomate** lah toh•maht | tomato |

## Fruit

| | |
|---|---|
| **l'abricot** lah•bree•koh | apricot |
| **la banane** lah bah•nahn | banana |
| **le citron** luh see•trohN | lemon |
| **la fraise** lah frehz | strawberry |
| **l'orange** loh•rawNzh | orange |
| **la pêche** lah pehsh | peach |
| **la poire** lah pwahr | pear |
| **la pomme** lah pohm | apple |
| **le raisin** luh reh•zehN | grape |

## Cheese

| | |
|---|---|
| **le brie** luh bree | soft cheese, ranging in strength and flavors |
| **le camembert** luh kah•mawN•behr | soft, raw cow's milk cheese |
| **le fromage de chèvre** luh froh•mahzh duh sheh•vruh | goat's milk cheese |

## Dessert

| | |
|---|---|
| **la crêpe au sucre** lah krehp oh sew•kruh | thin pancake with sugar |
| **la mousse au chocolat** lah moos oh shoh•koh•lah | chocolate mousse |
| **la poire belle-hélène** lah pwahr behl•ehl•ehn | poached pears with ice cream and chocolate sauce |
| **la tarte aux fruits** lah tahrt oh frwee | fruit pie or tart |
| **la tarte tatin** lah tahrt tah•tehN | upside down baked apple tart |

# *Drinks*

| | |
|---|---|
| The *wine list/drink menu*, please. | **La carte des *vins/boissons*, s'il vous plaît.** lah kahrt day *vehN/bwah•sohN* seel voo play |
| I'd like a *bottle/glass of red/white* wine. | **Je voudrais *une bouteille/un verre* de vin *rouge/blanc*.** zhuh voo•dray *ewn boo•tehy/uhN vehr* duh vehN *roozh/blawN* |
| Another *bottle/glass*, please. | ***Une autre bouteille/Un autre verre*, s'il vous plaît.** *ewn oh•truh boo•tehy/uhN noh•truh vehr* seel voo play |
| I'd like a local beer. | **Je voudrais une bière locale.** zhuh voo•dray ewn beeyehr loh•kahl |
| Cheers! | **Santé!** sawN•tay |
| A *coffee/tea*, please. | **Un *café/thé*, s'il vous plaît.** uhN *kah•fay/tay* seel voo play |
| Black. | **Noir.** nwahr |
| With… | **Avec…** ah•vehk… |
| – milk | **– du lait** dew lay |
| – sugar | **– du sucre** dew sew•kruh |
| – artificial sweetener | **– de l'édulcorant** duh lay•dewl•koh•rawN |

| | |
|---|---|
| A…, please. | **Un…, s'il vous plaît.** uhN…seel voo play |
| – juice | **– jus de fruit** zhew duh frwee |
| – soda | **– soda** soh•dah |
| – (sparkling/still) water | **– de l'eau (gazeuse/plate)** duh loh (gah•zuhz/plaht) |

## Apéritifs, Cocktails and Liqueurs

| | |
|---|---|
| **le cognac** luh koh•nyahk | brandy |
| **le rhum** luh ruhm | rum |
| **le whisky** luh wees•kee | whisky |

# *Talking*

| | |
|---|---|
| Hello!/Hi! | **Bonjour!/Salut!** bohN•zhoor/sah•lew |
| Good afternoon. | **Bon après-midi.** bohN nah•pray•mee•dee |
| Good evening. | **Bonsoir.** bohN•swahr |
| How are you? | **Comment allez-vous?** koh•mawN tah•lay•voo |
| Fine, thanks. | **Bien, merci.** beeyehN mehr•see |
| Excuse me! | **Excusez-moi!** ehk•skew•zay•mwah |
| What's your name? | **Comment vous appelez-vous?** koh•mawN voo zah•puh•lay•voo |
| My name is… | **Je m'appelle…** zhuh mah•pehl… |
| Nice to meet you. | **Enchanté♂/Enchantée♀.** awN•shawN•tay |
| Where are you from? | **D'où êtes-vous?** doo eht•voo |
| I'm from the *U.K./U.S.* | **Je viens *du Royaume-Uni/des États-Unis.*** zhuh veeyehN *dew rwah•yohm•ew•nee/day zay•tah•zew•nee* |
| Goodbye. | **Au revoir.** oh ruh•vwahr |
| See you later. | **À bientôt.** ah beeyehN•toh |

When addressing someone, it is polite to include a title: **monsieur** for a man or **madame** for a woman, even if you suspect she is not married. **Mademoiselle** is used only when addressing young girls.

## Communication Difficulties

| | |
|---|---|
| Do you speak English? | **Parlez-vous anglais?** pahr•lay•voo zawN•glay |
| I don't speak (much) French. | **Je ne parle pas (bien le) français.** zhuh nuh pahrl pah (beeyehN luh) frawN•say |
| Can you speak more slowly? | **Pouvez-vous parler plus lentement?** poo•vay•voo pahr•lay plew lawN•tuh•mawN |
| I don't understand. | **Je ne comprends pas.** zhuh nuh kohN•prawN pah |

# *Sightseeing*

| | |
|---|---|
| Where's the tourist information office? | **Où est l'office de tourisme?** oo ay loh•fees duh too•ree•smuh |
| Do you offer tours in English? | **Proposez-vous des visites en anglais?** Proh•poh•zay•voo day vee•zeet awN nawN•glay |
| Can I have a *map/guide*? | **Puis-je avoir *une carte/un guide*?** pwee•zhuh ah•vwahr *ewn kahrt/uhN geed* |

## Sights

| | |
|---|---|
| Where's...? | **Où est...?** oo ay... |
| – the cathedral | **– la cathédrale** lah kah•tay•drahl |
| – the castle | **– le château** luh shah•toh |
| – the downtown area | **– le centre-ville** luh sawN•truh•veel |
| – the museum | **– le musée** luh mew•zay |
| – the shopping area | **– le quartier commercial** luh kahr•teeyay koh•mehr•seeyahl |

## Shopping

| | |
|---|---|
| Where's the *market/ mall [shopping centre]*? | **Où est le *marché/centre commercial*?** oo ay luh *mahr•shay/sawN•truh koh•mehr•seeyahl* |
| I'm just looking. | **Je regarde seulement.** zhuh ruh•gahrd suhl•mawN |
| Can you help me? | **Pouvez-vous m'aider?** poo•vay•voo meh•day |
| I'm being helped. | **On s'occupe de moi.** ohN soh•kewp duh mwah |
| How much? | **Combien ça coûte?** kohN•beeyehN sah koot |
| That one, please. | **Celui-ci♂/Celle-ci♀, s'il vous plaît.** suh•lwee•see♂/sehl see♀ seel voo play |
| That's all. | **C'est tout.** say too |
| Where can I pay? | **Où puis-je payer?** oo pwee•zhuh pay•yay |
| I'll pay *in cash/by credit card.* | **Je paierai *en espèces/par carte de crédit.*** zhuh pay•ray *awN neh•spehs/pahr kahrt duh kray•dee* |
| A receipt, please. | **Un reçu, s'il vous plaît.** uhN ruh•sew seel voo play |

### Stores

| | |
|---|---|
| Where's...? | **Où est...** oo ay... |
| – the bakery | **– la boulangerie** lah boo•lawN•zhuh•ree |
| – the bookstore | **– la librairie** lah lee•breh•ree |
| – the department store | **– le grand magasin** luh grawN mah•gah•zehN |

– the pastry shop – **la pâtisserie** lah pah•tee•suh•ree

– the pharmacy [chemist] – **la pharmacie** lah fahr•mah•see

– the supermarket – **le supermarché** luh sew•pehr•mahr•shay

## Clothing

I'd like… **Je voudrais…** zhuh voo•dray…

Can I try this on? **Puis-je essayer ceci?** pwee•zhuh eh•say•yay suh•see

It doesn't fit. **Ça ne va pas.** sah nuh vah pah

Do you have this in a *bigger/smaller* size? **Avez-vous ceci en plus *grand/petit*?** ah•vay•voo suh•see awN plew *grawN/puh•tee*

### Color

I'd like something… **Je voudrais quelque chose de…** zhuh voo•dray kehl•kuh shohz duh…

– black – **noir** nwahr

– blue – **bleu** bluh

– brown – **marron** mah•rohN

– green – **vert** vehr

– orange – **orange** oh•rawNzh

– red – **rouge** roozh

– white – **blanc** blawN

– yellow – **jaune** zhohn

# *Sports and Leisure*

Where's…? **Où est…?** oo ay…

– the beach – **la plage** lah plazh

– the park – **le parc** luh pahrk

– the pool – **la piscine** lah pee•seen

Can I rent [hire] clubs? **Puis-je louer des clubs?** pwee•zhuh looway day kluhb

## Culture and Nightlife

| | |
|---|---|
| Do you have a program of events? | **Avez-vous un programme des festivités?** ah•vay•voo uhN proh•grahm day fehs•tee•vee•tay |
| Where's...? | **Où est...?** oo ay... |
| – the downtown area | **– le centre-ville** luh sawN•truh veel |
| – the bar | **– le bar** luh bahr |
| – the dance club | **– la discothèque** lah dees•koh•tehk |

## Business Travel

| | |
|---|---|
| I'm here on business. | **Je suis ici pour affaires.** zhuh swee zee•see poo rah•fehr |
| Here's my card. | **Voici ma carte.** vwah•see mah kahrt |
| Can I have your card? | **Puis-je avoir votre carte?** pwee•zhuh ah•vwahr voh•truh kahrt |
| I have a meeting with... | **J'ai une réunion avec...** zhay ewn ray•ew•neeyohN ah•vehk... |
| Where's...? | **Où est...?** oo ay... |
| – the business center | **– le centre d'affaires** luh sawN•truh dah•fehr |
| – the convention hall | **– le palais des congrès** luh pah•lay day kohN•greh |
| – the meeting room | **– la salle de réunion** lah sahl duh ray•ew•neeyohN |

## Travel with Children

| | |
|---|---|
| Is there a discount for kids? | **Y-a-t-il une remise pour les enfants?** yah•teel ewn ruh•meez poor lay zawN•fawN |
| Can you recommend a babysitter? | **Pouvez-vous me recommander une baby-sitter?** poo•vay•voo muh ruh•koh•mawN•day ewn bah•bee•see•tuhr |
| Do you have *a child's seat/highchair*? | **Avez-vous *un siège enfant/une chaise haute*?** ah•vay•voo *zuhN seeyehzh awN•fawN/ zewn shehz oht* |
| Where can I change the baby? | **Où puis-je changer le bébé?** oo pwee•zhuh shawN•zhay luh bay•bay |

## For the Disabled

| | |
|---|---|
| Is there...? | **Y-a-t-il...?** yah•teel... |
| – access for the disabled | **– un accès pour handicapés** uhN nahk•seh poor awN•dee•kah•pay |
| – a wheelchair ramp | **– un accès pour chaises roulantes** uhN nahk•say poor shehz roo•lawNt |
| – a handicapped- [disabled-] accessible toilet | **– des toilettes accessibles aux handicapés** day twah•leht ahk•seh•see•bluh oh zawN•dee•kah•pay |
| I need... | **J'ai besoin...** zhay buh•zwehN... |
| – assistance | **– d'aide** dehd |
| – an elevator [a lift] | **– d'un ascenseur** duhN nah•sawN•suhr |

## Emergencies

| | |
|---|---|
| Help! | **Au secours!** oh suh•koor |
| Go away! | **Allez-vous en!** ah•lay•voo zawN |
| Stop, thief! | **Arrêtez, au voleur!** ah•reh•tay oh voh•luhr |
| Get a doctor! | **Allez chercher un docteur!** ah•lay shehr•shay uhN dohk•tuhr |
| Fire! | **Au feu!** oh fuh |
| I'm lost. | **Je suis perdu♂/perdue♀.** zhuh swee pehr•dew |
| Can you help me? | **Pouvez-vous m'aider?** poo•vay•voo may•day |
| Call the police! | **Appelez la police!** ah•puh•lay lah poh•lees |

## Health

| | |
|---|---|
| I'm sick [ill]. | **Je suis malade.** zhuh swee mah•lahd |
| I need an English-speaking doctor. | **J'ai besoin d'un docteur qui parle anglais.** zhay buh•zwehN duhN dohk•tuhr kee pahrl awN•glay |
| It hurts here. | **Ça fait mal ici.** sah fay mahl ee•see |

# Reference

## Numbers

0 **zéro** zay•roh
1 **un** uhN
2 **deux** duh
3 **trois** trwah
4 **quatre** kah•truh
5 **cinq** sehNk
6 **six** sees
7 **sept** seht
8 **huit** weet
9 **neuf** nuhf
10 **dix** dees
11 **onze** ohNz
12 **douze** dooz
13 **treize** trehz
14 **quatorze** kah•tohrz
15 **quinze** kehNz
16 **seize** sehz
17 **dix-sept** dee•seht
18 **dix-huit** deez•weet
19 **dix-neuf** deez•nuhf
20 **vingt** vehN
21 **vingt et un** vehN•tay•uhN
22 **vingt-deux** vehN•duh
30 **trente** trawNt
31 **trente et un** trawN•tay•uhN
40 **quarante** kah•rawNt
50 **cinquante** sehN•kawNt
60 **soixante** swah•zawNt
70 **soixante-dix** swah•zawNt•dees
80 **quatre-vingts** kah•truh•vehN
90 **quatre-vingt-dix** kah•truh•vehN•dees
100 **cent** sawN
101 **cent-un** sawN•uhN
200 **deux cents** duh•sawN
500 **cinq cents** sehNk•sawN
1,000 **mille** meel
10,000 **dix mille** dee meel
1,000,000 **un million** uhN meel•yohN

## Time

What time is it? **Quelle heure est-il?** kehl uhr ay•teel

From one o'clock to two o'clock. **D'une heure à deux heures.** dewn nuhr ah duh zuhr

| | |
|---|---|
| 5:30 *a.m./p.m.* | **Cinq heures et demi *du matin/de l'après-midi.*** sehN kuhr eh duh•mee *dew mah•tehN/ duh lah•preh•mee•dee* |

## Days

| | |
|---|---|
| Monday | **lundi** luhN•dee |
| Tuesday | **mardi** mahr•dee |
| Wednesday | **mercredi** mehr•kruh•dee |
| Thursday | **jeudi** zhuh•dee |
| Friday | **vendredi** vawN•druh•dee |
| Saturday | **samedi** sahm•dee |
| Sunday | **dimanche** dee•mawNsh |

## Dates

| | |
|---|---|
| yesterday | **hier** eeyehr |
| today | **aujourd'hui** oh•zhoor•dwee |
| tomorrow | **demain** duh•mehN |

## Months

| | |
|---|---|
| January | **janvier** zhawN•veeyay |
| February | **février** fay•vreeyay |
| March | **mars** mahrs |
| April | **avril** ah•vreel |
| May | **mai** may |
| June | **juin** zhwehN |
| July | **juillet** zhwee•yay |
| August | **août** oot |
| September | **septembre** sehp•tawN•bruh |
| October | **octobre** ohk•toh•bruh |
| November | **novembre** noh•vawN•bruh |
| December | **décembre** day•sawN•bruh |

# German
## Pronunciation

The German alphabet is the same as English, with the addition of the letter **ß**. Some vowels appear with an **Umlaut**: **ä**, **ü** and **ö**. Of note, German recently underwent a spelling reform. The letter **ß** is now shown as **ss** after a short vowel, but is unchanged after a long vowel or diphthong. In print and dated material, you may still see the **ß**; e.g., formerly **Kuß**, now **Kuss**.

Stress has been indicated in the phonetic transcription: the underlined letters should be pronounced with more stress than others, e.g., **Adresse, ah-drehs-uh**.

### Consonants

| Letter | Approximate Pronunciation | Symbol | Example | Pronunciation |
|---|---|---|---|---|
| b | 1. at the end of a word or between a vowel and a consonant, like p in up | p | **ab** | ahp |
| | 2. elsewhere, as in English | b | **bis** | bihs |
| c | 1. before e, i, ä and ö, like ts in hits | ts | **Celsius** | tsehl·see·oos |
| | 2. elsewhere, like c in cat | k | **Café** | kah·feh |
| ch | 1. like k in kit | k | **Wachs** | vahks |
| | 2. after vowels, like ch in Scottish loch | kh | **doch** | dohkh |
| d | 1. at the end of the word or before a consonant, like t in eat | t | **Rad** | raht |
| | 2. elsewhere, like d in do | d | **danke** | dahn·kuh |

| Letter | Approximate Pronunciation | Symbol | Example | Pronunciation |
|---|---|---|---|---|
| g | 1. at the end of a word, sounds like k | k | **fertig** | fehr•teek |
| | 2. like g in go | g | **gehen** | geh•uhn |
| j | like y in yes | y | **ja** | yah |
| qu | like k + v | kv | **Quark** | kvahrk |
| r | pronounced in the back of the mouth | r | **warum** | vah•room |
| s | 1. before or between vowels, like z in zoo | z | **sie** | zee |
| | 2. before p and t, like sh in shut | sh | **Sport** | shpohrt |
| | 3. elsewhere, like s in sit | s | **es ist** | ehs ihst |
| ß | like s in sit | s | **groß** | grohs |
| sch | like sh in shut | sh | **schnell** | shnehl |
| tsch | like ch in chip | ch | **deutsch** | doych |
| tz | like ts in hits | ts | **Platz** | plahts |
| v | 1. like f in for | f | **vier** | feer |
| | 2. in foreign words, like v in voice | v | **Vase** | vah•seh |
| w | like v in voice | v | **wie** | vee |
| z | like ts in hits | ts | **zeigen** | tsie•gehn |

Letters f, h, k, l, m, n, p, t and x are pronounced as in English.

## Vowels

| Letter | Approximate Pronunciation | Symbol | Example | Pronunciation |
|---|---|---|---|---|
| a | like a in father | ah | **Tag** | tahk |
| ä | 1. like e in let | eh | **Lärm** | lehrm |

| | | | | |
|---|---|---|---|---|
| | 2. like a in late | ay | **spät** | shpayt |
| e | 1. like e in let | eh | **schnell** | shnehl |
| | 2. at the end of a word, if the syllable is not stressed, like u in us | uh | **bitte** | biht·tuh |
| i | 1. like i in hit, before a doubled consonant | ih | **billig** | bih·leek |
| | 2. otherwise, like ee in meet | ee | **ihm** | eem |
| o | like o in home | oh | **voll** | fohl |
| ö | like er in fern | er | **schön** | shern |
| u | like oo in boot | oo | **Nuss** | noos |
| ü | like ew in new | ew | **über** | ew·behr |
| y | like ew in new | ew | **typisch** | tew·peesh |

### Combined Vowels

| | | | | |
|---|---|---|---|---|
| ai, ay, ei, ey | like ie in tie | ie | **nein** | nien |
| ao, au | like ow in now | ow | **auf** | owf |
| äu, eu, oy | like oy in boy | oy | **neu** | noy |

## Basic Expressions

| | |
|---|---|
| Hello. | **Hallo.** hah·loh |
| Goodbye. | **Auf Wiedersehen.** owf vee·dehr·zehn |
| Yes. | **Ja.** yah |
| No. | **Nein.** nien |
| OK. | **Okay.** oh·keh |
| Excuse me! (to get attention, to get past) | **Entschuldigung!** ehnt·shool·dee·goong |

| | |
|---|---|
| Please. | **Bitte.** biht•tuh |
| Thank you. | **Danke.** dahn•kuh |
| You're welcome. | **Gern geschehen.** gehrn guh•sheh•uhn |
| Where's the restroom [toilet]? | **Wo ist die Toilette?** voh ihst dee toy•leh•tuh |

## *Arrival and Departure*

| | |
|---|---|
| I'm on vacation [holiday]. | **Ich mache Urlaub.** eekh mahkh•uh oor•lowb |
| I'm on business. | **Ich bin auf Geschäftsreise.** eekh bihn owf guh•shehfts•rie•zuh |
| I'm going to... | **Ich reise nach ...** eekh rie•zuh nahkh... |
| I'm staying at the...Hotel. | **Ich übernachte im Hotel ...** eekh ew•buhr•nahkh•tuh ihm hoh•tehl... |

### Passport Control and Customs

| | |
|---|---|
| I'm just passing through. | **Ich bin auf der Durchreise.** eekh been owf dehr doorkh•rie•zuh |
| I'd like to declare... | **Ich möchte ... verzollen.** eekh merkh•tuh... fehr•tsoh•luhn |
| I have nothing to declare. | **Ich habe nichts zu verzollen.** eekh hah•buh neekhts tsoo fehr•tsoh•luhn |

# Money and Banking

| | |
|---|---|
| Where's…? | **Wo ist … ?** voh ihst… |
| – the ATM | **– der Bankautomat** dehr bahnk•ow•toh•maht |
| – the bank | **– die Bank** dee bahnk |
| – the currency exchange | **– die Wechselstube** dee vehkh•zuhl•shtoo•buh |
| When does the bank *open/close*? | **Wann *öffnet/schließt* die Bank?** vahn *erf•nuht/shleest* dee bahnk |
| I'd like to change *dollars/pounds* into euros. | **Ich möchte *Dollar/Pfund* in Euro wechseln.** eekh mehrkh•tuh *doh•lahr/pfoont* ihn oy•roh vehkh•zuhln |
| I'd like to cash traveler's checks [cheques]. | **Ich möchte Reiseschecks einlösen.** eekh mehrkh•tuh rie•zuh•shehks ien•ler•zuhn |

# Transportation

| | |
|---|---|
| How do I get to town? | **Wie komme ich in die Stadt?** vee koh•muh eekh ihn dee shtaht |
| Where's…? | **Wo ist … ?** voh ihst… |
| – the airport | **– der Flughafen** dehr flook•hah•fuhn |
| – the train [railway] station | **– der Bahnhof** dehr bahn•hohf |
| – the bus station | **– die Bushaltestelle** dee boos•hahl•tuh•shteh•luh |
| – the subway [underground] station | **– die U-Bahn-Haltestelle** dee oo•bahn•hahl•tuh•shteh•luh |
| How far is it? | **Wie weit ist es?** vee viet ihst ehs |
| Where do I buy a ticket? | **Wo kann ich eine Fahrkarte kaufen?** voh kahn eekh ie•nuh fahr•kahr•tuh kow•fuhn |
| A *one-way/round-trip [return]* ticket to… | ***Ein Einzelticket/Eine Fahrkarte für Hin-und Rückfahrt* nach …** *ien ien•tsehl•tee•kuht/ie•nuh fahr•kahr•tuh fewr hihn oond rewk•fahrt* nahkh… |

| | |
|---|---|
| How much? | **Wie viel kostet es?** vee feel kohs•tuht ehs |
| Which gate? | **Welches Gate?** vehl•khehs geht |
| Which line? | **Welche Linie?** vehl•khuh leen•yuh |
| Which platform? | **Welcher Bahnsteig?** vehl•khehr bahn•shtieg |
| Where can I get a taxi? | **Wo finde ich ein Taxi?** voh fihn•duh eekh ien tahk•see |
| Take me to this address, please. | **Bitte fahren Sie mich zu dieser Adresse.** biht•tuh fah•ruhn zee meekh tsoo dee•zehr ah•dreh•suh |
| Can I have a map, please? | **Können Sie mir bitte einen Stadtplan geben?** ker•nuhn zee mihr biht•tuh ien•uhn shtaht•plahn geh•behn |

## Asking Directions

| | |
|---|---|
| How far is it to…? | **Wie weit ist es bis … ?** vee viet ihst ehs bihs… |
| Where's…? | **Wo ist … ?** voh ihst… |
| – …Street | **– die … Straße** dee… shtrahs•suh |
| – this address | **– diese Adresse** deez•uh ah•drehs•uh |
| Can you show me on the map? | **Können Sie mir das auf der Karte zeigen?** kern•nuhn zee meer dahs owf dehr kahrt•uh tsieg•uhn |
| I'm lost. | **Ich habe mich verfahren.** eekh hahb•uh meekh fehr•fahr•uhn |

### You May Hear…

| | |
|---|---|
| **geradeaus** geh•rahd•uh•ows | straight ahead |
| **links** leenks | left |
| **rechts** rehkhts | right |
| ***an der/um die* Ecke** *ahn dehr/oom dee* eh•kuh | *on/around* the corner |
| **neben** nehb•uhn | next to |

| | |
|---|---|
| **nach** nahkh | after |
| **nördlich/südlich** nerd·leekh/zewd·leekh | north/south |
| **östlich/westlich** erst·leekh/vehst·leekh | east/west |

## Accommodations

| | |
|---|---|
| I have a reservation. | **Ich habe eine Reservierung.** eekh hahb·uh ien·uh rehz·ehr·veer·oong |
| My name is... | **Mein Name ist ...** mien nahm·uh ihst... |
| When's check-out? | **Wann ist der Check-out?** vahn ihst dehr tshehk·owt |
| Can I leave this in the safe? | **Kann ich das im Safe lassen?** kahn eekh dahs ihm sehf lahs·suhn |
| Can I leave my bags? | **Kann ich meine Taschen hierlassen?** kahn eekh mien·uh tahsh·uhn heer·lahs·suhn |
| Can I have *my bill/a receipt*? | **Kann ich *meine Rechnung/eine Quittung* haben?** kahn eekh *mien·uh rehkh·noong/ien·uh kveet·oong* hah·buhn |

## Internet and Communications

| | |
|---|---|
| Where's an internet cafe? | **Wo gibt es ein Internetcafé?** voh gihpt ehs ien ihnt·ehr·neht·kah·feh |
| Can I *access the internet/check e-mail*? | **Kann ich *das Internet benutzen/meine E-Mails lesen*?** kahn eekh *dahs ihnt·ehr·neht beh·noot·suhn/mien·uh ee·mehls lehz·uhn* |
| Can I have your phone number? | **Kann ich Ihre Telefonnummer haben?** kahn eekh eehr·uh tehl·uh·fohn·noom·ehr hah·buhn |
| Here's my *number/e-mail.* | **Hier ist meine *Telefonnummer/E-Mail.*** heer ihst mien·uh *tehl·uh·fohn·noom·ehr/ee·mehl* |
| Call me. | **Rufen Sie mich an.** roo·fuhn zee meekh ahn |
| E-mail me. | **Mailen Sie mir.** mehl·uhn zee meer |

| | |
|---|---|
| Hello. This is… | **Hallo. Hier ist …** hah·loh heer ihst… |
| Can I speak to…? | **Kann ich mit … sprechen?** kahn eekh miht… shprehkh·uhn |
| Could you repeat that, please? | **Könnten Sie das bitte wiederholen?** kern·tuhn zee dahs biht·tuh veed·ehr·hohl·uhn |
| I'll call back later. | **Ich rufe später zurück.** eekh roof·uh shpeht·ehr tsoo·rewkh |
| Bye. | **Auf Wiederhören.** owf veed·ehr·her·ruhn |
| Where's the post office? | **Wo ist die Post?** voh ihst dee pohst |

## Eating Out

| | |
|---|---|
| Can you recommend a good *restaurant/ bar*? | **Können Sie *ein gutes Restaurant/eine gute Bar* empfehlen?** ker·nuhn zee *ien goo·tuhs reh·stow·rahnt/ien·uh goo·tuh bahr* ehm·pfeh·luhn |
| Is there a *traditional German/inexpensive* restaurant nearby? | **Gibt es in der Nähe ein *typisch deutsches/preisgünstiges* Restaurant?** gihpt ehs ihn dehr neh·uh ien *tew·peesh doy·chuhs/pries·gewn·stee·guhs* reh·stow·rahnt |
| A table for…, please. | **Bitte einen Tisch für …** biht·tuh ien·uhn tihsh fewr… |
| A menu, please. | **Die Speisekarte, bitte.** dee shpie·zuh·kahr·tuh biht·tuh |
| What do you recommend? | **Was empfehlen Sie?** vahs ehm·pfeh·luhn zee |
| I'd like… | **Ich möchte …** eekh merkh·tuh… |
| Some more…, please. | **Etwas mehr … , bitte.** eht·vahs mehr… biht·tuh |
| Enjoy your meal! | **Guten Appetit!** goo·tuhn ah·puh·teet |
| The check [bill], please. | **Die Rechnung, bitte.** dee rehkh·noonk biht·tuh |
| Is service included? | **Ist die Bedienung im Preis enthalten?** ihst dee buh·dee·nung ihm pries ehnt·hahl·tuhn |

| | |
|---|---|
| Can I pay *by credit card/have a receipt*? | **Kann ich *mit Kreditkarte bezahlen/eine Quittung haben*?** kahn eekh *miht kreh·deet·kahr·tuh beht·sahl·uhn/ien·uh kvee·toonk hah·buhn* |

## Breakfast

| | |
|---|---|
| **der Aufschnitt** dehr owf·shniht | cold cuts [charcuterie] |
| **das Brot** dahs broht | bread |
| **die Butter** dee boo·tehr | butter |
| **das Ei** dahs ie | egg |
| **der Käse** dehr kay·zuh | cheese |
| **das Müsli** dahs mew·slee | granola [muesli] |

## Appetizers [Starters]

| | |
|---|---|
| **die Aufschnittplatte** dee owf·shniht·plah·tuh | cold cuts served with bread |
| **der gemischte Salat** dehr geh·meesh·tuh sah·laht | mixed salad |
| **die Käseplatte** dee kay·zuh·plah·tuh | cheese platter |
| **der Krabbencocktail** dehr krahb·behn·kohk·tayl | shrimp cocktail |
| **der Wurstsalat** dehr voorst·sah·laht | cold cuts with onion and oil |

## Soup

| | |
|---|---|
| **die Champignoncremesuppe** dee shahm·pee·nyohn·krehm·zoo·puh | cream of mushroom soup |
| **die Erbsensuppe** dee ehrb·zuhn·zoo·puh | pea soup |
| **die Gemüsesuppe** dee guh·mew· zuh·zoo·puh | vegetable soup |
| **die Gulaschsuppe** dee gool·ahsh·zoo·puh | stewed beef in a spicy soup |
| **die Hühnersuppe** dee hewn·ehr·zoo·puh | chicken soup |

## Fish and Seafood

| | |
|---|---|
| **die Forelle** dee foh•reh•luh | trout |
| **der Hering** dehr heh•rihng | herring |
| **der Lachs** dehr lahks | salmon |
| **die Muschel** dee moo•shuhl | clam |
| **die Scholle** dee shoh•luh | flounder |

## Meat and Poultry

| | |
|---|---|
| **die Ente** dee ehn•tuh | duck |
| **die Frikadelle** dee free•kah•dehl•luh | fried meatballs |
| **das Hühnchen** dahs hewn•khuhn | chicken |
| **das Kalbfleisch** dahs kahlb•fliesh | veal |
| **das Lamm** dahs lahm | lamb |
| **das Rindfleisch** dahs rihnt•fliesh | beef |
| **die Rouladen** dee roo•lah•dehn | stuffed beef slices, rolled and braised in brown gravy |
| **das Schweinefleisch** dahs shvien•uh•fliesh | pork |
| **das Wiener Schnitzel** dahs vee•nehr shniht•tzehl | veal cutlet |

| | |
|---|---|
| rare | **roh** roh |
| medium | **medium** meh•dee•uhm |
| well-done | **durchgebraten** doorkh•geh•brah•tuhn |

## Vegetables and Staples

| | |
|---|---|
| **die Bohnen** dee boh•nuhn | beans |
| **der Blumenkohl** dehr bloo•muhn•kohl | cauliflower |
| **die Erbse** dee ehrb•zuh | pea |
| **die Kartoffel** dee kahr•toh•fuhl | potato |
| **die Möhre** dee mer•ruh | carrot |
| **die Pasta** dee pah•stah | pasta |

| | |
|---|---|
| **der Reis** dehr ries | rice |
| **die Tomate** dee toh·mah·teh | tomato |

## Fruit

| | |
|---|---|
| **der Apfel** dehr ahp·fuhl | apple |
| **die Apfelsine** dee ah·pfehl·zee·nuh | orange |
| **die Banane** dee bah·nah·nuh | banana |
| **die Erdbeere** dee ehrd·beh·ruh | strawberry |
| **die Himbeere** dee hihm·beh·ruh | raspberry |
| **die Pflaume** dee pflow·muh | plum |
| **die Zitrone** dee tsee·troh·nuh | lemon |

## Dessert

| | |
|---|---|
| **der Apfelkuchen** dehr ah·pfuhl·kookh·uhn | apple pie or tart |
| **das Eis** dahs ies | ice cream |
| **der Käsekuchen** dehr kay·zuh·kookh·uhn | cheesecake |
| **der Obstsalat** dehr ohpst·sah·laht | fruit salad |
| **die Torte** dee tohr·tuh | cake |

# *Drinks*

| | |
|---|---|
| The *wine list/drink menu*, please. | **Die *Weinkarte/Getränkekarte*, bitte.** dee *vien·kahr·tuh/geh·trehnk·uh·kahr·tuh* biht·tuh |
| Another *bottle/glass*, please. | **Noch *eine Flasche/ein Glas*, bitte.** nohkh *ien·uh flah·shuh/ien glahs* biht·tuh |
| I'd like a local beer. | **Ich möchte gern ein Bier aus der Region.** eekh merkh·tuh gehrn ien beer ows dehr rehg·yohn |
| I'd like a *bottle/glass* of *red/white* wine. | **Ich möchte gern *eine Flasche/ein Glas Rotwein/Weißwein*.** eekh merkh·tuh gehrn *ien·uh flah·shuh/ien glahs roht·vien/vies·vien* |
| Cheers! | **Prost!** prohst |
| A *coffee/tea*, please. | **Einen *Kaffee/Tee*, bitte.** ien·uhn *kah·feh/tee* biht·tuh |
| Black. | **Schwarz.** shvahrts |

| | |
|---|---|
| With… | **Mit …** miht… |
| – milk | – **Milch** mihlkh |
| – sugar | – **Zucker** tsoo•kehr |
| – artificial sweetener | – **Süßstoff** zews•shtohf |
| …, please. | **… , bitte.** … biht•tuh |
| – A juice | – **Einen Saft** ien•uhn zahft |
| – A soda | – **Ein Sodawasser** ien zoh•dah•vah•sehr |
| – A *still/sparkling* water | – **Ein *stilles Wasser/Wasser mit Kohlensäure*** ien *shtihl•uhs vah•sehr/ vah•sehr miht kohl•ehn•zoy•ruh* |

## Aperitifs, Cocktails and Liqueurs

| | |
|---|---|
| **der Gin** dehr djihn | gin |
| **der Rum** dehr room | rum |
| **der Weinbrand** dehr vien•brahnt | brandy |
| **der Whisky** dehr vees•kee | whisky |
| **der Wodka** dehr voht•kah | vodka |

## *Talking*

| | |
|---|---|
| Hello! | **Hallo!** hah·loh |
| Good morning. | **Guten Morgen.** goo·tuhn mohr·guhn |
| Good afternoon. | **Guten Tag.** goo·tuhn tahk |
| Good evening. | **Guten Abend.** goo·tuhn ah·behnt |
| How are you? | **Wie geht es Ihnen?** vee geht ehs eehn·uhn |
| Fine, thanks. | **Gut, danke.** goot dahn·kuh |
| Excuse me! | **Entschuldigung!** ehnt·shool·dee·goong |
| What's your name? | **Wie heißen Sie?** vee hie·suhn zee |
| My name is… | **Mein Name ist …** mien nahm·uh ihst… |
| Nice to meet you. | **Schön, Sie kennenzulernen.** shern zee keh·nehn·tsoo·lehr·nehn |
| Where are you from? | **Woher kommen Sie?** voh·hehr koh·muhn zee |
| I'm from the *U.S./U.K.* | **Ich komme aus *den USA/Großbritannien.*** eekh koh·muh ows dehn *oo·ehs·ah/ grohs·bree·tah·nee·ehn* |
| Goodbye. | **Auf Wiedersehen.** owf vee·dehr·zehn |
| See you later. | **Bis bald.** bihs bahld |

When addressing anyone but a very close friend, it is polite to use a title: **Herr** (Mr.), **Frau** (Miss/Ms./Mrs.) or **Herr Dr.** (Dr.), and to speak to him or her using **Sie**, the formal form of "you", until you are asked to use the familiar **Du**.

## Communication Difficulties

| | |
|---|---|
| Do you speak English? | **Sprechen Sie Englisch?** shpreh·khehn zee ehn·gleesh |
| I don't speak (much) German. | **Ich spreche kein (nicht viel) Deutsch.** eekh shpreh·khuh kien (neekht feel) doych |

| | |
|---|---|
| Can you speak more slowly, please? | **Können Sie bitte langsamer sprechen?** ker•nuhn zee biht•tuh lahng•sahm•ehr shpreh•khuhn |
| I (don't) understand. | **Ich verstehe (nicht).** eekh fehr•shteh•uh (neekht) |

## *Sightseeing*

| | |
|---|---|
| Where's the tourist information office? | **Wo ist das Touristeninformationsbüro?** voh ihst dahs too•ree•stuhn•een•fohr•mah•syohns•bew•roh |
| Do you have tours in English? | **Haben Sie Führungen in Englisch?** hah•buhn zee few•roong•uhn ihn ehn•gleesh |
| Can I have a *map/guide*? | **Kann ich einen *Stadtplan/Reiseführer* haben?** kahn eekh ien•uhn *shtaht•plahn/rie•seh•fewhr•ehr* hah•buhn |

### Sights

| | |
|---|---|
| Where's...? | **Wo ist ... ?** voh ihst... |
| – the castle | **– das Schloss** dahs shlohs |
| – the cathedral | **– die Kathedrale** dee kah•teh•drahl•uh |
| – the downtown area | **– das Stadtzentrum** dahs shtadt•tsehnt•room |
| – the museum | **– das Museum** dahs moo•zeh•oom |
| – the shopping area | **– das Einkaufszentrum** dahs ien•kowfs•tsehn•troom |

## *Shopping*

| | |
|---|---|
| Where's the *market/ mall [shopping centre]*? | **Wo ist *der Markt/das Einkaufszentrum*?** voh ihst *dehr mahrkt/dahs ien•kowfs•tsehn•troom* |
| I'm just looking. | **Ich schaue mich nur um.** eekh show•uh meekh noor oom |
| Can you help me? | **Können Sie mir helfen?** kern•uhn zee meer hehlf•uhn |
| I'm being helped. | **Ich werde schon bedient.** eekh vehrd•uh shohn beh•deent |
| How much? | **Wie viel kostet das?** vee feel kohs•tuht dahs |
| That one, please. | **Dieses bitte.** dee•zuhs biht•tuh |
| That's all. | **Das ist alles.** dahs ihst ahl•uhs |
| Where can I pay? | **Wo kann ich bezahlen?** voh kahn eekh beh•tsahl•uhn |
| I'll pay *in cash/by credit card.* | **Ich zahle *bar/mit Kreditkarte.*** eekh tsahl•uh *bahr/miht kreh•deet•kahr•tuh* |
| A receipt, please. | **Eine Quittung, bitte.** ien•uh kvih•toong biht•tuh |

### Stores

| | |
|---|---|
| Where's...? | **Wo ist ... ?** voh ihst... |
| – the bakery | **– die Bäckerei** dee beh•keh•rie |
| – the bookstore | **– der Buchladen** dehr bookh•lahd•uhn |
| – the department store | **– das Kaufhaus** dahs kowf•hows |
| – the pastry shop | **– die Konditorei** dee kohn•dee•toh•rie |
| – the pharmacy [chemist] | **– die Apotheke** dee ah•poh•tehk•uh |
| – the supermarket | **– der Supermarkt** dehr zoo•pehr•mahrkt |

### Clothing

| | |
|---|---|
| I'd like... | **Ich möchte ...** eekh merkht•uh... |
| Can I try this on? | **Kann ich das anprobieren?** kahn eekh dahs ahn•proh•bee•ruhn |

| | |
|---|---|
| It doesn't fit. | **Es passt nicht.** ehs pahst neekht |
| Do you have this in a *bigger/ smaller* size? | **Haben Sie das in einer *größeren/ kleineren* Größe?** hah•buhn zee dahs ihn ien•ehr *grers•ehr•uhn/klien•uh•ruhn* grers•uh |

### Color

| | |
|---|---|
| I'd like something… | **Ich möchte etwas …** eekh merkht•uh eht•vahs… |
| – black | **– Schwarzes** shvahrtz•uhs |
| – blue | **– Blaues** blow•uhs |
| – brown | **– Braunes** brown•uhs |
| – green | **– Grünes** grewn•uhs |
| – orange | **– Oranges** oh•rahnj•uhs |
| – red | **– Rotes** roht•uhs |
| – white | **– Weißes** vies•uhs |
| – yellow | **– Gelbes** gehlb•uhs |

## Sports and Leisure

| | |
|---|---|
| Where's…? | **Wo ist … ?** voh ihst… |
| – the beach | **– der Strand** dehr shtrahnd |
| – the park | **– der Park** dehr pahrk |
| – the pool | **– der Pool** dehr pool |
| Can I rent [hire] golf clubs? | **Kann ich Golfschläger ausleihen?** kahn eekh gohlf•shlehg•uhr ows•lie•uhn |

## Culture and Nightlife

| | |
|---|---|
| Where's…? | **Wo ist … ?** voh ihst… |
| – the downtown area | **– das Stadtzentrum** dahs shtadt•tsehn•troom |
| – the bar | **– die Bar** dee bahr |
| – the dance club | **– der Tanzclub** dehr tahnts•kloop |
| Do you have a program of events? | **Haben Sie ein Veranstaltungsprogramm?** hah•buhn zee ien fehr•ahn•shtahlt•oongs•prohg•rahm |

## Business Travel

| | |
|---|---|
| I'm here on business. | **Ich bin geschäftlich hier.** eekh been guh•<u>shehft</u>•leekh heer |
| Here's my business card. | **Hier ist meine Visitenkarte.** heer ihst <u>mien</u>•uh vih•<u>zee</u>•tuhn•kahr•tuh |
| Can I have your card? | **Kann ich Ihre Karte haben?** kahn eekh <u>ihr</u>•uh <u>kahrt</u>•uh <u>hah</u>•buhn |
| I have a meeting with… | **Ich habe ein Meeting mit …** eekh <u>hahb</u>•uh ien <u>mee</u>•teeng miht… |
| Where's the *convention hall/ meeting room*? | **Wo ist *der Kongresssaal/das Konferenzzimmer*?** voh ihst *dehr kohn•<u>grehs</u>•sahl/dahs kohn•fehr•<u>ehnts</u>•tsihm•ehr* |

## Travel with Children

| | |
|---|---|
| Is there a discount for kids? | **Gibt es Ermäßigung für Kinder?** gihpt ehs ehr•<u>meh</u>•see•goong fewr <u>kihn</u>•dehr |
| Can you recommend a babysitter? | **Können Sie einen Babysitter empfehlen?** <u>kern</u>•uhn zee <u>ien</u>•uhn <u>beh</u>•bee•siht•ehr ehm•<u>pfeh</u>•luhn |
| Do you have a *child's seat/highchair*? | **Haben Sie einen *Kindersitz/Kinderstuhl*?** <u>hah</u>•buhn zee <u>ien</u>•uhn *<u>kihnd</u>•ehr•zihts/ <u>kihnd</u>•ehr•shtoohl* |
| Where can I change the baby? | **Wo kann ich das Baby wickeln?** voh kahn eekh dahs <u>beh</u>•bee <u>vihk</u>•uhln |

## For the Disabled

| | |
|---|---|
| Is there…? | **Gibt es … ?** gihpt ehs… |
| – access for the disabled | **– einen Zugang für Behinderte** <u>ien</u>•uhn <u>tsoo</u>•gahng fewr beh•<u>hihnd</u>•ehrt•uh |
| – a wheelchair ramp | **– eine Rollstuhlrampe** <u>ien</u>•uh <u>rohl</u>•shtool•rahm•puh |
| – a handicapped- [disabled-] accessible toilet | **– eine Behindertentoilette** <u>ien</u>•uh beh•<u>hihn</u>•dehrt•uhn•toy•leh•tuh |

| | |
|---|---|
| I need… | **Ich brauche …** eekh browkh•uh… |
| – assistance | **– Hilfe** hihlf•uh |
| – an elevator [a lift] | **– einen Fahrstuhl** ien•uhn fahr•shtoohl |

## Emergencies

| | |
|---|---|
| Help! | **Hilfe!** hihlf•uh |
| Go away! | **Gehen Sie weg!** geh•uhn zee vehk |
| Stop, thief! | **Haltet den Dieb!** hahlt•uht dehn deeb |
| Get a doctor! | **Holen Sie einen Arzt!** hohl•uhn zee ien•uhn ahrtst |
| Fire! | **Feuer!** foy•ehr |
| I'm lost. | **Ich habe mich verlaufen.** eekh hahb•uh meekh fehr•lowf•uhn |
| Can you help me? | **Können Sie mir helfen?** kern•uhn zee meer hehlf•uhn |
| Call the police! | **Rufen Sie die Polizei!** roof•uhn zee dee poh•leet•sie |

## Health

| | |
|---|---|
| I'm sick [ill]. | **Ich bin krank.** eekh bihn krahnk |
| I need an English-speaking doctor. | **Ich brauche einen englischsprechenden Arzt.** eekh browkh•uh ien•uhn ehng•glihsh•shprehkh•ehnd•uhn ahrtst |
| It hurts here. | **Es tut hier weh.** ehs toot heer veh |

## Reference

### Numbers

| | | | |
|---|---|---|---|
| 0 | **null** nool | 5 | **fünf** fewnf |
| 1 | **eins** iens | 6 | **sechs** zehks |
| 2 | **zwei** tsvie | 7 | **sieben** zeeb•uhn |
| 3 | **drei** drie | 8 | **acht** ahkht |
| 4 | **vier** feer | 9 | **neun** noyn |

10 **zehn** tsehn

11 **elf** ehlf

12 **zwölf** tsverlf

13 **dreizehn** drie•tsehn

14 **vierzehn** feer•tsehn

15 **fünfzehn** fewnf•tsehn

16 **sechszehn** zehk•tsehn

17 **siebzehn** zeep•tsehn

18 **achtzehn** ahkht•tsehn

19 **neunzehn** noyn•tsehn

20 **zwanzig** tsvahn•tseek

21 **einundzwanzig** ien•oond•tsvahn•tseek

22 **zweiundzwanzig** tsvie•oond•tsvahn•tseek

30 **dreißig** drie•seekh

31 **einunddreißig** ien•oont•drie•seekh

40 **vierzig** feer•tseek

50 **fünfzig** fewnf•tseeg

60 **sechzig** zehkht•seeg

70 **siebzig** zeeb•tseeg

80 **achtzig** ahkht•tseeg

90 **neunzig** noynt•seek

100 **einhundert** ien•hoon•dehrt

101 **einhunderteins** ien•hoon•dehrt•iens

200 **zweihundert** tsvie•hoon•dehrt

500 **fünfhundert** fewnf•hoon•dehrt

1,000 **eintausend** ien•tow•zuhnt

10,000 **zehntausend** tsehn•tow•zuhnt

1,000,000 **eine Million** ien•uh mihl•yohn

## Time

| | |
|---|---|
| From one o'clock to two o'clock. | **Von eins bis zwei.** fohn iens bihs tsvie |
| What time is it? | **Wie spät ist es?** vee shpayt ihst ehs |
| 5:30 a.m./5:30 p.m. | **Fünf Uhr dreißig/Siebzehn Uhr dreißig** fewnf oohr drie•seeg/zeeb•tsehn oohr drie•seeg |

## Days

| | |
|---|---|
| Monday | **Montag** mohn•tahk |
| Tuesday | **Dienstag** deens•tahk |
| Wednesday | **Mittwoch** miht•vohkh |
| Thursday | **Donnerstag** dohn•ehrs•tahk |

| | |
|---|---|
| Friday | **Freitag** frie·tahk |
| Saturday | **Samstag** zahms·tahk |
| Sunday | **Sonntag** zohn·tahk |

## Dates

| | |
|---|---|
| yesterday | **gestern** gehs·tehrn |
| today | **heute** hoy·tuh |
| tomorrow | **morgen** mohr·guhn |

## Months

| | | | |
|---|---|---|---|
| January | **Januar** yahn·wahr | July | **Juli** yoo·lee |
| February | **Februar** fehb·rooahr | August | **August** ow·goost |
| March | **März** mehrts | September | **September** zehp·tehm·behr |
| April | **April** ah·prihl | October | **Oktober** ohk·toh·behr |
| May | **Mai** mie | November | **November** noh·vehm·behr |
| June | **Juni** yoo·nee | December | **Dezember** deh·tsehm·behr |

# Greek
## Pronunciation

Stress is important in Greek, as often the meaning of the word changes depending upon which syllable is stressed. In written Greek, stress is indicated by a small mark (′) on the syllable to be stressed. In the Greek phonetic transcription, stress is indicated with an underline. Over the last 25 years, the Greek language has been greatly simplified, with the number of stress and breathing marks reduced; however, one may still encounter words written with the more elaborate stress marks, mainly in older Greek texts.

In the Greek language, the question mark is indicated by the semi-colon (;).

### Consonants

| Letter | Approximate Pronunciation | Symbol | Example | Pronunciation |
|---|---|---|---|---|
| β | like v in voice | v | **βάζο** | vah•zoh |
| δ | voiced th, like th in then | TH | **δεν** | THehn |
| ζ | like z in zoo | z | **ζω** | zoh |
| θ | unvoiced th, like th in thing | th | **θέλω** | theh•loh |
| κ | like k in key | k | **κότα** | koh•tah |
| λ | like l in lemon | l | **λεμόνι** | leh•moh•nee |
| μ | like m in man | m | **μαμά** | mah•mah |
| ν | like n in net | n | **νέο** | neh•oh |
| ξ | like x in fox | ks | **ξένος** | kseh•nohs |
| π | like p in pen | p | **πένα** | peh•nah |
| ρ | trilled like a Scottish r | r | **ώρα** | oh•rah |
| σ | like s in sit | s | **σε** | seh |
| ς* | like s in slim | s | **ήλιος** | ee•liohs |
| τ | like t in tea | t | **τι** | tee |

* This character is used instead of σ, when the latter falls at the end of a word.

| Letter | Approximate Pronunciation | Symbol | Example | Pronunciation |
|---|---|---|---|---|
| φ | like f in fun | f | φως | fohs |
| χ | like ch in Scottish loch | kh | χαρά | khah•rah |
| ψ | like ps in tops | ps | ψάρι | psah•ree |
| γ | like g + h | gh | γάλα | ghah•lah |
| γγ, γκ | like g in go, but in some cases a more nasal ng as in sing | g | γκαρσόν | gahr•sohn |
| μπ | like b in bath, but in some cases more like mp as in lamp | b | μπαρ | bahr |
| ντ | like d in do, but in some cases more like nd as in end | d | ντομάτα | doh•mah•tah |
| τζ | like j in jazz | j | τζατζίκι | jah•jee•kee |
| τσ | like ts in lets | ts | τσάντα | tsahn•dah |

## Vowels

| Letter | Approximate Pronunciation | Symbol | Example | Pronunciation |
|---|---|---|---|---|
| α | like a in father | ah | μα | mah |
| ε | like e in ten | eh | θέλω | theh•loh |
| η, ι, υ | like ee in keen | ee | πίνω | pee•noh |
| ο, ω | like o in top | oh | πότε | poh•teh |
| αι | like e in ten | eh | μπαίνω | beh•noh |
| οι, ει, υι | like ee in keen | ee | πλοίο | plee•oh |

## Vowel Combinations

| Letters | Approximate Pronunciation | Symbol | Example | Pronunciation |
|---|---|---|---|---|
| αυ | 1) when followed by θ, κ, ξ, π, σ, τ, φ, χ, ψ, like af in after | ahf | αυτός | ahf•tohs |

| Letters | Approximate Pronunciation | Symbol | Example | Pronunciation |
|---|---|---|---|---|
| | 2) in all other cases, like av in avocado | ahv | **αύρα** | ahv•rah |
| **ευ** | 1) when followed by θ, κ, ξ, π, σ, τ, φ, χ, ψ, like ef in effect | ehf | **λευκός** | lehf•kohs |
| | 2) in all other cases, like ev in ever | ehv | **νεύρο** | nehv•roh |
| **ου** | like oo in zoo | oo | **ούζο** | oo·zoh |
| **για, γεια** | like yah in yard | yah | **για** | yah |
| **γε, γιε** | like ye in yet | yeh | **γερό** | yeh•roh |
| **ειο, γιο** | like yo in yogurt | yoh | **γιος** | yohs |
| **γι, γυ, γη** | like yea in yeast | yee | **γύρω** | yee•roh |
| **ια, οια** | like ia in piano | iah | **ποια** | piah |

## Basic Expressions

Hello. **Χαίρετε.** kheh·reh·teh

Goodbye. **Γεια σας.** yah sahs

Yes. **Ναι.** neh

No. **Όχι.** oh·khee

Ok. **Εντάξει.** ehn·dah·ksee

Excuse me! (to get attention) **Παρακαλώ!** pah·rah·kah·loh

Excuse me. (to get past) **Συγνώμη.** see·ghnoh·mee

Please. **Παρακαλώ.** pah•rah•kah•loh

Thank you. **Ευχαριστώ.** ehf·khahr·ee·stoh

You're welcome. **Παρακαλώ.** pah•rah•kah•loh

Where is the restroom [toilet]? **Πού είναι η τουαλέτα;** poo ee•neh ee too·ah·leh·tah

# *Arrival and Departure*

| | |
|---|---|
| I'm here on *vacation [holiday]/business.* | **Είμαι εδώ για *διακοπές/δουλειά*.** ee·meh eh·THoh yah *THiah·koh·pehs/THoo·liah* |
| I'm going to… | **Θα…** thah… |
| I'm staying at the… Hotel. | **Μένω στο…ξενοδοχείο.** meh·noh stoh… kseh·noh·THoh·khee·oh |

## Passport Control and Customs

| | |
|---|---|
| I'm just passing through. | **Απλώς περνώ από εδώ.** ahp·lohs pehr·noh ah·poh eh·THoh |
| I would like to declare… | **Θα ήθελα να δηλώσω…** thah ee·theh·lah nah THee·loh·soh… |
| I have nothing to declare. | **Δεν έχω να δηλώσω τίποτα.** THehn eh·khoh nah THee·loh·soh tee·poh·tah |

# *Money and Banking*

| | |
|---|---|
| Where is…? | **Πού είναι…;** poo ee·neh… |
| –the ATM | **– το αυτόματο μηχάνημα ανάληψης** toh ahf·toh·mah·toh mee·khah·nee·mah ah·nah·lee·psees |
| –the bank | **– η τράπεζα** ee trah·peh·zah |
| –the currency exchange office | **– γραφείο ανταλλαγής συναλλάγματος** ghrah·fee·oh ahn·dah·lah·ghees see·nah·lahgh·mah·tohs |
| What time does the bank *open/close*? | **Τι ώρα *ανοίγει/κλείνει* η τράπεζα;** tee oh·rah *ah·nee·ghee/klee·nee* ee trah·peh·zah |
| I'd like to change *dollars/pounds* into euros. | **Θα ήθελα να αλλάξω *μερικά δολάρια/λίρες* σε ευρώ.** thah ee·theh·lah nah ah·lah·ksoh *meh·ree·kah THoh·lah·ree·ah/meh·ree·kehs lee·rehs* seh ehv·roh |
| I want to cash some traveler's checks [cheques]. | **Θα ήθελα να εξαργυρώσω μερικές ταξιδιωτικές επιταγές.** thah ee·theh·lah nah eh·ksahr·yee·roh·soh meh·ree·kehs tah·ksee·THee·oh·tee·kehs eh·pee·tah·yehs |

# Transportation

| | |
|---|---|
| How do I get to town? | **Πώς μπορώ να πάω στην πόλη;** pohs boh·roh nah pah·oh steen poh·lee |
| Where's...? | **Πού είναι...;** poo ee·neh... |
| –the airport | **– το αεροδρόμιο** toh ah·eh·roh·THroh·mee·oh |
| –the train [railway] station | **– ο σταθμός των τρένων** oh stahth·mohs ton treh·nohn |
| –the bus station | **– ο σταθμός των λεωφορείων** oh stahth·mohs tohn leh·oh·foh·ree·ohn |
| –the subway [underground] station | **– ο σταθμός του μετρό** oh stahth·mohs too meh·troh |
| How far is it? | **Πόσο απέχει;** poh·soh ah·peh·khee |
| Where can I buy tickets? | **Από πού μπορώ να αγοράσω εισιτήρια;** ah·poh poo boh·roh nah ah·ghoh·rah·soh ee·see·tee·ree·ah |
| A *one-way [single]/ round-trip [return]* ticket. | **Ένα *απλό εισιτήριο/εισιτήριο με επιστροφή*.** eh·nah *ahp·loh ee·see·tee·ree·oh/ ee·see·tee·ree·oh meh eh·pees·troh·fee* |
| How much? | **Πόσο;** poh·soh |
| Is there a discount? | **Υπάρχει μειωμένο ειστήριο;** ee·pahr·khee mee·oh·meh·noh ee·see·tee·ree·oh |
| Which...? | **Ποια...;** piah... |
| –gate | **– είσοδος** ee·soh·THohs |
| –line | **– γραμμή** ghrah·mee |
| –platform | **– πλατφόρμα** plaht·fohr·mah |
| Where can I get a taxi? | **Πού μπορώ να βρω ταξί;** poo boh·roh nah vroh tah·ksee |

| | |
|---|---|
| Please take me to this address. | **Παρακαλώ πηγαίνετέ με σε αυτή τη διεύθυνση.** pah•rah•kah•loh pee•yeh•neh•teh meh seh ahf•tee tee THee•ehf•theen•see |
| Where can I rent [hire] a car? | **Πού μπορώ να νοικιάσω ένα αυτοκίνητο;** poo boh•roh nah nee•kee•ah•soh eh•nah ahf•toh•kee•nee•toh |
| Can I have a map? | **Μπορώ να έχω ένα χάρτη;** boh•roh nah eh•khoh eh•nah khahr•tee |

## Asking Directions

| | |
|---|---|
| How far is it to...? | **Πόσο μακριά είναι για...;** poh•soh mahk•ree•ah ee•neh yah... |
| Where's...? | **Πού είναι...;** poo ee•neh... |
| –...Street | **– η οδός...** ee oh•THohs... |
| –this address | **– αυτή η διεύθυνση** ahf•tee ee THee•ehf•theen•see |
| Can you show me on the map? | **Μπορείτε να μου δείξετε στο χάρτη;** boh•ree•teh nah moo THee•kseh•teh stoh khahr•tee |
| I'm lost. | **Έχω χαθεί.** eh•hoh khah•thee |

### You May Hear...

| | |
|---|---|
| **ευθεία/ίσια** ehf•thee•ah/ee•see•ah | straight ahead |
| **στα αριστερά** stah ah•rees•teh•rah | on the left |
| **στα δεξιά** stah THeh•ksee•ah | on the right |
| ***στη/μετά τη* γωνία** *stee/meh•tah* tee ghoh•nee•ah | *on/around* the corner |
| **δίπλα** THee•plah | next to |
| **μετά** meh•tah | after |
| **βόρεια/νότεια** voh•ree•ah/noh•tee•ah | north/south |
| **ανατολικά/δυτικά** ah•nah•toh•lee•kah/THee•tee•kah | east/west |

## Accommodations

| | |
|---|---|
| I have a reservation. | **Έχω κλείσει δωμάτιο.** eh•khoh klee•see THoh•mah•tee•oh |
| My name is… | **Λέγομαι…** leh•ghoh•meh… |
| When's check-out? | **Τι ώρα πρέπει να αδειάσουμε το δωμάτιο;** tee oh•rah preh•pee nah ah•THee•ah•soo•meh toh THoh•mah•tee•oh |
| Can I leave this in the safe? | **Μπορώ να αφήσω αυτό στη θυρίδα;** boh•roh nah ah•fee•soh ahf•toh stee thee•ree•THah |
| Could we leave our baggage here until…? | **Μπορούμε να αφήσουμε τα πράγματά μας εδώ ως τις…;** boh•roo•meh nah ah•fee•soo•meh tah prahgh•mah•tah mahs eh•THoh ohs tees… |
| Could I have *the bill/a receipt*? | **Μπορώ να έχω *τον λογαριασμό/μια απόδειξη*;** boh•roh nah eh•hoh *tohn loh•ghahr•yahs•moh/miah ah•poh•THee•ksee* |

## Internet and Communications

| | |
|---|---|
| Where's an internet cafe? | **Πού υπάρχει internet cafe;** poo ee•pahr•khee een•tehr•neht kah•feh |
| Can I *access the internet/check e-mail* here? | **Μπορώ *να μπω στο internet/να ελέγξω τα e-mail μου* εδώ;** boh•roh *nah boh stoh een•tehr•neht/nah eh•lehng•ksoh tah ee•meh•eel moo* eh•THoh |
| Can I have your phone number? | **Μπορώ να έχω τον αριθμό τηλεφώνου σας;** boh•roh nah eh•hoh tohn ah•reeth•moh tee•leh•foh•noo sahs |
| Here's my *number/e-mail address.* | **Ορίστε το *τηλέφωνό μου/e-mail μου.*** oh•rees•teh toh *tee•leh•foh•noh moo/ee•meh•eel moo* |
| Call me. | **Πάρτε με τηλέφωνο.** pahr•teh meh tee•leh•foh•noh |
| E-mail me. | **Στείλτε μου e-mail.** steel•teh moo ee•meh•eel |
| Hello. This is… | **Εμπρός. Είμαι…** ehm•brohs ee•meh… |
| I'd like to speak to… | **Θα ήθελα να μιλήσω με…** thah ee•theh•lah nah mee•lee•soh meh… |

| | |
|---|---|
| Repeat that, please. | **Επαναλάβετέ το, παρακαλώ.** eh•pah•nah•lah•veh•teh toh pah•rah•kah•loh |
| I'll be in touch. | **Θα επικοινωνήσω μαζί σας.** thah eh•pee•kee•noh•nee•soh mah•zee sahs |
| Bye. | **Αντίο.** ah•dee•oh |
| Where is the *nearest/main* post office? | **Πού είναι το *κοντινότερο/κεντρικό* ταχυδρομείο;** poo ee•neh toh *koh•ndee•noh•teh•roh/kehn•dree•koh* tah•khee•THroh•mee•oh |

## Eating Out

| | |
|---|---|
| Can you recommend a good *restaurant/bar*? | **Μπορείτε να συστήσετε ένα καλό *εστιατόριο/μπαρ*;** boh•ree•teh nah sees•tee•seh•teh eh•nah kah•loh *ehs•tee•ah•toh•ree•oh/bahr* |
| Is there a *traditional Greek/an inexpensive* restaurant near here? | **Υπάρχει κανένα *ελληνικό/φθηνό* εστιατόριο εδώ κοντά;** ee•pahr•khee kah•neh•nah *eh•lee•nee•koh/fthee•noh* ehs•tee•ah•toh•ree•oh eh•THoh kohn•dah |
| A table for..., please. | **Ένα τραπέζι για..., παρακαλώ.** eh•nah trah•peh•zee yah...pah•rah•kah•loh |
| A menu, please. | **Έναν κατάλογο, παρακαλώ.** eh•nahn kah•tah•loh•ghoh pah•rah•kah•loh |
| What do you recommend? | **Τι προτείνετε;** tee proh•tee•neh•teh |
| I'd like... | **Θα ήθελα...** thah ee•theh•lah... |
| Some more..., please. | **Λίγο ακόμη..., παρακαλώ.** lee•ghoh ah•koh•mee...pah•rah•kah•loh |
| Enjoy your meal! | **Καλή όρεξη!** kah•lee oh•reh•ksee |
| The check [bill], please. | **Τον λογαριασμό, παρακαλώ.** tohn loh•ghah•riahs•moh pah•rah•kah•loh |
| Is service included? | **Συμπεριλαμβάνεται και το φιλοδώρημα;** seem•beh•ree•lahm•vah•neh•teh keh toh fee•loh•THoh•ree•mah |

| | |
|---|---|
| Can I have a receipt? | **Μπορώ να έχω απόδειξη;** boh·roh nah eh·khoh ah·poh·THee·ksee |

## Breakfast

| | |
|---|---|
| bread | **ψωμί** psoh·mee |
| butter | **βούτυρο** voo·tee·roh |
| cereal (*cold/hot*) | **δημητριακά με (*ζεστό/κρύο*) γάλα** THee·meet·ree·ah·kah meh (*zehs·toh/kree·oh*) ghah·lah |
| roll | **ψωμάκι** psoh·mah·kee |
| yogurt (with honey) | **γιαούρτι (με μέλι)** yah·oor·tee (meh meh·lee) |

## Appetizers [Starters]

| | |
|---|---|
| fried baby squid | **καλαμαράκια** kah·lah·mah·rah·kiah |
| fried meatballs | **κεφτεδάκια** kef·teh·THah·kiah |
| spinach and feta in pastry dough | **σπανακόπιτα** spah·nah·koh·pee·tah |
| stuffed grape leaves | **ντολμαδάκι** dohl·mah·THah·kee |
| yogurt, garlic and cucumber dip | **τζατζίκι** jah·jee·kee |

## Soup

| | |
|---|---|
| bean soup with tomatoes and parsley | **φασολάδα** fah·soh·lah·THah |

| | |
|---|---|
| chicken soup | **κοτόσουπα** koh·toh·soo·pah |
| fish soup thickened with egg and lemon | **ψαρόσουπα αυγολέμονο** psah·roh·soo·pah ahv·ghoh·leh·moh·noh |
| meat soup | **κρεατόσουπα** kreh·ah·toh·soo·pah |
| tripe soup | **πατσάς** pah·tsahs |

## Fish and Seafood

| | |
|---|---|
| fresh cod | **μπακαλιάρος** bah·kah·liah·rohs |
| mussel | **μύδι** mee·THee |
| octopus | **χταπόδι** khtah·poh·THee |
| red mullet | **μπαρμπούνι** bahr·boo·nee |
| swordfish | **ξιφίας** ksee·fee·ahs |

## Meat and Poultry

| | |
|---|---|
| beef | **βοδινό** voh·THee·noh |
| Greek burger | **μπιφτέκι** beef·teh·kee |
| chicken | **κοτόπουλο** koh·toh·poo·loh |
| duck | **πάπια** pah·piah |
| goat | **κατσικάκι** kah·tsee·kah·kee |
| lamb | **αρνί** ahr·nee |
| skewered pork or lamb, well seasoned and cooked over charcoal | **κοντοσούβλι** koh·ndoh·soov·lee dohs |
| veal | **μοσχάρι** mohs·khah·ree |

## Vegetables

| | |
|---|---|
| cauliflower | **κουνουπίδι** koo·noo·pee·THee |
| cucumber | **αγγούρι** ahn·goo·ree |
| eggplant [aubergine] | **μελιτζάνα** meh·lee·jah·nah |

| | |
|---|---|
| spinach | **σπανάκι** spah·nah·kee |
| tomato | **ντομάτα** ndoh·mah·tah |
| zucchini [courgette] | **κολοκυθάκι** koh·loh·kee·thah·kee |

## Fruit

| | |
|---|---|
| apple | **μήλο** mee·loh |
| banana | **μπανάνα** bah·nah·nah |
| fig | **σύκο** see·koh |
| grape | **σταφύλι** stah·fee·lee |
| lemon | **λεμόνι** leh·moh·nee |
| orange | **πορτοκάλι** pohr·toh·kah·lee |
| pear | **αχλάδι** akh·lah·THee |
| watermelon | **καρπούζι** kahr·poo·zee |

## Dessert

| | |
|---|---|
| baklava, flaky pastry with nut filling | **μπακλαβάς** bah·klah·vahs |
| rice pudding | **ρυζόγαλο** ree·zoh·ghah·loh |
| walnut cake | **καρυδόπιτα** kah·ree·THoh·pee·tah |

# *Drinks*

| | |
|---|---|
| May I see the *wine list/drink menu*? | **Μπορώ να δω τον κατάλογο με τα *κρασιά/ποτά*;** boh·roh nah THoh tohn kah·tah·loh·ghoh meh tah *krah·siah/poh·tah* |
| I'd like a *bottle/glass* of *red/white* wine. | **Θα ήθελα ένα *μπουκάλι/ποτήρι κόκκινο/λευκό* κρασί.** thah ee·theh·lah eh·nah *boo·kah·lee/poh·tee·ree koh·kee·noh/lehf·koh* krah·see |
| Another *bottle/glass*, please. | **Άλλο ένα *μπουκάλι/ποτήρι*, παρακαλώ.** ah·loh eh·nah *boo·kah·lee/poh·tee·ree* pah·rah·kah·loh |

| | |
|---|---|
| I'd like a local beer. | **Θα ήθελα μια τοπική μπύρα.** thah ee•theh•lah miah toh•pee•kee bee•rah |
| Cheers! | **Στην υγειά σας!** steen ee•ghiah sahs |
| A *coffee/tea*, please. | ***Έναν καφέ/Ένα τσάι*, παρακαλώ.** *eh•nahn kah•feh/eh•nah tsah•ee* pah•rah•kah•loh |
| Black. | **Σκέτος.** skeh•tohs |
| With... | **Με...** meh... |
| – milk | **– γάλα** ghah•lah |
| – sugar | **– ζάχαρη** zah•khah•ree |
| – artificial sweetener | **– ζαχαρίνη** zah•khah•ree•nee |
| ..., please. | **..., παρακαλώ.** ...pah•rah•kah•loh |
| – A juice | **– Ένα χυμό** eh•nah khee•moh |
| – A soda | **– Μία σόδα** mee•ah soh•THah |
| – A sparkling water | **– Ένα ανθρακούχο νερό** eh•nah ahn•thrah•koo•khoh neh•roh |
| – A still water | **– Ένα νερό χωρίς ανθρακικό** eh•nah neh•roh khoh•rees ahn•thrah•kee•koh |

## Aperitifs, Cocktails and Liqueurs

| | |
|---|---|
| Greek brandy | **Μεταξά** meh•tah•ksah |
| kumquat liqueur (Corfu) | **κουμ-κουάτ** koom•koo•aht |
| ouzo | **ούζο** oo•zoh |

# *Talking*

| | |
|---|---|
| Hello. | **Χαίρετε.** kheh•reh•teh |
| Good morning. | **Καλημέρα.** kah•lee•meh•rah |
| Good *afternoon/evening*. | **Καλησπέρα.** kah•lee•speh•rah |
| Good night. | **Καληνύχτα.** kah•lee•neekh•tah |
| How are you? | **Πώς είστε;** pohs ee•steh |

| | |
|---|---|
| Fine, thanks. And you? | **Καλά, ευχαριστώ. Εσείς;** kah·lah ehf·khah·ree·stoh eh·sees |
| Excuse me! | **Συγγνώμη!** seegh·noh·mee |
| What's your name? | **Πώς λέγεστε;** pohs leh·yeh·steh |
| My name is... | **Λέγομαι...** leh·ghoh·meh... |
| Nice to meet you. | **Χαίρω πολύ.** kheh·roh poh·lee |
| Where are you from? | **Από πού είστε;** ah·poh poo ee·steh |
| I'm from the *U.S./U.K.* | **Είμαι από *τις Ηνωμένες Πολιτείες/το Ηνωμένο Βασίλειο*.** ee·meh ah·poh *tees ee·noh·meh·nehs poh·lee·tee·ehs/toh ee·noh·meh·noh vah·see·lee·oh* |
| Goodbye. | **Γεια σας.** yah sahs |
| See you later. | **Τα λέμε αργότερα.** tah leh·meh ahr·ghoh·teh·rah |

In Greek, Mrs. is **κυρία** (kee·ree·ah), Mr. is **κύριος** (kee·ree·ohs) and Miss is **δεσποινίς** (THehs·pee·nees).
Greek has a formal and an informal form of "you": **γεια σας** (yah sahs) and **γεια σου** (yah soo), respectively. The informal is used between friends or when addressing children. Use the formal **γεια σας** unless prompted to do otherwise.

## Communication Difficulties

| | |
|---|---|
| Do you speak English? | **Μιλάτε Αγγλικά;** mee·lah·teh ahng·lee·kah |
| I don't speak Greek. | **Δεν μιλώ Ελληνικά.** THehn mee·loh eh·lee·nee·kah |
| Could you speak more slowly? | **Μπορείτε να μιλάτε πιο αργά;** boh·ree·teh nah mee·lah·teh pioh ahr·ghah |
| I (don't) understand. | **(Δεν) Καταλαβαίνω.** (THehn) kah·tah·lah·veh·noh |

# Sightseeing

| | |
|---|---|
| Where's the tourist information office? | **Πού είναι το γραφείο τουρισμού;** poo ee•neh toh ghrah•fee•oh too•reez•moo |
| Do you have tours in English? | **Γίνονται ξεναγήσεις στα αγγλικά;** ghee•nohn•deh kseh•nah•ghee•sees stah ahng•lee•kah |
| Could I have a *map/guide*? | **Μπορώ να έχω ένα *χάρτη/οδηγό*;** boh•roh nah eh•khoh eh•nah *khahr•tee/oh•THee•ghoh* |

## Sights

| | |
|---|---|
| Where is...? | **Πού είναι...;** poo ee•neh... |
| – the castle | – **το κάστρο** toh kahs•troh |
| – the downtown area | – **το κέντρο της πόλης** toh kehn•droh tees poh•lees |
| – the museum | – **το μουσείο** toh moo•see•oh |
| – the shopping area | – **η εμπορική περιοχή** ee ehm•boh•ree•kee peh•ree•oh•khee |

# Shopping

| | |
|---|---|
| Where is the *market/mall [shopping centre]*? | **Πού είναι *η αγορά/το εμπορικό κέντρο*;** poo ee•neh *ee ah•ghoh•rah/toh ehm•boh•ree•koh kehn•droh* |
| I'm just looking. | **Απλώς κοιτάω.** ahp•lohs kee•tah•oh |
| Can you help me? | **Μπορείτε να με βοηθήσετε;** boh•ree•teh nah meh voh•ee•thee•seh•teh |
| I'm being helped. | **Με εξυπηρετούν.** meh eh•ksee•pee•reh•toon |
| How much? | **Πόσο;** poh•soh |
| *This/That* one, thanks. | ***Αυτό/Εκείνο*, παρακαλώ.** *ahf•toh/eh•kee•noh* pah•rah•kah•loh |
| That's all, thanks. | **Τίποτε άλλο, ευχαριστώ.** tee•poh•teh ah•loh ehf•khah•rees•toh |
| Where do I pay? | **Πού πληρώνω;** poo plee•roh•noh |

| | |
|---|---|
| I'll pay *in cash/by credit card.* | **Θα πληρώσω *τοις μετρητοίς/με πιστωτική κάρτα.*** thah plee•roh•soh *tees meht•ree•tees/ meh pees•toh•tee•kee kahr•tah* |
| A receipt, please. | **Μια απόδειξη, παρακαλώ.** miah ah•poh•THee•ksee pah•rah•kah•loh |

## Stores

| | |
|---|---|
| Where is...? | **Πού είναι...;** poo ee•neh... |
| –the bakery | **– το αρτοποιείο** toh ahr•toh•pee•ee•oh |
| –the bookstore | **– το βιβλιοπωλείο** toh veev•lee•oh•poh•lee•oh |
| –the department store | **– το πολυκατάστημα** toh poh•lee•kah•tahs•tee•mah |
| –the pharmacy [chemist's] | **– το φαρμακείο** toh fahr•mah•kee•oh |
| –the supermarket | **– το σουπερμάρκετ** toh soo•pehr mahr•keht |

## Clothing

| | |
|---|---|
| Can I try this on? | **Μπορώ να το δοκιμάσω;** boh•roh nah toh THoh•kee•mah•soh |
| It doesn't fit. | **Δεν μου κάνει.** THehn moo kah•nee |

| | |
|---|---|
| Do you have this in a *bigger/smaller* size? | **Το έχετε σε *μεγαλύτερο/μικρότερο* μέγεθος;** toh eh•kheh•teh seh *meh•ghah•lee•teh•roh/ meek•roh•teh•roh* meh•gheh•thohs |

## Color

| | |
|---|---|
| I'm looking for something in... | **Ψάχνω κάτι σε...** psahkh•noh kah•tee seh... |
| –black | **- μαύρο** mahv•roh |
| –blue | **- μπλε** bleh |
| –brown | **- καφέ** kah•feh |
| –green | **- πράσινο** prah•see•noh |
| –orange | **- πορτοκαλί** pohr•toh•kah•lee |
| –red | **- κόκκινο** koh•kee•noh |
| –white | **- άσπρο** ahs•proh |
| –yellow | **- κίτρινο** keet•ree•noh |

# *Sports and Leisure*

| | |
|---|---|
| Where's...? | **Πού είναι...;** poo ee•neh... |
| –the beach | **- η παραλία** ee pah•rah•lee•ah |
| –the park | **- το πάρκο** toh pahr•koh |
| –the pool | **- η πισίνα** ee pee•see•nah |
| Can I rent [hire] golf clubs? | **Μπορώ να νοικιάσω μπαστούνια του γκόλφ;** boh•roh nah nee•kiah•soh bahs•too•niah too gohlf |

# *Culture and Nightlife*

| | |
|---|---|
| Do you have a program of events? | **Έχετε ένα πρόγραμμα εκδηλώσεων;** eh•kheh•teh eh•nah prohgh•rah•mah ehk•THee•loh•seh•ohn |
| Where's...? | **Πού είναι...;** poo ee•neh... |
| –the downtown area | **- το κέντρο της πόλης** toh kehn•droh tees poh•lees |

| | |
|---|---|
| – the bar | **– το μπαρ** toh bahr |
| – the dance club | **– η ντισκοτέκ** ee dees•koh•tehk |

## Business Travel

| | |
|---|---|
| I'm here on business. | **Είμαι εδώ για δουλειά.** ee•meh eh•THoh yah THoo•lee•ah |
| Here's my business card. | **Ορίστε η κάρτα μου.** oh•rees•teh ee kahr•tah moo |
| Can I have your card? | **Μου δίνετε την κάρτα σας;** moo THee•neh•teh teen kahr•tah sahs |
| I have a meeting with… | **Έχω μια συνάντηση με...** eh•khoh miah see•nahn•dee•see me… |
| Where's…? | **Πού είναι...;** poo ee•neh… |
| – the business center | **– το επαγγελματικό κέντρο** toh eh•pah•gehl•mah•tee•koh kehn•droh |
| – the convention hall | **– η αίθουσα συνεδριάσεων** ee eh•thoo•sah see•nehTH•ree•ah•seh•ohn |
| – the meeting room | **– η αίθουσα συσκέψεων** ee eh•thoo•sah sees•keh•pseh•ohn |

## Travel with Children

| | |
|---|---|
| Is there a discount for children? | **Υπάρχει μειωμένο εισιτήριο για παιδιά;** ee•pahr•khee mee•oh•meh•noh ee•see•tee•ree•oh yah peh•THyah |
| Can you recommend a babysitter? | **Μπορείτε να συστήσετε μια υπεύθυνη μπέιμπυ-σίτερ;** boh•ree•teh nah sees•tee•seh•teh miah ee•pehf•thee•nee beh•ee•bee see•tehr |
| Could I have a *child's seat/ highchair*? | **Μπορούμε να έχουμε *ένα παιδικό καθισματάκι/ μια καρέκλα μωρού*;** boh•roo•meh nah eh•khoo•meh *eh-nah peh•THee•koh kah•theez•mah•tah•kee/miah kah•reh•klah moh•roo* |

| | |
|---|---|
| Where can I change the baby? | **Πού μπορώ να αλλάξω το μωρό;** poo boh•roh nah ah•lah•ksoh toh moh•roh |

## *For the Disabled*

| | |
|---|---|
| Is there...? | **Υπάρχει...;** ee•pahr•khee... |
| –access for the disabled | **- πρόσβαση για άτομα με ειδικές ανάγκες;** prohz•vah•see yah ah•toh•mah meh ee•THee•kehs ah•nahn•gehs |
| –a wheelchair ramp | **- ράμπα για αναπηρικό καρότσι** rahm•bah yah ah•nah•pee•ree•koh kah•roh•tsee |
| –a handicapped-[disabled-] accessible toilet | **- προσβάσιμη τουαλέτα για ανάπηρους** prohs•vah•see•mee too•ah•leh•tah yah ah•nah•pee•roos |
| I need... | **Χρειάζομαι...** khree•ah•zoh•meh... |
| –assistance | **- βοήθεια** voh•ee•thiah |
| –an elevator [lift] | **- ασανσέρ** ah•sahn•sehr |

## *Emergencies*

| | |
|---|---|
| Help! | **Βοήθεια!** voh•ee•thee•ah |
| Go away! | **Φύγετε!** fee•yeh•teh |
| Stop, thief! | **Σταματήστε τον κλέφτη!** stah•mah•tees•teh tohn klehf•tee |
| Get a doctor! | **Φωνάξτε ένα γιατρό!** foh•nahks•teh eh•nah yaht•roh |
| Fire! | **Φωτιά!** foh•tiah |
| I'm lost. | **Έχω χαθεί.** eh•khoh khah•thee |
| Can you help me? | **Μπορείτε να με βοηθήσετε;** boh•ree•teh nah meh voh•ee•thee•seh•teh |
| Call the police! | **Φωνάξτε την αστυνομία!** foh•nahks•teh teen ahs•tee•noh•mee•ah |

# Health

| | |
|---|---|
| I'm sick [ill]. | **Είμαι άρρωστος.** ee·meh ah·rohs·tohs |
| I need an English-speaking doctor. | **Χρειάζομαι ένα γιατρό που να μιλάει αγγλικά.** khree·ah·zoh·meh eh·nah yaht·roh poo nah mee·lah·ee ang·lee·kah |
| It hurts here. | **Με πονάει εδώ.** meh poh·nah·ee eh·THoh |

# Reference

## Numbers

| | |
|---|---|
| 0 | **μηδέν** mee·THehn |
| 1 | **ένας** eh·nahs |
| 2 | **δύο** THee·oh |
| 3 | **τρεις** trees |
| 4 | **τέσσερις** teh·seh·rees |
| 5 | **πέντε** pehn·deh |
| 6 | **έξι** eh·ksee |
| 7 | **επτά** eh·ptah |
| 8 | **οκτώ** oh·ktoh |
| 9 | **εννέα** eh·neh·ah |
| 10 | **δέκα** THeh·kah |
| 11 | **έντεκα** ehn·deh·kah |
| 12 | **δώδεκα** THoh·THeh·kah |
| 13 | **δεκατρία** THeh·kah·tree·ah |
| 14 | **δεκατέσσερα** THeh·kah·teh·seh·rah |
| 15 | **δεκαπέντε** THeh·kah·pehn·deh |
| 16 | **δεκαέξι** THeh·kah·eh·ksee |
| 17 | **δεκαεπτά** THeh·kah·eh·ptah |
| 18 | **δεκαοκτώ** THeh·kah·oh·ktoh |
| 19 | **δεκαεννέα** THeh·kah·eh·neh·ah |
| 20 | **είκοσι** ee·koh·see |
| 21 | **είκοσι ένα** ee·koh·see eh·nah |
| 22 | **είκοσι δύο** ee·koh·see THee·oh |
| 30 | **τριάντα** tree·ahn·dah |
| 31 | **τριάντα ένα** tree·ahn·dah eh·nah |
| 40 | **σαράντα** sah·rahn·dah |
| 50 | **πενήντα** peh·neen·dah |
| 60 | **εξήντα** eh·kseen·dah |
| 70 | **εβδομήντα** ehv·THoh·meen·dah |
| 80 | **ογδόντα** ohgh·THohn·dah |
| 90 | **ενενήντα** eh·neh·neen·dah |
| 100 | **εκατό** eh·kah·toh |
| 101 | **εκατόν ένα** eh·kah·tohn eh·nah |
| 200 | **διακόσια** THee·ah·koh·siah |
| 500 | **πεντακόσια** pehn·dah·koh·siah |
| 1,000 | **χίλια** khee·liah |
| 10,000 | **δέκα χιλιάδες** THeh·kah khee·liah·THehs |
| 1,000,000 | **ένα εκατομμύριο** eh·nah eh·kah·toh·mee·ree·oh |

## Time

| | |
|---|---|
| What time is it? | **Τι ώρα είναι;** tee <u>oh</u>•rah <u>ee</u>•neh |
| From nine o'clock to five o'clock. | **Από τις εννέα ως τις πέντε.** ah•<u>poh</u> tees eh•<u>neh</u>•ah ohs tees <u>pehn</u>•deh |
| 5:30 *a.m./p.m.* | **Πεντέμιση *π.μ./μ.μ.*** pehn•<u>deh</u>•mee•see *proh meh•seem•<u>vree</u>•ahs/ meh•<u>tah</u> meh•seem•<u>vree</u>•ahs* |

## Days

| | |
|---|---|
| Monday | **Δευτέρα** THehf•<u>teh</u>•rah |
| Tuesday | **Τρίτη** <u>tree</u>•tee |
| Wednesday | **Τετάρτη** teh•<u>tahr</u>•tee |
| Thursday | **Πέμπτη** <u>pehm</u>•tee |
| Friday | **Παρασκευή** pah•rahs•keh•<u>vee</u> |
| Saturday | **Σάββατο** <u>sah</u>•vah•toh |
| Sunday | **Κυριακή** keer•yah•<u>kee</u> |

## Dates

| | |
|---|---|
| yesterday | **χτες** khtehs |
| today | **σήμερα** <u>see</u>•meh•rah |
| tomorrow | **αύριο** <u>ahv</u>•ree•oh |

## Months

| | |
|---|---|
| January | **Ιανουάριος** ee•ah•noo•<u>ah</u>•ree•ohs |
| February | **Φεβρουάριος** fehv•roo•<u>ah</u>•ree•ohs |
| March | **Μάρτιος** <u>mahr</u>•tee•ohs |
| April | **Απρίλιος** ahp•<u>ree</u>•lee•ohs |
| May | **Μάιος** <u>mah</u>•ee•ohs |
| June | **Ιούνιος** ee•<u>oo</u>•nee•ohs |
| July | **Ιούλιος** ee•<u>oo</u>•lee•ohs |
| August | **Αύγουστος** <u>ahv</u>•ghoo•stohs |
| September | **Σεπτέμβριος** sehp•<u>tehm</u>•vree•ohs |
| October | **Οκτώβριος** ohk•<u>toh</u>•vree•ohs |
| November | **Νοέμβριος** noh•<u>ehm</u>•vree•ohs |
| December | **Δεκέμβριος** THeh•<u>kehm</u>•vree•ohs |

# Italian

## Pronunciation

Stress has been indicated in the phonetic pronunciations by underlining. These letters should be pronounced with more emphasis. Generally, the vowel of the next to last syllable is stressed. When a final vowel is stressed, it has an accent.

### Consonants

| Letter(s) | Approximate Pronunciation | Symbol | Example | Pronunciation |
|---|---|---|---|---|
| c | 1. before e and i, ch as in chip | ch | **cerco** | chehr•koh |
| | 2. elsewhere, c as in cat | k | **conto** | kohn•toh |
| ch | c as in cat | k | **che** | keh |
| g | 1. before e and i, like j in jet | j | **valigia** | vah•lee•jyah |
| | 2. elsewhere, g as in go | g | **grande** | grahn•deh |
| gg | pronounced more intensely | dj | **viaggio** | vyah•djoh |
| gh | g as in go | gh | **ghiaccio** | ghyah•chyoh |
| gli | lli as in million | lly | **bagaglio** | bah•gah•llyoh |
| gn | like the first n in onion | ny | **bagno** | bah•nyoh |
| h | always silent | | **ha** | ah |
| r | rolled in the back of the mouth | r | **Roma** | roh•mah |
| s | 1. generally s as in sit | s | **salsa** | sahl•sah |

| Letter(s) | Approximate Pronunciation | Symbol | Example | Pronunciation |
|---|---|---|---|---|
| | 2. sometimes z as in zoo | z | **casa** | kah·zah |
| sc | 1. before e and i, sh as in shut | sh | **uscita** | oo·shee·tah |
| | 2. elsewhere, sk as in skin | sk | **scarpa** | skahr·pah |
| z/zz | 1. generally ts as in hits | ts | **grazie** | grah·tsyeh |
| | 2. sometimes a little softer, like dz | dz | **zero** | dzeh·roh |

The letters b, d, f, k, l, m, n, p, q, t and v are pronounced as in English. The letters j, k, w, x and y are not true members of the Italian alphabet and appear only in foreign words or names.

## Vowels

| Letter | Approximate Pronunciation | Symbol | Example | Pronunciation |
|---|---|---|---|---|
| a | short, as in father | ah | **gatto** | gaht·toh |
| e | 1. like e as in get | eh | **destra** | deh·strah |
| | 2. before a single consonant, sometimes like e in they | ay | **sete** | say·teh |
| i | ee as in meet | ee | **vini** | vee·nee |
| o | o as in so | oh | **sole** | soh·leh |
| u | oo as in boot | oo | **fumo** | foo·moh |

### Vowel Combinations

| Letter | Symbol | Example | Pronunciation |
|---|---|---|---|
| ae | ah·eh | **paese** | pah·eh·zeh |
| ao | ah·oh | **Paolo** | pah·oh·loh |
| au | ow | **auto** | ow·toh |
| eo | eh·oh | **museo** | moo·zeh·oh |
| eu | eh·oo | **euro** | eh·oo·roh |
| ei | ay | **lei** | lay |
| ia | yah | **piazza** | pyah·tsah |
| ie | yeh | **piede** | pyeh·deh |
| io | yoh | **piove** | pyoh·veh |
| iu | yoo | **più** | pyoo |
| ua | wah | **quale** | kwah·leh |
| ue | weh | **questo** | kweh·stoh |
| ui | wee | **qui** | kwee |
| uo | woh | **può** | pwoh |

## *Basic Expressions*

| | |
|---|---|
| Hello. | **Salve.** sahl·veh |
| Goodbye. | **Arrivederla.** ahr·ree·veh·dehr·lah |
| Yes. | **Sì.** see |
| No. | **No.** noh |
| OK. | **OK.** oh·kay |
| Excuse me! (to get attention) | **Scusi!** skoo·zee |
| Excuse me. (to get past) | **Permesso.** pehr·mehs·soh |
| I'm sorry. | **Mi dispiace.** mee dees·pyah·cheh |
| Please. | **Per favore.** pehr fah·voh·reh |
| Thank you. | **Grazie.** grah·tsyeh |

| | |
|---|---|
| You're welcome. | **Prego.** preh•goh |
| Where's the restroom [toilet]? | **Dov'è la toilette?** doh•veh lah twah•leht |

## Arrival and Departure

| | |
|---|---|
| I'm on *vacation [holiday]/business.* | **Sono in *vacanza/viaggio d'affari.*** soh•noh een *vah•kahn•tsah/vyah•djoh dahf•fah•ree* |
| I'm going to... | **Vado a...** vah•doh ah... |
| I'm staying at the...Hotel. | **Sono all'hotel...** soh•noh ahl•loh•tehl... |

### Passport Control and Customs

| | |
|---|---|
| I'm just passing through. | **Sono solo di passaggio.** soh•noh soh•loh dee pahs•sah•djoh |
| I'd like to declare... | **Vorrei dichiarare...** vohr•ray dee•kyah•rah•reh... |
| I have nothing to declare. | **Non ho nulla da dichiarare.** nohn oh nool•lah dah dee•kyah•rah•reh |

## Money and Banking

| | |
|---|---|
| Where's...? | **Dov'è...?** doh•veh... |
| – the ATM | **– il bancomat** eel bahn•koh•maht |

| | |
|---|---|
| – the bank | **– la banca** lah bahn•kah |
| – the currency exchange office | **– l'ufficio di cambio** loof•fee•chyoh dee kahm•byoh |
| When does the bank *open/close*? | **A che ora *apre/chiude* la banca?** ah keh oh•rah *ah•preh/kyoo•deh* lah bahn•kah |
| I'd like to change *dollars/pounds* into euros. | **Vorrei cambiare *dei dollari/delle sterline* in euro.** vohr•ray kahm•byah•reh *day dohl•lah•ree/dehl•leh stehr•lee•neh* een eh•oo•roh |
| I'd like to cash traveler's checks [cheques]. | **Vorrei riscuotere dei travellers cheques.** vohr•ray ree•skwoh•teh•reh day trah•vehl•lehrs chehks |

## *Transportation*

| | |
|---|---|
| How do I get to town? | **Come si arriva in città?** koh•meh see ahr•ree•vah een cheet•tah |
| Where's…? | **Dov'è…?** doh•veh… |
| – the airport | **– l'aeroporto** lah•eh•roh•pohr•toh |
| – the train [railway] station | **– la stazione ferroviaria** lah stah•tsyoh•neh fehr•roh•vyah•ryah |
| – the bus station | **– la stazione degli autobus** lah stah•tsyoh•neh deh•llyee ow•toh•boos |
| – the subway [underground] station | **– la stazione della metropolitana** lah stah•tsyoh•neh dehl•lah meh•troh•poh•lee•tah•nah |
| How far is it? | **Quanto dista?** kwahn•toh dees•tah |
| Where do I buy a ticket? | **Dove si comprano i biglietti?** doh•veh see kohm•prah•noh ee bee•llyeht•tee |
| A *one-way/round-trip [return]* ticket to… | **Un biglietto *di andata/di andata e ritorno* per…** oon bee•llyeht•toh *dee ahn•dah•tah/dee ahn•dah•tah eh ree•tohr•noh* pehr… |
| How much? | **Quant'è?** kwahn•teh |
| Is there a discount? | **C'è uno sconto?** cheh oon•oh skohn•toh |

| | |
|---|---|
| Which…? | **Quale…?** kwah•leh… |
| – gate | **– uscita** oo•shee•tah |
| – line | **– linea** lee•neh•ah |
| – platform | **– binario** bee•nah•ryoh |
| Where can I get a taxi? | **Dove posso trovare un taxi?** doh•veh pohs•soh troh•vah•reh oon tah•ksee |
| Take me to this address. | **Mi porti a questo indirizzo.** mee pohr•tee ah kweh•stoh een•dee•ree•tsoh |
| Where's the car rental [hire]? | **Dov'è un autonoleggio?** doh•veh oon ow•toh•noh•leh•djoh |
| Can I have a map? | **Può darmi una cartina?** pwoh dahr•mee oo•nah kahr•tee•nah |

## Asking Directions

| | |
|---|---|
| How far is it to…? | **Quanto dista…?** kwahn•toh dees•tah… |
| Where's…? | **Dov'è…?** doh•veh… |
| – …Street | **– Via…** vee•ah… |
| – this address | **– questo indirizzo** kweh•stoh een•dee•ree•tsoh |
| Can you show me on the map? | **Può indicarmelo sulla cartina?** pwoh een•dee•kahr•meh•loh sool•lah kahr•tee•nah |
| I'm lost. | **Mi sono perso♂/persa♀.** mee soh•noh pehr•soh♂/pehr•sah♀ |

### You May Hear…

| | |
|---|---|
| **sempre dritto** sehm•preh dreet•toh | straight ahead |
| **a sinistra** ah see•nee•strah | left |
| **a destra** ah deh•strah | right |
| **all'angolo/dietro l'angolo** ahl•lahn•goh•loh/dyeh•troh lahn•goh•loh | on the corner/around the corner |
| **accanto a** ahk•kahn•toh ah | next to |

| | |
|---|---|
| **dopo** doh•poh | after |
| a ***nord/sud*** ah *nohrd/sood* | north/south |
| a ***est/ovest*** ah *ehst/oh•vehst* | east/west |

## Accommodations

| | |
|---|---|
| I have a reservation. | **Ho una prenotazione.** oh oo•nah preh•noh•tah•tsyoh•neh |
| My name is… | **Mi chiamo…** mee kyah•moh… |
| When's check-out? | **A che ora devo lasciare la camera?** ah keh oh•rah deh•voh lah•shah•reh lah kah•meh•rah |
| Can I leave this in the safe? | **Posso lasciare questo nella cassaforte?** pohs•soh lah•shah•reh kweh•stoh nehl•lah kahs•sah•fohr•teh |
| Can I leave my bags? | **Posso lasciare le valigie?** pohs•soh lah•shah•reh leh vah•lee•jyeh |
| I'd like the *bill/receipt*. | **Vorrei *il conto/la ricevuta.*** vohr•ray *eel kohn•toh/lah ree•cheh•voo•tah* |

## Internet and Communications

| | |
|---|---|
| Where's an internet cafe? | **Dov'è un Internet caffè?** doh•veh oon een•tehr•neht kahf•feh |
| Can I *access the internet/check e-mail*? | **Posso *collegarmi a Internet/controllare le e-mail*?** pohs•soh *kohl•leh•gahr•mee ah een•tehr•neht/kohn•trohl•lah•reh leh ee•mayl* |
| Can I have your number, please? | **Mi può dare il suo numero, per favore?** mee pwoh dah•reh eel soo•oh noo•meh•roh pehr fah•voh•reh |
| Here's my *number/e-mail*. | **Ecco *il mio numero/la mia e-mail*.** ehk•koh *eel mee•oh noo•meh•roh/lah mee•ah ee•mayl* |
| *Call/E-mail* me. | **Mi *chiami/mandi una e-mail*.** mee *kyah•mee/mahn•dee oo•nah ee•mayl* |
| Hello. This is... | **Pronto. Sono...** prohn•toh soh•noh... |
| Can I speak to...? | **Posso parlare con...?** pohs•soh pahr•lah•reh kohn... |
| Can you repeat that? | **Può ripetere?** pwoh ree•peh•teh•reh |
| I'll call back later. | **Richiamo più tardi.** ree•kyah•moh pyoo tahr•dee |
| Bye. | **Arrivederla.** ahr•ree•veh•dehr•lah |
| Where's the post office? | **Dov'è un ufficio postale?** doh•veh oon oof•fee•chyoh poh•stah•leh |

## Eating Out

| | |
|---|---|
| Can you recommend a good *restaurant/bar*? | **Può consigliarmi un buon *ristorante/bar*?** pwoh kohn•see•llyahr•mee oon bwohn *ree•stoh•rahn•teh/bahr* |
| Is there a *traditional/inexpensive* restaurant nearby? | **C'è un ristorante *tipico/economico* qui vicino?** cheh oon ree•stoh•rahn•teh *tee•pee•koh/eh•koh•noh•mee•koh* kwee vee•chee•noh |
| A table for..., please. | **Un tavolo per..., per favore.** oon tah•voh•loh pehr...pehr fah•voh•reh |

| | |
|---|---|
| The menu, please. | **Il menù, per favore.** eel meh•noo pehr fah•voh•reh |
| What do you recommend? | **Cosa mi consiglia?** koh•zah mee kohn•see•llyah |
| I'd like… | **Vorrei…** vohr•ray… |
| Enjoy your meal! | **Buon appetito!** bwohn ahp•peh•tee•toh |
| The check [bill], please. | **Il conto, per favore.** eel kohn•toh pehr fah•voh•reh |
| Is service included? | **Il servizio è compreso?** eel sehr•vee•tsyoh eh kohm•preh•zoh |
| Can I *pay by credit card/have a receipt*? | **Posso *pagare con carta di credito/avere una ricevuta*?** pohs•soh *pah•gah•reh kohn kahr•tah dee kreh•dee•toh/ah•veh•reh oo•nah ree•cheh•voo•tah* |

## Breakfast

| | |
|---|---|
| **il burro** eel boor•roh | butter |
| **il pane** eel pah•neh | bread |
| **i cereali** ee cheh•reh•ah•lee | cereal |
| **la marmellata** lah mahr•mehl•lah•tah | jam |
| **il panino** eel pah•nee•noh | roll |
| **la salsiccia** lah sahl•see•chyah | sausage |
| **l'uovo** lwoh•voh | egg |

## Appetizers [Starters]

| | |
|---|---|
| **l'affettato** lahf•feht•tah•toh | platter of cold cuts |
| **l'antipasto misto** lahn•tee•pah•stoh mee•stoh | assorted appetizers |
| **i crostini** ee kroh•stee•nee | toast topped with a variety of ingredients, including tomatoes, sardines and cheese |

**l'insalata di frutti di mare** leen•sah•lah•tah dee froot•tee dee mah•reh — seafood salad

**il prosciutto crudo di Parma** eel proh•shyoot•toh kroo•doh dee pahr•mah — cured ham from Parma

## Soup

**la crema di legumi** lah kreh•mah dee leh•goo•mee — vegetable cream soup

**il minestrone** eel mee•neh•stroh•neh — mixed vegetable and bean soup

**la zuppa di fagioli** lah dzoop•pah dee fah•jyoh•lee — bean soup

**la zuppa di vongole** lah dzoop•pah dee vohn•goh•leh — clam and white wine soup

## Fish and Seafood

**il baccalà** eel bahk•kah•lah — salted, dried cod

**il branzino** eel brahn•dzee•noh — sea bass

**i calamari** ee kah•lah•mah•ree — squid

**le cozze** leh koh•tseh — mussels

**il merluzzo** eel mehr•loo•tsoh — cod

**la sogliola** lah soh•llyoh•lah — sole

**il tonno** eel tohn•noh — tuna

## Meat and Poultry

**la braciola** lah brah•chyoh•lah — grilled pork chop

**l'agnello** lah•nyehl•loh — lamb

**l'anatra** lah•nah•trah — duck

**la bistecca** lah bee•stehk•kah — steak

**gli involtini** llyee een•vohl•tee•nee — thin slices of meat rolled and stuffed

**il maiale** eel mah•yah•leh — pork

| | |
|---|---|
| **il manzo** eel mahn•dzoh | beef |
| **il pollo** eel pohl•loh | chicken |
| **il tacchino** eel tahk•kee•noh | turkey |
| **il vitello** eel vee•tehl•loh | veal |

| | |
|---|---|
| rare | **al sangue** ahl sahn•gweh |
| medium | **mediamente cotta** meh•dyah•mehn•teh koht•tah |
| well-done | **ben cotta** behn koht•tah |

## Pasta

| | |
|---|---|
| **i cannelloni** ee kahn•nehl•loh•nee | stuffed pasta tubes, topped with sauce |
| **le fettuccine** leh feht•too•chee•neh | broad, long pasta made from eggs and flour |
| **gli gnocchi** llyee nyohk•kee | small potato dumplings |
| **le lasagne** leh lah•sah•nyeh | thin pasta strips layered with tomato or white sauce, meat and cheese |

## Pasta Sauces

| | |
|---|---|
| **all'amatriciana** ahl•lah•mah•tree•chyah•nah | bacon and tomato |
| **alla bolognese** ahl•lah boh•loh•nyeh•seh | ground meat and tomato |
| **alla carbonara** ahl•lah kahr•boh•nah•rah | bacon and egg |
| **al pomodoro** ahl poh•moh•doh•roh | simple tomato sauce |

## Vegetables

| | |
|---|---|
| **la bietole** lah byeh•toh•lah | swiss chard |
| **i broccoli** ee brohk•koh•lee | broccoli |
| **il carciofo** eel kahr•chyoh•foh | artichoke |
| **i funghi** ee foon•ghee | mushrooms |

**la melanzana** lah meh•lahn•tsah•nah — eggplant [aubergine]

**il peperone *rosso/verde*** eel peh•peh•roh•neh *rohs•soh/vehr•deh* — *red/green* pepper

## Fruit

**l'arancia** lah•rahn•chah — orange

**la banana** lah bah•nah•nah — banana

**la fragola** lah frah•goh•lah — strawberry

**il limone** eel lee•moh•neh — lemon

**la mela** lah meh•lah — apple

**la pesca** lah peh•skah — peach

**l'uva** loo•vah — grape

## Dessert

**il gelato** eel jeh•lah•toh — ice cream

**la panna cotta** lah pahn•nah koht•tah — molded chilled cream pudding

**il tiramisù** eel tee•rah•mee•soo — coffee- and rum-flavored layered dessert

**la torta** lah tohr•tah — cake

# *Drinks*

The *wine/drink* menu, please.
**La *carta dei vini/lista delle bevande*, per favore.** lah *kahr•tah day vee•nee/lee•stah dehl•leh beh•vahn•deh* pehr fah•voh•reh

I'd like *a bottle/glass* of *red/white* wine.
**Vorrei *una bottiglia/un bicchiere* di vino *rosso/bianco*.** vohr•ray *oo•nah boht•tee•llyah/oon beek•kyeh•reh* dee vee•noh *rohs•soh/byahn•koh*

Another *bottle/glass*, please.
***Un'altra bottiglia/Un altro bicchiere*, per favore.** *oo•nahl•trah boht•tee•llyah/oo•nahl•troh beek•kyeh•reh* pehr fah•voh•reh

| | |
|---|---|
| I'd like a local beer. | **Vorrei una birra locale.** vohr·ray oo·nah beer·rah loh·kah·leh |
| Cheers! | **Salute!** sah·loo·teh |
| A *coffee/tea*, please. | **Un *caffè/tè*, per favore.** oon *kahf·feh/teh* pehr fah·voh·reh |
| Black. | **Nero.** neh·roh |
| With… | **Con…** kohn… |
| – some milk | **– un po' di latte** oon poh dee laht·teh |
| – sugar | **– lo zucchero** loh dzook·keh·roh |
| – artificial sweetener | **– il dolcificante** eel dohl·chee·fee·kahn·teh |
| …, please. | **…, per favore.** …pehr fah·voh·reh |
| – A juice | **– Un succo** oon sook·koh |
| – A soda | **– Una bibita** oo·nah bee·bee·tah |
| – A (sparkling/still) water | **– Un bicchiere d'acqua (frizzante/ naturale)** oon beek·kyeh·reh dah·kwah (free·dzahn·teh/nah·too·rah·leh) |

## Aperitifs, Cocktails and Liqueurs

| | |
|---|---|
| **l'amaretto** lah·mah·reht·toh | almond liqueur |
| **l'amaro** lah·mah·roh | bitter |
| **la sambuca** lah sahm·boo·kah | aniseed-flavored liqueur |
| **il digestivo** eel dee·jehs·tee·voh | after-dinner drink |

# *Talking*

| | |
|---|---|
| Hello! | **Salve!** sahl·veh |
| Hi! | **Ciao!** chah·oh |
| Good morning. | **Buongiorno.** bwohn·jyohr·noh |
| Good afternoon. | **Buon pomeriggio.** bwohn poh·meh·ree·djoh |
| Good evening. | **Buonasera.** bwoh·nah·seh·rah |
| How are you? | **Come sta?** koh·meh stah |

| | |
|---|---|
| Fine, thanks. | **Bene, grazie.** beh•neh grah•tsyeh |
| Excuse me! | **Scusi!** skoo•zee |
| What's your name? | **Come si chiama?** koh•meh see kyah•mah |
| My name is... | **Mi chiamo...** mee kyah•moh... |
| Nice to meet you. | **Piacere.** pyah•cheh•reh |
| Where are you from? | **Di dov'è?** dee doh•veh |
| I'm American. | **Sono americano ♂/americana ♀.** soh•noh ah•meh•ree•kah•noh ♂/ah•meh•ree•kah•nah ♀ |
| I'm British. | **Sono inglese.** soh•noh een•gleh•zeh |
| Goodbye. | **Arrivederla.** ahr•ree•veh•dehr•lah |
| See you later. | **A dopo.** ah doh•poh |

**Signore** (Mr.), **Signora** (Mrs.), **Signorina** (Miss) and professional titles—**Dottore** (Dr.), **Professore** (Professor)—are frequently used, even when you don't know the person's last name. When trying to get someone's attention, you don't have to include his or her title; a simple **Scusi!** (formal) or **Scusa!** (informal) is sufficient.

## Communication Difficulties

| | |
|---|---|
| Do you speak English? | **Parla inglese?** pahr•lah een•gleh•zeh |
| I don't speak (much) Italian. | **Non parlo (molto bene l') italiano.** nohn pahr•loh (mohl•toh beh•neh l) ee•tah•lyah•noh |
| Can you speak more slowly? | **Può parlare più lentamente?** pwoh pahr•lah•reh pyoo lehn•tah•mehn•teh |
| I (don't) understand. | **(Non) capisco.** (nohn) kah•pee•skoh |

# *Sightseeing*

| | |
|---|---|
| Where's the tourist information office? | **Dov'è l'ufficio informazioni turistiche?** doh•veh loof•fee•chyoh een•fohr•mah•tsyoh•nee too•ree•stee•keh |

| | |
|---|---|
| Do you have tours in English? | **Ci sono visite guidate in inglese?** chee soh•noh vee•zee•teh gwee•dah•teh een een•gleh•zeh |
| Can I have a *map/guide*? | **Mi può dare una *cartina/guida*?** mee pwoh dah•reh oo•nah *kahr•tee•nah/gwee•dah* |

## Sights

| | |
|---|---|
| Where *is/are*...? | ***Dov'è/Dove* sono...?** *doh•veh/doh•veh* soh•noh... |
| – the castle | **– il castello** eel kah•stehl•loh |
| – the cathedral | **– la cattedrale** lah kaht•teh•drah•leh |
| – the downtown area | **– il centro** eel chehn•troh |
| – the museum | **– il museo** eel moo•zeh•oh |
| – the shopping area | **– i negozi** ee neh•goh•tzee |

# *Shopping*

| | |
|---|---|
| Where's the *market/ mall [shopping centre]*? | **Dov'è il *mercato/centro commerciale*?** doh•veh eel *mehr•kah•toh/chehn•troh kohm•mehr•chyah•leh* |
| I'm just looking. | **Sto solo guardando.** stoh soh•loh gwahr•dahn•doh |
| Can you help me? | **Può aiutarmi?** pwoh ah•yoo•tahr•mee |
| I'm being helped. | **Mi stanno servendo.** mee stahn•noh sehr•vehn•doh |
| How much? | **Quant'è?** kwahn•teh |
| That one, please. | **Quello, per favore.** kwehl•loh pehr fah•voh•reh |
| That's all. | **Basta così.** bah•stah koh•zee |
| Where can I pay? | **Dove posso pagare?** doh•veh pohs•soh pah•gah•reh |
| I'll pay *in cash/by credit card*. | **Pago *in contanti/con carta di credito*.** pah•goh *een kohn•tahn•tee/kohn kahr•tah dee kreh•dee•toh* |
| A receipt, please. | **Una ricevuta, per favore.** oo•nah ree•cheh•voo•tah pehr fah•voh•reh |

## Stores

| | |
|---|---|
| Where's…? | **Dov'è…?** doh·veh… |
| – the bakery | **– una panetteria** oo·nah pah·neht·teh·ree·ah |
| – the bookstore | **– una libreria** oo·nah lee·breh·ree·ah |
| – the department store | **– un grande magazzino** oon grahn·deh mah·gah·dzee·noh |
| – the pharmacy [chemist] | **– una farmacia** oo·nah fahr·mah·chee·ah |
| – the supermarket | **– un supermercato** oon soo·pehr·mehr·kah·toh |

## Clothing

| | |
|---|---|
| I'd like… | **Vorrei…** vohr·ray… |
| Can I try this on? | **Posso provarlo?** pohs·soh proh·vahr·loh |
| It doesn't fit. | **Non mi va bene.** nohn mee vah beh·neh |
| Do you have this in a *bigger/smaller* size? | **Non c'è in una taglia più *grande/piccola*?** nohn cheh een oo·nah tah·llyah pyoo *grahn·deh/peek·koh·lah* |

### Color

| | |
|---|---|
| I'd like something… | **Vorrei qualcosa di…** vohr·ray kwahl·koh·zah dee… |
| – black | **– nero** neh·roh |
| – blue | **– blu** bloo |
| – brown | **– marrone** mahr·roh·neh |
| – green | **– verde** vehr·deh |
| – orange | **– arancione** ahr·ahn·chyoh·neh |
| – red | **– rosso** rohs·soh |
| – white | **– bianco** byahn·koh |
| – yellow | **– giallo** jyahl·loh |

## Sports and Leisure

| | |
|---|---|
| Where's…? | **Dov'è…?** doh•veh… |
| – the beach | **– la spiaggia** lah spyah•djah |
| – the park | **– il parco** eel pahr•koh |
| – the pool | **– la piscina** lah pee•shee•nah |
| Can I rent [hire] golf clubs? | **Posso noleggiare delle mazze?** pohs•soh noh•leh•djah•reh dehl•leh mah•tseh |

## Culture and Nightlife

| | |
|---|---|
| Do you have a program of events? | **Mi può dare un calendario degli eventi?** mee pwoh dah•reh oon kah•lehn•dah•ryoh deh•llyee eh•vehn•tee |
| Where's…? | **Dov'è…?** doh•veh… |
| – the downtown area | **– il centro** eel chehn•troh |
| – the bar | **– il bar** eel bahr |
| – the dance club | **– la discoteca** lah dee•skoh•teh•kah |

## Business Travel

| | |
|---|---|
| I'm here on business. | **Sono qui per lavoro.** soh•noh kwee pehr lah•voh•roh |
| Here's my business card. | **Ecco il mio biglietto da visita.** ehk•koh eel mee•oh bee•llyeht•toh dah vee•zee•tah |
| Can I have your card? | **Mi può dare il suo biglietto da visita?** mee pwoh dah•reh eel soo•oh bee•llyeht•toh dah vee•zee•tah |
| I have a meeting with… | **Ho una riunione con…** oh oo•nah ryoo•nyoh•neh kohn… |
| Where's…? | **Dov'è…?** doh•veh… |
| – the business center | **– il centro business** eel chehn•troh bees•nehs |

| | |
|---|---|
| – the convention hall | – **la sala congressi** lah sah•lah kohn•grehs•see |
| – the meeting room | – **la sala riunioni** lah sah•lah ryoo•nyoh•nee |

## Travel with Children

| | |
|---|---|
| Is there a discount for kids? | **È previsto uno sconto per bambini?** eh preh•vee•stoh oo•noh skohn•toh pehr bahm•bee•nee |
| Can you recommend a babysitter? | **Può consigliarmi una babysitter?** pwoh kohn•see•llyahr•mee oo•nah bah•bee•seet•tehr |
| Do you have a child's *seat/highchair*? | **Avete un *seggiolino/seggiolone* per bambini?** ah•veh•teh oon *seh•djoh•lee•noh/ seh•djoh•loh•neh* pehr bahm•bee•nee |
| Where can I change the baby? | **Dove posso cambiare il bambino?** doh•veh poh•soh kahm•byah•reh eel bahm•bee•noh |

## For the Disabled

| | |
|---|---|
| Is there…? | **C'è…?** cheh… |
| – access for the disabled | – **l'accesso per disabili** lah•cheh•soh pehr dee•zah•bee•lee |
| – a wheelchair ramp | – **la rampa per le sedie a rotelle** lah rahm•pah pehr leh seh•dyeh ah roh•tehl•leh |
| – a handicapped- [disabled-] accessible restroom | – **la toilette per i disabili** lah twah•leht pehr ee dee•zah•bee•lee |
| I need… | **Mi serve…** mee sehr•veh… |
| – assistance | – **assistenza** ah•see•stehn•tsah |
| – an elevator [a lift] | – **un ascensore** oon ah•shehn•soh•reh |
| – a ground-floor room | – **una stanza al pianterreno** oo•nah stahn•tsah ahl pyahn•tehr•reh•noh |

# Emergencies

| | |
|---|---|
| Help! | **Aiuto!** ah•yoo•toh |
| Go away! | **Se ne vada!** seh neh vah•dah |
| Stop, thief! | **Fermi, al ladro!** fehr•mee ahl lah•droh |
| Get a doctor! | **Un medico!** oon meh•dee•koh |
| Fire! | **Al fuoco!** ahl fwoh•koh |
| I'm lost. | **Mi sono perso♂/persa♀.** mee soh•noh pehr•soh♂/pehr•sah♀ |
| Can you help me? | **Può aiutarmi?** pwoh ah•yoo•tahr•mee |
| Call the police! | **Chiami la polizia!** kyah•mee lah poh•lee•tsee•ah |

# Health

| | |
|---|---|
| I'm sick [ill]. | **Sto male.** stoh mah•leh |
| I need an English-speaking doctor. | **Ho bisogno di un medico che parli inglese.** oh bee•soh•nyoh dee oon meh•dee•koh keh pahr•lee een•gleh•zeh |
| It hurts here. | **Mi fa male qui.** mee fah mah•leh kwee |

# Reference

## Numbers

0 **zero** dzeh•roh
1 **uno** oo•noh
2 **due** doo•eh
3 **tre** treh
4 **quattro** kwaht•troh
5 **cinque** cheen•kweh
6 **sei** say
7 **sette** seht•teh
8 **otto** oht•toh
9 **nove** noh•veh
10 **dieci** dyeh•chee
11 **undici** oon•dee•chee
12 **dodici** doh•dee•chee
13 **tredici** treh•dee•chee
14 **quattordici** kwaht•tohr•dee•chee
15 **quindici** kween•dee•chee

16 **sedici** seh•dee•chee

17 **diciassette** dee•chyahs•seht•teh

18 **diciotto** dee•chyoht•toh

19 **diciannove** dee•chyahn•noh•veh

20 **venti** vehn•tee

21 **ventuno** vehn•too•noh

22 **ventidue** vehn•tee•doo•eh

30 **trenta** trehn•tah

31 **trentuno** trehn•too•noh

40 **quaranta** kwah•rahn•tah

50 **cinquanta** cheen•kwahn•tah

60 **sessanta** sehs•sahn•tah

70 **settanta** seht•tahn•tah

80 **ottanta** oht•tahn•tah

90 **novanta** noh•vahn•tah

100 **cento** chehn•toh

101 **centouno** chen•toh•oo•noh

200 **duecento** doo•eh•chehn•toh

500 **cinquecento** cheen•kweh•chehn•toh

1,000 **mille** meel•leh

10,000 **diecimila** dyeh•chee•mee•lah

1,000,000 **milione** mee•lyoh•neh

## Time

What time is it? — **Che *ore sono*?** keh *oh•reh soh•noh*

From one o'clock to two o'clock. — **Dall'una alle due.** dahl•loo•nah ahl•leh doo•eh

5:30 a.m./5:30 p.m. — **le cinque e mezzo/le diciassette e trenta** leh cheen•kweh eh meh•dzoh/leh dee•chyahs•seht•teh eh trehn•tah

## Days

Monday — **lunedì** loon•eh•dee

Tuesday — **martedì** mahr•teh•dee

Wednesday — **mercoledì** mehr•koh•leh•dee

Thursday — **giovedì** jyoh•veh•dee

Friday — **venerdì** veh•nehr•dee

Saturday — **sabato** sah•bah•toh

Sunday — **domenica** doh•meh•nee•kah

## Dates

| | |
|---|---|
| yesterday | **ieri** yeh•ree |
| today | **oggi** oh•djee |
| tomorrow | **domani** doh•mah•nee |

## Months

| | | | |
|---|---|---|---|
| January | **gennaio** jehn•nah•yoh | July | **luglio** loo•llyoh |
| February | **febbraio** fehb•brah•yoh | August | **agosto** ah•goh•stoh |
| March | **marzo** mahr•tsoh | September | **settembre** seht•tehm•breh |
| April | **aprile** ah•pree•leh | October | **ottobre** oht•toh•breh |
| May | **maggio** mah•djoh | November | **novembre** noh•vehm•breh |
| June | **giugno** jyoo•nyoh | December | **dicembre** dee•chem•breh |

# Norwegian

## Pronunciation

This section is designed to make you familiar with the sounds of Norwegian—the Oslo accent—by using our simplified phonetic transcription. You'll find the pronunciation of the Norwegian letters explained below, together with their "imitated" equivalents (the Norwegian alphabet is the same as in English, with the addition of the letters **æ**, **ø** and **å**).

Stress has been indicated in the phonetic transcription with underlining, tone with the accent marks and long vowels with bold.

▶ For more on Norwegian tone, see page 11.

▶ For more on Norwegian vowels, see page 9.

### Consonants

| Letter | Approximate Pronunciation | Symbol | Example | Pronunciation |
|---|---|---|---|---|
| g | 1. before i and y, (sometimes before ei) like y in yes | y | **gi** | y**ee** |
| | 2. elsewhere, like g in go | g | **gått** | goht |
| gj | like y in yes | y | **gjest** | yehst |
| j | like y in yes | y | **ja** | y**ah** |
| k | 1. before i, y and ei like h in hue, but with the tongue raised a little higher | kh | **kino** | kh**ee**´·nu |
| | 2. elsewhere, like k in kit | k | **kaffe** | kahf´·fuh |
| kj | like h in hue, but with the tongue raised a little higher | kh | **kjøre** | kh**ur**`·ruh |

| Letter | Approximate Pronunciation | Symbol | Example | Pronunciation |
|---|---|---|---|---|
| r | rolled near the front of the mouth | r | **rare** | rah`·ruh |
| s | like s in sit | s | **spise** | spee`·suh |
| sj | like sh in shut | sh | **stasjon** | stah·shoo´n |
| sk | 1. before i and y (sometimes before øy), like sh in shut | sh | **ski** | shee |
| | 2. elsewhere, like sk in skate | sk | **skole** | skoo`·luh |
| skj | like sh in shut | sh | **skje** | sheh |
| w | like v in vice | v | **whisky** | vihs´·kih |
| z | like s in sit | s | **zoom** | soom |

Letters b, c, d, f, h, l, m, n, p, q, t, v, x are generally pronounced as in English.

In Norwegian, consonants are silent in the following situations:
1. The letter **d** is generally silent after **l**, **n** or **r** (e.g. **holde**, **land**, **gård**), and sometimes at the end of words (e.g. **god**, **med**).
2. The letter **g** is silent in the endings **-lig** and **-ig**.
3. The letter **h** is silent when followed by a consonant (e.g. **hjem**, **hva**).
4. The letter **t** is silent in the definite form ("the") of neuter nouns (e.g., **eplet**) and in the pronoun **det**.
5. The letter **v** is silent in certain words (e.g. **selv**, **tolv**, **halv**).
6. In the eastern part of Norway the letter **r** is silent when followed by **l**, **n**, **s**, **t** (and sometimes **d**). These consonants then are pronounced with the tip of the tongue turned up well behind the front teeth. The **r** then ceases to be pronounced, but influences the tone of the following consonant. This "retroflex" pronunciation also occurs in words ending with an **r** if the following word begins with a **d**, **l**, **n**, **s** or **t**.

## Vowels

| Letter | Approximate Pronunciation | Symbol | Example | Pronunciation |
|---|---|---|---|---|
| a | 1. like a in father, but longer | ah | **tak** | tahk |
| | 2. like a in father | ah | **takk** | tahk |
| e | 1. like e in get, but longer | eh | **sent** | sehnt |
| | 2. like e in get | eh | **penn** | pehn |
| | 3. like a in bad | a | **her** | har |
| | 4. before r, like a in bad | a | **herre** | ha`·ruh |
| | 5. like u in uncle | uh | **sitte** | sih`·tuh |
| i | 1. like ee in bee | ee | **hit** | heet |
| | 2. like i in sit | ih | **sitt** | siht |
| o | 1. like oo in soon, with lips tightly rounded | oo | **ord** | oor |
| | 2. like aw in saw | aw | **tog** | tawg |
| | 3. like u in put, with lips tightly rounded | u | **ost** | ust |
| | 4. like o in cloth | oh | **stoppe** | stohp`·puh |
| | 5. before r, like oo in soon | oo | **hvor** | voor |
| u | 1. like ew in few, but longer | ew | **mur** | mewr |
| | 2. like ew in few | ew | **busk** | bewsk |
| | 3. like u in put, with lips tightly rounded | u | **bukk** | buk |
| y | 1. like ui in fruit, but longer | ui | **myr** | muir |
| | 2. like ui in fruit | ui | **bygge** | buig`·guh |

| Letter | Approximate Pronunciation | Symbol | Example | Pronunciation |
|---|---|---|---|---|
| æ | 1. like a in bad, but longer | a | **lære** | la`·ruh |
| | 2. like a in bad | a | **færre** | far´·ruh |
| ø | 1. like ur in fur, but longer and with lips rounded | ur | **blø** | bl**ur** |
| | 2. like ur in fur, with lips rounded | ur | **sønn** | surn |
| å | 1. like aw in saw, but longer | aw | **såpe** | s**aw**`·puh |
| | 2. like o in cloth | oh | **gått** | goht |

## Vowel Combinations

| Letter | Approximate Pronunciation | Symbol | Example | Pronunciation |
|---|---|---|---|---|
| ai | like ie in tie | ie | **mais** | mies |
| au | like ev in ever | ev | **sau** | sev |
| ei | like ay in say | ay | **geit** | yayt |
| eg | at the end of a word and before n, like ay in say | ay | **jeg** | yay |
| oi | like oi in oil | oi | **koie** | koi`·uh |
| øy | like ur + y | ury | **høy** | hury |

In Norwegian, vowel length distinguishes meaning. All vowels come in two lengths, long and short. Long vowels are in bold throughout the phonetics.
Norwegian is a tonal language. This means that tone is used to distinguish between certain words, which otherwise would sound the same. For example:
**hender** (hehn´·nuhr), tone 1 = plural of **hånd** (hand)
**hender** (hehn`·nuhr), tone 2 = present tense of **hende** (happen)

In the phonetics, tone 1, which is a rising tone (i.e., starts low and rises in pitch) is marked with the acute accent (´); tone 2, which is a falling tone (i.e., starts high and lowers in pitch), with the grave accent (`).

## Basic Expressions

| | |
|---|---|
| Hello/Hi! | **Hallo/Hei!** hah•loo´/hay |
| Goodbye. | **Adjø.** ahd•yur´ |
| Yes. | **Ja.** yah |
| No. | **Nei.** nay |
| OK. | **OK.** u•kaw´ |
| Excuse me. | **Unnskyld.** ewn´•shewl |
| Sorry! | **Beklager!** buh•klah´•guhr |
| Please. | **Vær så snill.** var saw snihl |
| Thank you. | **Takk.** tahk |
| You're welcome. | **Ingen årsak.** ihng`•uhn awr`•sahk |
| Where is the restroom [toilet]? | **Hvor er toalettet?** voor ar tu•ah•leh´•tuh |

## *Arrival and Departure*

| | |
|---|---|
| I'm here on *vacation [holiday]/business.* | **Jeg er her *på ferie/i forretninger.*** yay **a**r h**a**r *paw feh´r•yuh/ih fohr•reht´•nihng•uhr* |
| I'm going to… | **Jeg reiser til…** yay rays`•uhr tihl… |
| I'm staying at the… Hotel. | **Jeg bor på Hotell…** yay b**oo**r paw hu•tehl´… |

## Passport Control and Customs

| | |
|---|---|
| I'm just passing through. | **Jeg er bare på gjennomreise.** yay **a**r b**ah**`•ruh paw yehn`•nohm•ray•suh |
| I would like to declare… | **Jeg vil gjerne fortolle…** yay vihl ya`r•nuh fohr•tohl´•luh… |
| I have nothing to declare. | **Jeg har ingenting å fortolle.** yay h**ah**r ihng`•uhn•tihng aw fohr•tohl´•luh |

## *Money and Banking*

| | |
|---|---|
| Where's…? | **Hvor er det…?** voor **a**r deh… |
| – the ATM | **– en minibank** ehn m**ee**´•nih•bangk |
| – the bank | **– en bank** ehn bahngk |
| – the currency exchange office | **– et vekslingskontor** eht vehk`s•lihngs•kun•t**oo**r |
| What time does the bank *open/close*? | **Når *åpner/stenger* banken?** nohr ***aw**`p•nuhr/stehng`•uhr* bahng´•kuhn |
| I'd like to change some *dollars/pounds.* | **Jeg vil gjerne veksle noen *dollar/pund.*** yay vihl y**a**`r•nuh vehk`s•luh n**oo**`•uhn *dohl´•lahr/pewn* |
| I'd like to cash a traveler's check [cheque]. | **Jeg vil gjerne løse inn en reisesjekk.** yay vihl y**a**`r•nuh l**ur**`•suh ihn ehn ray`•suh•shehk |

## *Transportation*

| | |
|---|---|
| How do I get to town? | **Hvordan kommer jeg til byen?** voor´•dahn kohm´•muhr yay tihl b**ui**´•uhn |
| Where is…? | **Hvor er…?** voor **a**r… |

| | |
|---|---|
| – the airport | **– flyplassen** flui´•plahs•suhn |
| – the train [railway] station | **– jernbanestasjonen** ya`rn•bah•nuh•stah•shoon•uhn |
| – the bus station | **– busstasjonen** bews´•stah•shoon•uhn |
| – the subway [underground] station | **– T-banestasjonen** teh´•bah•nuh•stah•shoon•uhn |
| How far is it? | **Hvor langt er det?** voor lahngt ar deh |
| Where can I buy tickets? | **Hvor kan jeg kjøpe billetter?** voor kahn yay khur`•puh bihl•leht´•tuhr |
| A *one-way [single]/ round-trip [return]* ticket. | **En *enveisbillett/tur-returbillett.*** ehn *ehn´•vays•bihl•leht/tewr•reh•tew´r•bil•leht* |
| How much? | **Hvor mye koster det?** voor mui`•uh kohs`•tuhr deh |
| Are there any discounts? | **Er det noen rabatter?** ar deh noo`•uhn rah•baht´•tuhr |
| Which...? | **Hvilken...?** vihl´•kuhn... |
| – gate | **– utgang** ew`t•gahng |
| – line | **– linje** lihn`•yuh |
| – platform | **– perrong** pehr•rohng´ |
| Where can I get a taxi? | **Hvor kan jeg få tak i en drosje?** voor kahn yay faw tahk ih ehn drohsh`•uh |
| Can you take me to this address? | **Kan du kjøre meg til denne adressen?** kahn dew khur`•ruh may tihl dehn`•nuh ahd•rehs´•suhn |
| Where can I rent a car? | **Hvor kan jeg leie bil?** voor kahn yay lay`•uh beel |
| Can I have a map? | **Kan jeg få et kart?** kahn yay faw eht kahrt |

## Asking Directions

| | |
|---|---|
| How far is it to...? | **Hvor langt er det til...?** voor lahngt ar deh tihl... |
| Where's...? | **Hvor er...?** voor ar... |

| | |
|---|---|
| – …Street | **– …gate** …gah`·tuh |
| – this address | **– denne adressen** dehn`·nuh ahd·rehs´·suhn |
| Can you show me where I am on the map? | **Kan du vise meg på kartet hvor jeg er?** kahn dew vee`·suh may paw kahr´·tuh voor yay ar |
| I'm lost. | **Jeg har gått meg vill.** yay hahr goht may vihl |

## You May Hear…

| | |
|---|---|
| **rett frem** reht frehm | straight ahead |
| **på venstre side** poh vehn´·struh see`·duh | on the left |
| **på høyre side** poh hury´·ruh see`·duh | on the right |
| ***på/rundt* hjørnet** *poh/rewnt* yurr`·nuh | *on/around* the corner |
| **ved siden av…** veh see`·duhn ah… | next to… |
| **etter…** eht`·tuhr… | after… |
| **nord/sør** noor/surr | north/south |
| **øst/vest** urst/vehst | east/west |

## Accommodations

| | |
|---|---|
| I have a reservation. | **Jeg har bestilt rom.** yay hahr buh·stihlt´ rum |
| My name is… | **Jeg heter…** yay heh`·tuhr… |
| When's check-out? | **Når må jeg sjekke ut?** nohr maw yay shehk`·kuh ewt |
| Can I leave my bags? | **Kan jeg sette igjen bagasjen?** kahn yay seht`·tuh ih·yehn´ bah·gah´·shuhn |
| Can I have *the bill/ a receipt*? | **Kan jeg få *regningen/en kvittering*?** kahn yay faw *ray`·ning·uhn/ehn kviht·teh´·rihng* |

## Internet and Communications

Where's an internet cafe? — **Hvor finner jeg en internettkafé?** voor fihn´•nuhr yay ehn ihn´•tuhr•neht•kah•feh

Can I access *the internet/check e-mail*? — **Kan jeg *bruke internett/sjekke e-post*?** kahn yay *brew`•kuh ihn´•tuhr•neht/shehk`•kuh eh´•pohst*

Can I have your phone number? — **Kan jeg få telefonnummeret ditt?** kahn yay faw teh•luh•foon´•num•muhr•uh diht

Here's my *number/e-mail address.* — **Her har du *nummeret mitt/e-postadressen min.*** har hahr dew *num´•muhr•uh miht/eh´•pohst•ahd•rehs•suhn mihn*

Call me. — **Ring meg.** rihng may

E-mail me. — **Send meg en e-post.** sehn may ehn eh´•pohst

Where's the post office? — **Hvor er postkontoret?** voor ar pohst´•kun•toor•uh

## Eating Out

Can you recommend a good *restaurant/bar*? — **Kan du anbefale en bra *restaurant/bar*?** kahn dew ahn´•buh•fah•luh ehn brah *rehs•tew•rahng´/bahr*

Is there *a traditional Norwegian/an inexpensive* restaurant near here? — **Fins det en *typisk norsk/billig* restaurant i nærheten?** fihns deh ehn *tui´•pihsk nohrsk/bihl`•lih* rehs•tew•rahng´ ih nar´•heh•tuhn

A table for… — **Et bord til…** eht boor tihl…

Can I have a menu? — **Kan jeg få se menyen?** kahn yay faw seh meh•nui´•uhn

What do you recommend? — **Hva kan du anbefale?** vah kahn dew ahn´•buh•fah•luh

I'd like… — **Jeg vil gjerne ha…** yay vihl ya`r•nuh hah…

Can I have more…? — **Kan jeg få litt mer…?** kahn yay faw liht mehr…

Enjoy your meal! — **God appetitt!** gu ahp•puh•tiht´

| | |
|---|---|
| Can I have the check [bill]? | **Kan jeg få regningen?** kahn yay faw ray`•nihng•uhn |
| Is service included? | **Er service inkludert?** ar surr´•vihs ing•klew•dehrt´ |
| Can I have a receipt? | **Kan jeg få kvittering?** kahn yay faw kviht•teh´•rihng |

## Breakfast

| | |
|---|---|
| **brød** brur | bread |
| **eggerøre** ehg`•guh•rur•ruh | scrambled eggs |
| **frokostblanding** froo´•kohst•blahn•nihng | cereal |
| **havregrøt** hahv`•ruh•grurt | oatmeal [porridge] |
| **smør** smurr | butter |
| **syltetøy** suil`•tuh•tury | jam |
| **yoghurt** yoo´•gewrt | yogurt |

## Appetizers [Starters]

| | |
|---|---|
| **fenalår** feh`•nah•lawr | cured leg of mutton |
| **ferske reker** fehrs`•kuh reh`•kuhr | unshelled shrimp [prawns] |
| **gravlaks** grahv`•lahks | cured salmon flavored with dill |
| **kamskjell** kahm`•shehl | scallop |
| **røkelaks** rur`•kuh•lahks | smoked salmon |

## Soup

| | |
|---|---|
| **fiskesuppe** fihs`•kuh•sewp•puh | fish soup |
| **gul ertesuppe** gewl ar`•tuh•sewp•puh | yellow pea soup |
| **kjøttsuppe** khurt`•sewp•puh | meat soup |
| **soppsuppe** sohp`•sewp•puh | field mushroom soup |

## Fish and Seafood

| | |
|---|---|
| **hummer** hum´•muhr | lobster |
| **kveite** kvay`•tuh | halibut |
| **laks** lahks | salmon |

**reker** reh`•kuhr — shrimp [prawns]

**torsk** tohrsk — cod

## Meat and Poultry

**and** ahn — duck

**elg** ehlg — moose

**hjort** yohrt — deer

**kalvekjøtt** kahl`•vuh•khurt — veal

**kylling** khuil`•lihng — chicken

**lammekjøtt** lahm`•muh•khurt — lamb

**oksekjøtt** ohk`•suh•khurt — beef

**reinsdyr** rayns´•duir — reindeer

**svinekjøtt** svee`•nuh•khurt — pork

| | |
|---|---|
| rare | **råstekt** raw`•stehkt |
| medium | **medium stekt** meh´•dih•ewm stehkt |
| well-done | **godt stekt** goht stehkt |

## Vegetables and Staples

| | |
|---|---|
| **agurk** ah•gewr´k | cucumber |
| **blomkål** blohm´•kawl | cauliflower |
| **erter** ar´•tuhr | peas |
| **gulrøtter** gew`l•rurt•tuhr | carrots |
| **kål** kawl | cabbage |
| **potet** pu•teh´t | potato |
| **tomater** tu•maht´•uhr | tomatoes |

## Fruit

| | |
|---|---|
| **appelsin** ahp•puhl•see´n | orange |
| **banan** bah•nah´n | banana |
| **eple** ehp`•luh | apple |
| **jordbær** yoo´r•bar | strawberries |
| **molter/multer** mohl`•tuhr/mewl`•tuhr | arctic cloudberries |
| **tyttebær** tuit´•tuh•bar | lingonberry |

## Dessert

| | |
|---|---|
| **is** ees | ice cream |
| **karamellpudding** kah•rah•mehl´•pewd•dihng | creme caramel |
| **pannekaker** pahn`•nuh•kah•kuhr | pancakes |
| **tilslørte bondepiker** tihl´•slurr•tuh bun´•nuh•pee•kuhr | layers of stewed apples, cookie [biscuit] crumbs, and whipped cream |
| **varm eplekake med krem** vahrm ehp`•luh•kah•kuh meh krehm | hot apple pie with whipped cream |

# *Drinks*

| | |
|---|---|
| Can I have the *wine list/drink menu*? | **Kan jeg få se *vinkartet/drikkekartet*?** kahn yay faw seh *veen`•kahr•tuh/drihk`•kuh•kahr•tuh* |
| Can I have the house wine? | **Kan jeg få husets vin?** kahn yay faw hew´s•uhs veen |

| | |
|---|---|
| Cheers! | **Skål!** skawl |
| A *coffee/tea*, please. | **En *kaffe/te*, takk.** ehn *kahf´·fuh/teh* tahk |
| Black. | **Svart.** svahrt |
| With… | **Med…** meh… |
| – milk | **– melk** mehlk |
| – sugar | **– sukker** suk´·kuhr |
| – artificial sweetener | **– søtningsmiddel** sur`t·nihngs·mihd·duhl |
| A glass of…, please. | **Et glass…, takk.** eht glahs…tahk |
| – juice | **– juice** yews |
| – soda | **– soda** soo´·dah |
| – (*sparkling/still*) water | **– vann (*med kullsyre/uten kullsyre*)** vahn (*meh kewl`·sui·ruh/ew`·tuhn kewl`·sui·ruh*) |
| red wine | **rødvin** rur´·veen |
| white wine | **hvitvin** veet´·veen |
| *light/dark* beer | ***lyst/mørkt* øl** *luist/murrkt* url |
| aquavit | **akevitt** ah·kuh·viht´ |
| cognac | **konjakk** kohn·yahk´ |

## Talking

| | |
|---|---|
| Hello/Hi! | **Hallo/Hei!** hah·loo´/hay |
| Good morning. | **God morgen.** gum·maw`·ruhn |
| Good afternoon. | **God dag.** gud·dah´g |
| Good evening. | **God aften/God kveld.** gu·ahf`·tuhn/guk·kvehl´ |
| How are you? | **Hvordan står det til?** voor´·dahn stawr deh tihl |
| Fine, thanks. | **Bare bra, takk.** bah`·ruh brah tahk |
| Excuse me. | **Unnskyld.** ewn´·shewl |
| What's your name? | **Hva heter du?** vah heh`·tuhr dew |
| My name is… | **Jeg heter…** yay heh`·tuhr… |
| Nice to meet you! | **Hyggelig å treffes!** huig`·guh·lih aw trehf`·fuhs |
| Where are you from? | **Hvor kommer du fra?** voor kohm´·muhr dew frah |

| | |
|---|---|
| I'm from *the U.S./ the U.K.* | **Jeg er fra *USA/Storbritannia*.** yay ar frah *ew·ehs·ah´/stoo´r·brih·tahn·yah* |
| Goodbye. | **Adjø.** ahd·yur´ |
| See you later. | **Vi ses.** vee seh`·uhs |

> **i** **De** (the formal form of "you") is generally no longer used to address strangers, but is restricted to written works and addressing older people. As a general rule, **du** can be used in all situations without offending anyone.

## Communication Difficulties

| | |
|---|---|
| Do you speak English? | **Snakker du engelsk?** snahk`·kuhr dew ehng´·uhlsk |
| I don't speak (much) Norwegian. | **Jeg snakker ikke (så bra) norsk.** yay snahk`·kuhr ihk`·kuh (saw brah) norsk |
| Could you speak more slowly? | **Kan du snakke litt langsommere?** kahn dew snahk`·kuh liht lahng`·sohm·muh·ruh |
| I (don't) understand. | **Jeg forstår (ikke).** yay for·staw´r (ihk`·kuh) |

# *Sightseeing*

| | |
|---|---|
| Where's the tourist information office? | **Hvor er turistkontoret?** voor ar tew·rihst´·kun·too·ruh |
| Do you have tours in English? | **Har dere omvisninger på engelsk?** hahr deh`·ruh ohm´·vihs·nihng·uhr poh ehng´·uhlsk |
| Can I have a *map/ guide*? | **Kan jeg få *et kart/en guide*?** kahn yay faw *eht kahrt/ehn gied* |

## Sights

| | |
|---|---|
| Where *is/are*...? | **Hvor er...?** voor ar... |
| – the castle | **– slottet** slot´·tuh |
| – the downtown area | **– sentrum** sehn´·trewm |
| – the museum | **– museet** mew·seh´·uh |
| – the shopping area | **– handlestrøket** hahn`d·luh·strur·kuh |

## Shopping

| | |
|---|---|
| Where is the *market/ mall [shopping centre]*? | **Hvor er *torget/kjøpesenteret*?** voor ar *tohr´•guh/khur`•puh•sehn•truh* |
| I'm just looking. | **Jeg bare ser meg omkring.** yay bah`•ruh sehr may ohm•krihng´ |
| Can you help me? | **Kan du hjelpe meg?** kahn dew yehl`•puh may |
| I'm being helped. | **Jeg får hjelp.** yay fawr yehlp |
| How much? | **Hvor mye koster det?** voor mew`•uh kohs`•tuhr deh |
| That one. | **Den der.** dehn dar |
| No, thanks. That's all. | **Nei takk. Det var alt.** nay tahk deh vahr ahlt |
| Where do I pay? | **Hvor betaler man?** voor buh•tah´•luhr mahn |
| I'll pay *in cash/by credit card*. | **Jeg betaler *kontant/med kredittkort*.** yay buh•tah´•luhr *kun•tahn´t/meh kreh•diht´•kohrt* |
| Could I have a receipt? | **Kan jeg få kvittering?** kahn yay faw kviht•teh´•rihng |

### Stores

| | |
|---|---|
| Where is...? | **Hvor er det...?** voor ar deh... |
| – the bakery | **– et bakeri** eht bah•kuhr•ee´ |
| – the bookstore | **– en bokhandel** ehn book`•hahn•duhl |

– the department store – **et stormagasin** eht stoor`·mah·gah·seen
– the pharmacy [chemist] – **et apotek** eht ah·pu·teh´k
– the supermarket – **et supermarked** eht sew´·puhr·mahr·kuhd

## Clothing

Can I try this on? **Kan jeg prøve den?** kahn yay prur`·vuh dehn
It doesn't fit. **Den passer ikke.** dehn pahs`·suhr ihk`·kuh
Do you have this in size...? **Har du denne i størrelse...?** hahr dew dehn`·nuh ih sturr`·rehl·suh...

▶For numbers, see page 141.

### Color

I'd like something in... **Jeg vil gjerne ha noe i...** yay vihl yar`·nuh hah noo`·uh ih...
– black – **svart** svahrt
– blue – **blått** bloht
– brown – **brunt** brewnt
– green – **grønt** grurnt
– orange – **oransje** u·rahng´·shuh
– red – **rødt** rurt
– white – **hvitt** viht
– yellow – **gult** gewlt

# *Sports and Leisure*

Where's...? **Hvor er...?** voor ar...
– the beach – **stranden** strahn´·nuhn
– the park – **parken** pahr´·kuhn
– the swimming pool – **svømmebassenget** svurm`·muh·bahs·sehng·uh
Can I rent [hire] golf clubs? **Kan jeg leie golfkøller?** kahn yay lay`·uh gohlf´·kurl·luhr

## Culture and Nightlife

| | |
|---|---|
| Do you have a program of events? | **Har du en oversikt over ting som skjer?** hahr dew ehn aw`·vuhr·sihkt aw´·vuhr tihng sohm shehr |
| Where's…? | **Hvor er…?** voor ar… |
| – the downtown area | – **sentrum** sehn´·trewm |
| – the bar | – **baren** bahr´·uhn |
| – the dance club | – **diskoteket** dihs·ku·teh´·kuh |

## Business Travel

| | |
|---|---|
| I'm here on business. | **Jeg er her i forretninger.** yay ar har ih fohr·reht´·ning·uhr |
| Here's my business card. | **Her har du visittkortet mitt.** har hahr dew vih·siht´·kor·tuh miht |
| Can I have your card? | **Kan jeg få kortet ditt?** kahn yay faw kor´·tuh diht |
| I have a meeting with… | **Jeg har et møte med…** yay hahr eht mur`·tuh meh… |
| Where's…? | **Hvor er…?** voor ar… |
| – the business center | – **forretningssenteret** fohr·reht´·nihngs·sehn·tuhr·uh |
| – the convention hall | – **konferansesenteret** kohn·fehr·ahng´·suh·sehn·tuhr·uh |
| – the meeting room | – **møterommet** mur`·tuh·rum·muh |

## Travel with Children

| | |
|---|---|
| Is there any discount for children? | **Er det reduksjon for barn?** ar deh reh·dewk·shoo´n fohr bahrn |
| Can you recommend a babysitter? | **Kan du anbefale en barnevakt?** kahn dew ahn´·buh·fah·luh ehn bahr`·nuh·vahkt |
| Could we have a *child's seat/highchair*? | **Kan vi få en *barnestol/babystol*?** kahn vee faw ehn *bahr`·nuh·stool/beh´·bih·stool* |
| Where can I change the baby? | **Hvor kan jeg bytte på babyen?** voor kahn yay buit`·tuh poh beh´·bih·uhn |

## For the Disabled

| | |
|---|---|
| Is there...? | **Er det...?** ar deh... |
| – access for the disabled | **– adkomst for bevegelseshemmede** ahd`•kohmst fohr buh•veh´•guhl•suhs•hem•muhd•uh |
| – a wheelchair ramp | **– en rullestolsrampe** ehn rewl`•luh•stools•rahm•puh |
| – a handicapped-[disabled-] accessible toilet | **– et handikaptoalett** eht hehn´•dih•kehp•tu•ah•leht |
| I need... | **Jeg trenger...** yay trehng´•uhr... |
| – assistance | **– hjelp** yehlp |
| – an elevator [lift] | **– en heis** ehn hays |
| – a ground-floor room | **– et rom i første etasje** eht rum ih furr`•stuh eh•tah´•shuh |

## Emergencies

| | |
|---|---|
| Help! | **Hjelp!** yehlp |
| Go away! | **Gå vekk!** gaw vehk |
| Stop, thief! | **Stopp tyven!** stohp tui´•vuhn |
| Get a doctor! | **Hent en lege!** hehnt ehn leh`•guh |
| Fire! | **Brann!** brahn |
| I'm lost. | **Jeg har gått meg bort.** yay hahr goht may boort |
| Can you help me? | **Kan du hjelpe meg?** kahn dew yehl`•puh may |
| Call the police! | **Ring politiet!** ring pu•lih•tee´•uh |

## Health

| | |
|---|---|
| I'm sick [ill]. | **Jeg er syk.** yay ar suik |
| I need an English-speaking doctor. | **Jeg trenger en lege som snakker engelsk.** yay trehng´•uhr ehn leh`•guh sohm snahk`•kuhr ehng´•ehlsk |
| It hurts here. | **Det gjør vondt her.** deh yurr vunt har |

# Reference

## Numbers

| | |
|---|---|
| 0 **null** newl | 19 **nitten** niht`·tuhn |
| 1 **en** ehn | 20 **tjue** khew`·uh |
| 2 **to** too | 21 **tjueen** khew·uh·eh´n |
| 3 **tre** treh | 22 **tjueto** khew·uh·too´ |
| 4 **fire** fee`·ruh | 30 **tretti** treht´·tih |
| 5 **fem** fehm | 31 **trettien** treht·tih·eh´n |
| 6 **seks** sehks | 40 **førti** furr´·tih |
| 7 **sju** shew | 50 **femti** fehm´·tih |
| 8 **åtte** oht`·tuh | 60 **seksti** sehks´·tih |
| 9 **ni** nee | 70 **sytti** surt´·tih |
| 10 **ti** tee | 80 **åtti** oht´·tih |
| 11 **elleve** ehl`·vuh | 90 **nitti** niht´·tih |
| 12 **tolv** tohl | 100 **hundre** hewn`·druh |
| 13 **tretten** treh`t·tuhn | 101 **hundreogen** hewn·druh·oh·eh´n |
| 14 **fjorten** fyu`·rtuhn | 200 **to hundre** too hewn`·druh |
| 15 **femten** fehm`·tuhn | 500 **fem hundre** fehm hewn`·druh |
| 16 **seksten** says`·tuhn | 1,000 **tusen** tew´·suhn |
| 17 **sytten** surt`·tuhn | 10,000 **ti tusen** tee tew´·suhn |
| 18 **atten** aht`·tuhn | 1,000,000 **en million** ehn mihl·yoo´n |

## Time

What time is it? **Hvor mye er klokken?** voor mui`·uh ar klohk`·kuhn

From nine o'clock to five o'clock. **Fra klokken ni til klokken fem.** fra klohk`·kuhn nee tihl klohk`·kuhn fehm

5:30 a.m./p.m. **Fem tretti/Sytten tretti.** fehm treht´·tih/surt`·tuhn treht´·tih

## Days

| | |
|---|---|
| Monday | **mandag** mahn´·dahg |
| Tuesday | **tirsdag** teers´·dahg |
| Wednesday | **onsdag** uns´·dahg |
| Thursday | **torsdag** tawrs´·dahg |
| Friday | **fredag** freh´·dahg |
| Saturday | **lørdag** lurr´·dahg |
| Sunday | **søndag** surn´·dahg |

## Dates

| | |
|---|---|
| yesterday | **i går** ih gawr |
| today | **i dag** ih dahg |
| tomorrow | **i morgen** ih mawr`·uhn |

## Months

| | | | |
|---|---|---|---|
| January | **januar** yah·new·ah´r | July | **juli** yew´·lee |
| February | **februar** feh·brew·ah´r | August | **august** ev·gews´t |
| March | **mars** mahrs | September | **september** sehp·tehm´·buhr |
| April | **april** ahp·ree´l | October | **oktober** ohk·taw´·buhr |
| May | **mai** mie | November | **november** nu·vehm´·buhr |
| June | **juni** yew´·nee | December | **desember** deh·sehm´·buhr |

# Portuguese

## Pronunciation

Stressed syllables are indicated by underlining in the phonetics. Portuguese has four accent marks; acute (´), grave (`), circumflex (ˆ), and tilde (˜). Accent marks are used to indicate a stressed syllable, or to distinguish between words with the same spelling but with a different pronunciation and meaning: for example, **é** pronounced "eh" (meaning is) and **e** pronounced "ee" (meaning and).

There are some differences in vocabulary and pronunciation between the Portuguese spoken in Portugal and that spoken in Brazil, although people in either country can easily understand the other. This section is specifically geared to travelers in Portugal.

### Consonants

| Letter(s) | Approximate Pronunciation | Symbol | Example | Pronunciation |
|---|---|---|---|---|
| b | 1. as in English | b | **bota** | baw•tuh |
| | 2. between vowels, as in English but softer | b | **bebida** | beh•bee•duh |
| c | 1. before e or i, like s in same | s | **centro** | sehn•troh |
| | 2. like k in kit | k | **como** | koh•moh |
| ç | like s in same | s | **cabeça** | kuh•beh•suh |
| ch | like sh in shower | sh | **chave** | shahv |
| d | 1. as in English | d | **diário** | dee•ah•ree•oo |
| | 2. like th in theater | th | **medo** | meh•thoo |
| g | 1. before e or i, like s in pleasure | zs | **gelo** | zseh•loo |

| Letter(s) | Approximate Pronunciation | Symbol | Example | Pronunciation |
|---|---|---|---|---|
| | 2. before a, o or u, as in English | g | **guerra** | geh•rruh |
| h | always silent | | **história** | ee•staw•ree•uh |
| j | like s in pleasure | zs | **juiz** | zsoo•eezs |
| l | 1. as in English | l | **luz** | looz |
| | 2. before h (lh), like ll in millions | ly | **milho** | mee•lyoo |
| m | 1. as in English | m | **camera** | cuh•meh•ruh |
| | 2. at the end of a word, m is nasalized: see p. 146 | | | |
| n | 1. as in English | n | **caneta** | kuh•neh•tah |
| | 2. before h (nh), like ny in canyon | ny | **banho** | buh•nyoo |
| qu | 1. before e and i, like k in kite | k | **quente** | kint |
| | 2. before a and o like qu in queen | kw | **qualidade** | kwah•lee•dahd |
| r | 1. strongly trilled | rr | **rio** | rree•oo |
| | 2. lightly trilled | r | **para** | puh•ruh |
| s | 1. like s in same | s | **sua** | soo•uh |
| | 2. between vowels, like z in zebra | z | **camisa** | kuh•mee•zuh |
| x | 1. like sh in sheep | sh | **peixe** | paysh |
| | 2. like s in same | s | **próximo** | praw•see•moo |
| | 3. like z in lazy | z | **exame** | ee•zuhm |

Letters f, m, p, t and z are pronounced as in English. Letters k, w and y are used only in foreign loan words.

## Vowels

| Letter(s) | Approximate Pronunciation | Symbol | Example | Pronunciation |
|---|---|---|---|---|
| a, ã, â | like a in about | uh | **anos** | <u>uh</u>•nooz |
| á, à | like a in father | ah | **farmácia** | fuhr•<u>mah</u>•see•uh |
| e | 1. like e in get | eh | **esta** | <u>eh</u>•stuh |
| | 2. like ee in eel | ee | **exame** | ee•<u>zuhm</u> |
| | 3. silent at the end of a word | | **leite** | layt |
| | 4. occasionally, like i in inn | i | **antes** | <u>ahn</u>•tis |
| | 5. when combined with the letter I, like ay in say | ay | **leite** | layt |
| é | like e in get | eh | **esta** | <u>eh</u>•stuh |
| ê | like i in inn | i | **mês** | miz |
| i, í | like ee in eel | ee | **sim** | seeng |
| o | 1. like au in caught | au | **onda** | <u>aun</u>•duh |
| | 2. at the end of a word, like oo in boo | oo | **gato** | <u>gah</u>•too |
| oi | like oy in coy | oy | **doi** | doy |
| ó | like aw in paw | aw | **história** | ee•<u>staw</u>•ree•uh |
| ô | like u in put | oah | **avô** | uh•<u>voah</u> |
| u | 1. like oo in boo | oo | **uva** | <u>oo</u>•vuh |
| | 2. silent after g and q | | **guerra** | <u>geh</u>•rruh |
| ú | like oo in boo | oo | **úmido** | <u>oo</u>•mee•thoo |

When a vowel has an accent, you must stress the syllable in the word that contains the accented vowel.

## Nasal Sounds

Some nasal sounds are produced when a vowel is followed by the letter m. This nasal sound is also found when a combination of certain vowels are used (ãe, ão, õe). These nasal sounds produce either an ng sound (e.g., tying) or an oam sound (e.g., foam) with the speaker barely pronouncing the g or m.

| Letter(s) | Approximate Pronunciation | Symbol | Example | Pronunciation |
|---|---|---|---|---|
| ãe | like ayin in saying | eng | **mãe** | meng |
| ão | like oam in foam | ohm | **cão** | kohm |
| õe | like oing in boing | oing | **milhões** | mee·lyoings |
| am | at the end of a word, like oam in foam otherwise not nasal: see page 144 | ohm | **falam** | fah·loam |
| om | like ong in gong | ohng | **som** | sohng |
| em | like aying in saying | eng | **bem** | beng |
| im | like ing in tying | ing | **assim** | uh·sing |

# *Basic Expressions*

| | |
|---|---|
| Hello. | **Olá.** aw·lah |
| Goodbye. | **Adeus.** uh·dehoosh |
| Yes. | **Sim.** seeng |
| No. | **Não.** nohm |
| OK. | **O.K.** aw·kay |
| Excuse me! (to get attention) | **Desculpe!** deh·skoolp |
| Excuse me. (to get past) | **Com licença.** kohng lee·sehn·suh |
| Sorry! | **Perdão!** pehr·dohm |
| Please. | **Se faz favor.** seh fahz fuh·vaur |

| | |
|---|---|
| Thank you. | **Obrigado♂/Obrigada♀.** aw•bree•gah•doo♂/aw•bree•gah•duh♀ |
| You're welcome. | **De nada.** deh nah•duh |
| Where are the restrooms [toilets]? | **Onde são as casas de banho?** aund sohm uhz kah•zuhz deh buh•nyoo |

## *Arrival and Departure*

| | |
|---|---|
| I'm on *vacation [holiday]/business.* | **Estou** ***de férias/em negócios.*** ee•stawoo *deh feh•ree•uhz/eng neh•gaw•see•yooz* |
| I'm going to... | **Vou para...** vawoo puh•ruh... |
| I'm staying at the... Hotel. | **Permaneço no hotel...** pehr•muh•neh•soo noo aw•tehl... |

### Passport Control and Customs

| | |
|---|---|
| I'm just passing through. | **Estou só de passagem.** ee•stawoo saw deh puh•sah•zheng |
| I would like to declare... | **Queria declarar...** keh•ree•uh deh•kluh•rahr... |
| I have nothing to declare. | **Não tenho nada a declarar.** nohm teh•nyoo nah•duh uh deh•kluh•rahr |

## *Money and Banking*

| | |
|---|---|
| Where's...? | **Onde é...?** aund eh... |
| – the ATM | **– o multibanco** oo mool•tee•buhn•koo |
| – the bank | **– o banco** oo buhn•koo |
| – the currency exchange office | **– o câmbio** oo kuhm•bee•oo |
| What time does the bank *open/close*? | **A que horas é que o banco** ***abre/fecha*?** uh keh aw•ruhz eh keh oo buhn•koo *ah•breh/feh•shuh* |
| I'd like to change *dollars/pounds* into *euros.* | **Queria trocar** ***dólares/libras*** **em** ***euros.*** keh•ree•uh troo•kahr *daw•luhrz/lee•bruhz* eng *ehoo•rooz* |

I want to cash some traveler's checks [cheques]. **Quero cobrar cheques de viagem.** keh•roo koo•brahr sheh•kehz deh vee•ah•zseng

## *Transportation*

How do I get to the city center? **Como é que vou para o centro da cidade?** kau•moo eh keh vawoo puh•ruh oo sehn•troo duh see•dahd

Where's...? **Onde é...?** aund eh...

– the airport **– o aeroporto** oo uh•eh•rau•paur•too

– the train station [the railway station] **– a estação de caminho de ferro** uh ee•stuh•sohm deh kuh•mee•nyoo deh feh•rroo

– the bus station **– a estação de camionetas** uh ee•stuh•sohm deh kah•meeoo•neh•tuhz

– the subway [underground] station **– a estação de metro** uh ee•stuh•sohm deh meh•troo

How far is it? **A que distância fica?** uh keh dee•stuhn•see•uh fee•kuh

Where can I buy tickets? **Onde posso comprar bilhetes?** aund paw•soo kaum•prahr bee•lyehtz

A *one-way [single]/ round-trip [return]* ticket to... **Um bilhete *de ida/de ida e volta* para...** oong bee•lyeht *deh ee•thuh/deh ee•thuh ee vaul•tuh* puh•ruh...

How much? **Quanto custa?** kwuhn•too koo•stuh

Are there any discounts? **Há descontos?** ah dehs•caun•tooz

Which...? **Qual...?** kwahl...

– gate **– porta** port•uh

– line **– linha** lee•nyuh

– platform **– plataforma** plah•tuh•fawr•muh

| | |
|---|---|
| Where can I get a taxi? | **Onde posso apanhar um táxi?** aund paw•soo uh•puh•nyar oong tahk•see |
| Please take me to this address. | **Leve-me a esta morada.** leh•veh•meh uh eh•stuh maw•rah•duh |
| Where can I rent a car? | **Onde posso alugar um carro?** aund paw•soo uh•loo•gahr oong kah•rroo |
| Could I have a map? | **Pode dar-me um mapa?** pawd dahr•meh oong mah•puh |

## Asking Directions

| | |
|---|---|
| How far is it to...? | **A que distância fica...?** uh keh dee•stuhn•see•uh fee•kuh... |
| Where's...? | **Onde fica...?** aund fee•kuh... |
| – ...Street | **– a rua...** uh rroo•uh... |
| – this address | **– esta morada** eh•stuh maw•rah•duh |
| Can you show me on the map? | **Pode-me indicar no mapa?** pawd meh een•dee•kahr noo mah•puh |
| I'm lost. | **Estou perdido ♂ /perdida ♀.** ee•stawoo pehr•dee•doo ♂ /pehr•dee•duh ♀ |

### You May Hear...

| | |
|---|---|
| **sempre em frente** sehm•preh eng frehn•teh | straight ahead |
| **à esquerda** ah ee•skehr•duh | on the left |
| **à direita** ah dee•ray•tuh | on the right |
| **a seguir ao ♂ /à ♀** uh seh•geer ahoo ♂ /ah ♀ | next to |
| **depois do ♂ /da ♀** deh•poyz thoo ♂ /duh ♀ | after |
| **norte/sul** nawrt/sool | north/south |
| **leste/oeste** lehs•the/aw•ehs•teh | east/west |
| ***depois de*/*ao* dobrar da esquina** *deh•poyz deh*/*ahoo* doo•brahr duh ees•kee•nuh | *on*/*around* the corner |

## Accommodations

| | |
|---|---|
| I have a reservation. | **Tenho uma reserva.** teh•nyoo oo•muh reh•zehr•vuh |
| My name is… | **Chamo-me…** shuh•moo•meh… |
| What time is check-out? | **A que horas temos de deixar o quarto?** uh kee aw•ruhz teh•mooz deh thay•shahr oo kwahr•too |
| Can I leave this in the safe? | **Posso deixar isto no cofre?** paw•soo thay•shahr ee•stoo noo kaw•freh |
| Can I leave my bags? | **Posso deixar a minha bagagem?** paw•soo day•shahr uh mee•nyuh buh•gah•geng |
| Can I have *the bill/ a receipt*? | **Pode dar-me *a conta/uma factura*?** pawd dahr•meh *uh kaum•tuh/oo•muh fah•too•ruh* |

## Internet and Communications

| | |
|---|---|
| Where's an internet café? | **Onde fica um internet café?** aund fee•kuh oong een•tehr•neht kuh•feh |
| Can I access the Internet here? | **Tenho acesso à internet aqui?** teh•nyoo uh•seh•soo ah een•tehr•neht uh•kee |
| Can I check e-mail here? | **Posso ler o meu e-mail aqui?** paw•soo lehr oo mehoo ee•mehl uh•khee |
| Can I have your phone number? | **Pode dar-me o seu número de telefone?** pawd dahr•meh oo sehoo noo•meh•roo deh tehl•fawn |
| Here's my *number/ e-mail address*. | **Este é o meu *número/e-mail*.** ehst eh oo mehoo *noo•meh•roo/ee•mehl* |
| Call me. | **Telefone-me.** tehl•fawn•eh•meh |
| E-mail me. | **Envie-me um e-mail.** ehn•vee•eh meh oong ee•mehl |
| Hello. This is… | **Estou. Fala…** ee•stawoo. fah•luh… |
| I'd like to speak to… | **Queria falar com…** keh•ree•uh fuh•lahr kaum… |

| | |
|---|---|
| Could you repeat that, please? | **Importa-se de repetir, por favor?** eem•pawr•tuh•seh deh reh•peh•teer poor fuh•vaur |
| I'll call back later. | **Chamo mais tarde.** shuh•moo meyez tahr•deh |
| Bye. | **Adeus.** uh•deeoosh |
| Where's the post office? | **Onde são os correios?** aund sohm ooz koo•rray•ooz |

## Eating Out

| | |
|---|---|
| Can you recommend a good *restaurant/ bar*? | **Pode recomendar-me um bom *restaurante/ bar*?** pawd reh•kaw•mehn•dahr•meh oong bohng *reh•stahoo•ruhnt/bar* |
| Is there a(n) *traditional Portuguese/ inexpensive* restaurant near here? | **Há um restaurante *tradicional português/barato* perto daqui?** ah oong reh•stuhoo•ruhnt *truh•dee•see•oo•nahl por•too•gehz/buh•rah•too* pehr•too duh•kee |
| A table for..., please. | **Uma mesa para..., se faz favor.** oo•muh meh•zuh puh•ruh...seh fahz fuh•vaur |
| A menu, please. | **Uma ementa, por favor.** oo•muh ee•mehn•tuh poor fuh•vaur |
| What do you recommend? | **O que é que me recomenda?** oo keh eh keh meh reh•koo•mehn•duh |
| I'd like... | **Queria...** keh•ree•uh... |
| Some more..., please. | **Mais..., se faz favor.** meyez...seh fahz fuh•vaur |
| Enjoy your meal. | **Bom apetite.** bohng uh•peh•tee•teh |
| The check [bill], please. | **A conta, por favor.** uh kaum•tuh poor fuh•vaur |
| Is service included? | **O serviço está incluído?** oo sehr•vee•soo ee•stah een•kloo•ee•thoo |
| Could I have a receipt, please? | **Pode dar-me uma factura, por favor?** pawd dahr•meh oo•muh fah•too•ruh poor fuh•vaur |

## Breakfast

| | |
|---|---|
| **o cereal (*frio/quente*)** oo seh•ree•ahl (*free•oo/kehnt*) | (*cold/hot*) cereal |
| **o doce de fruta** oo dau•seh deh froo•tuh | jam |
| **a manteiga** uh muhn•tay•guh | butter |
| **o pão** oo pohm | bread |
| **as salsichas** uhz sahl•see•shuhz | sausages |
| **o yogurte** oo yaw•goort | yogurt |

## Appetizers [Starters]

| | |
|---|---|
| **as carnes frias** uhz kahr•nehz free•uhz | cold cuts |
| **as lulas à milanesa** uhz loo•luhz ah mee•luh•neh•zuh | squid |
| **o paio** oo peye•oo | smoked pork fillet |
| **o chouriço** oo shauoo•ree•soo | sausage |
| **o pipis** oo pee•peez | spicy chicken stew |

## Soup

| | |
|---|---|
| **o caldo verde** oo kahl•doo vehrd | potato and kale soup with sausage |
| **o gaspacho** oo guhz•pah•shoo | chilled soup with tomatoes, sweet peppers, onions, cucumbers and croutons |
| **a sopa transmontana** a sau•puh truhnz•moo•tuh•nuh | vegetable soup with bacon and bread |

## Fish and Seafood

| | |
|---|---|
| **o atum** oo uh•toong | tuna |
| **os camarões** ooz kuh•muh•roings | shrimp [prawns] |
| **a lagosta** uh luh•gau•stuh | lobster |

**o linguado** oo leeng·gwah·thoo | sole
**as lulas** uhz loo·luhz | squid

## Meat and Poultry

| | |
|---|---|
| **o arroz de frango** oo uh·rrauz deh fruhn·goo | chicken with white wine, ham and rice |
| **o bife na frigideira** oo beef nuh free·zsuh·day·ruh | steak fried in butter, white wine and garlic |
| **o borrego** oo boo·rreh·goo | lamb |
| **a carne de porco** uh kahrn deh paur·koo | pork |
| **a carne de vaca** uh kahrn deh vah·kuh | beef |
| **o carneiro guisado** oo kuhrr·nay·roo gee·zah·thoo | mutton with tomatoes, garlic and herbs |
| **o cozido à Portuguesa** oo koo·zee·doo ah poor·too·geh·zuh | boiled beef, bacon, smoked sausage and vegetables |
| **o frango** oo fruhn·goo | chicken |
| **a vitela** uh vee·tehl·uh | veal |

| | |
|---|---|
| rare | **mal passado ♂/passada ♀** mahl puh·sah·thoo ♂/puh·sah·thuh ♀ |
| medium | **meio passado ♂/passada ♀** may·oo puh·sah·thoo ♂/puh·sah·thuh ♀ |
| well-done | **bem passado ♂/passada ♀** beng puh·sah·thoo ♂/puh·sah·thuh ♀ |

## Vegetables and Staples

| | |
|---|---|
| **a alface** uh ahl·fah·seh | lettuce |
| **as cebolas** uhz seh·bau·luhz | onions |
| **os cogumelos** ooz koo·goo·meh·looz | mushrooms |
| **as ervilhas** uhz eer·vee·lyuhz | peas |
| **as favas** uhz fah·vuhz | broad beans |

| | |
|---|---|
| **o feijão** oo fay·zsohm | kidney beans |
| **o feijão verde** oo fay·zsohm vehrd | green beans |
| **os pimentos** ooz pee·mehn·tooz | peppers |

## Fruit

| | |
|---|---|
| **as ameixas** uhz uh·may·shuhz | plums |
| **a laranja** uh luh·ruhn·zsuh | orange |
| **o limão** oo lee·mohm | lemon |
| **a maçã** uh muh·suh | apple |
| **a melancia** uh meh·luhn·see·uh | watermelon |
| **o pêssego** oo pay·seh·goo | peach |
| **as uvas** uhz oo·vuhz | grapes |

## Dessert

| | |
|---|---|
| **a arrufada de Coimbra** uh uh·rroo·fah·duh deh kooeem·bruh | cinnamon dough cake |
| **o bolo podre** oo bau·loo pau·dreh | honey and cinnamon cake |
| **o pastel de Tentúgal** oo puhz·tehl deh tehn·too·gahl | pastry filled with egg yolks cooked in syrup |
| **o pudim flan** oo poo·deeng fluhn | caramel custard |

## *Drinks*

| | |
|---|---|
| The *wine list/drink menu*, please. | **A *carta dos vinhos/ementa de bebidas*, se faz favor.** uh *kahr·tuh dooz vee·nyooz/ ee·mehn·tuh deh beh·bee·duhz* seh fahz fuh·vaur |
| I'd like a *bottle/glass* of *red/white* wine. | **Queria *uma garrafa/um copo* de vinho *tinto/branco*.** keh·ree·uh *oo·muh guh·rrah·fuh/ oong kaw·poo* deh vee·nyoo *teen·too/bruhn·koo* |
| Another *bottle/glass*, please. | ***Outra garrafa/Outro copo*, se faz favor.** *auoo·truh guh·rrah·fuh/auoo·troo kaw·poo* ser fahz fuh·vaur |
| I'd like a local beer. | **Gostaria de uma cerveja local.** goo·stuh·ree·uh deh oo·muh sehr·vay·zsuh loo·kahl |
| Cheers! | **Viva!** vee·vuh |
| A *coffee/tea*, please. | **Um *café/chá*, se faz favor.** oong *kuh·feh/ shah* seh fahz fuh·vaur |
| Black. | **Bica.** bee·kuh |
| With… | **com…** kaum… |
| – milk | **– leite** layt |
| – sugar | **– açúcar** uh·soo·kuhr |
| – artificial sweetener | **– adoçante** uh·doo·suhnty |
| …, please. | **…, se faz favor.** …seh fahz fuh·vaur |
| – A juice | **– Um sumo** oong soo·moo |
| – A soda | **– Um refresco** oong reh·freh·skoo |
| – A *sparkling/still* water | **– Uma água *com/sem* gás** oo-muh ah·gwuh *kaum/sehm* gahz |

## Aperitifs, Cocktails and Liqueurs

| | |
|---|---|
| **velha** veh·lyuh | brandy |
| **a ginjinha** uh zseeng·zsee·nyuh | spirit distilled from morello cherries |
| **a vodca** uh vaw·dee·kuh | vodka |

## Talking

| | |
|---|---|
| Hello. | **Olá.** aw·lah |
| Good morning. | **Bom dia.** bong dee·uh |
| Good afternoon. | **Boa tarde.** baw·uh tahrd |
| Good evening. | **Boa noite.** baw·uh noyt |
| How are you? | **Como está?** kau·moo ee·stah |
| Fine, thanks. | **Bem, obrigado♂/obrigada♀.** behm aw·bree·gah·doo♂/aw·bree·gah·duh♀ |
| Excuse me! (*to get attention*) | **Desculpe!** dehz·kool·peh |
| What's your name? | **Como se chama?** kau·moo seh shuh·muh |
| My name is… | **Chamo-me…** shuh·moo meh… |
| Nice to meet you. | **Muito prazer.** mooee·too pruh·zehr |
| Where are you from? | **De onde é?** deh aund eh |
| I'm from the *U.S./U.K.* | **Sou *dos Estados Unidos/da Inglaterra*.** soh *dooz ee·stah·dooz oo·nee·dooz/ duh eeng·luh·teh·rruh* |
| Goodbye. | **Adeus.** uh·deeooz |
| See you later. | **Até mais tarde.** uh·teh meyez tahrd |

In Portuguese, there are a number of forms for "you" (taking different verb forms): **tu** (singular) and **vós** (plural) are used when talking to relatives, close friends and children; **você** (singular) and **vocês** (plural) are used in all other cases. If in doubt, use **você/vocês**.

## Communication Difficulties

| | |
|---|---|
| Do you speak English? | **Fala inglês?** fah·luh eeng·lehz |
| I don't speak (much) Portuguese. | **Não falo (muito) português.** nohm fah·loo (mooee·too) poor·too·gehz |

| | |
|---|---|
| Could you speak more slowly? | **Pode falar mais devagar?** pawd fuh·lahr meyez deh·vuh·gahr |
| I (don't) understand. | **(Não) compreendo.** nohm kaum·pree·ehn·doo |

## *Sightseeing*

| | |
|---|---|
| Where's the tourist office? | **Onde é o posto de turismo ?** aund eh oo pau·stoo deh too·reez·moo |
| Do you have tours in English? | **Tem excursões em inglês?** teng ee·skoor·soings eng eng·lehz |
| Can I have a *map/ guide*? | **Pode dar-me um *mapa/ guia*?** pawd dahr·meh oong *mah·puh/ gee·uh* |

### Sights

| | |
|---|---|
| Where is...? | **Onde é...?** aund eh... |
| – the castle | **– o castelo** oo kuhz·teh·loo |
| – the cathedral | **– a catedral** uh keh·teh·drahl |
| – the downtown area | **– o centro da cidade** oo sehn·troo duh see·dahd |
| – the museum | **– o museu** oo moo·zehoo |
| – the shopping area | **– a zona comercial** uh zau·nuh koo·mehr·see·ahl |

# Shopping

| | |
|---|---|
| Where is the *market/ mall* [*shopping center*]? | **Onde é *o mercado/o centro comercial*?** aund eh *oo mehr•kah•thoo/oo sehn•troo koo•mehr•see•ahl* |
| I'm just looking. | **Estou só a ver.** ee•stawoo saw uh vehr |
| Can you help me? | **Pode ajudar-me?** pawd uh•zsoo•dahr•meh |
| I'm being helped. | **Alguém está a ajudar-me.** ahl•gehng ee•stah uh uh•zsoo•dahr•meh |
| How much is it? | **Quanto é?** kwuhn•too eh |
| That one, please. | **Aquele♂/Aquela♀, por favor.** uh•kehl♂/ uh•keh•luh♀ poor fuh•vaur |
| That's all, thanks. | **É tudo, obrigado♂/obrigada♀.** eh too•doo aw•bree•gah•doo♂/aw•bree•gah•thuh♀ |
| Where can I pay? | **Onde pago?** aund pah•goo |
| I'll pay *in cash/by credit card.* | **Pago *com dinheiro/com o cartão de crédito*.** pah•goo *kaum dee•nyay•roo/kaum oo kuhr•tohm deh kreh•dee•too* |
| A receipt, please. | **Um recibo, se faz favor.** oong reh•see•boo seh fahz fuh•vaur |

## Stores

| | |
|---|---|
| Where is…? | **Onde é…?** aund eh… |
| – the bakery | – **a padaria** uh pah•deh•ree•uh |
| – the bookstore | – **a livraria** uh lee•vreh•ree•uh |
| – the department store | – **o grande armazém** oo gruhnd uhr•muh•zeng |
| – the pastry shop | – **a pastelaria** uh puh•stuh•luh•ree•uh |
| – the pharmacy [chemist] | – **a farmácia** uh fuhr•mah•see•uh |
| – the supermarket | – **o supermercado** oo soo•pehr•mehr•kah•thoo |

## Clothing

| | |
|---|---|
| Can I try this on? | **Posso provar isto?** paw•soo proo•vahr ee•stoo |
| It doesn't fit. | **Não me serve.** nohm meh sehrv |
| Do you have this in a *bigger/smaller* size? | **Tem isto num tamanho *maior/mais pequeno*?** teng ee•stoo noong tuh•muh•nyoo *meye•awr/meyez peh•kehn•oo* |

### Color

| | |
|---|---|
| I'd like something... | **Queria algo...** keh•ree•uh ahl•goo... |
| – black | **– em preto** eng preh•too |
| – blue | **– em azul** eng uh•zool |
| – brown | **– em castanho** eng kuhz•tay•nyoo |
| – green | **– em verde** eng vehrd |
| – orange | **– em cor-de-laranja** eng kaur deh luh•ruhn•zsuh |
| – red | **– em vermelho** eng vehr•meh•lyoo |
| – white | **– em branco** eng bruhn•koo |
| – yellow | **– em amarelo** eng uh•meh•reh•loo |

## *Sports and Leisure*

| | |
|---|---|
| Where's...? | **Onde é...?** aund eh... |
| – the beach | **– a praia** uh preye•uh |
| – the park | **– o parque** oo pahr•keh |
| – the pool | **– a piscina** uh pee•see•nuh |
| Can I rent [hire] golf clubs? | **Posso alugar tacos?** paw•soo uh•loo•gahr tah•kooz |

## *Culture and Nightlife*

| | |
|---|---|
| Do you have a program of events? | **Tem um programa dos espectáculos?** teng oong proo•gruh•muh dooz ee•spehk•tah•koo•looz |

| | |
|---|---|
| Where's...? | **Onde é...?** aund eh... |
| – the downtown area | **– o centro** oo sehn•troo |
| – the bar | **– o bar** oo bar |
| – the dance club | **– a discoteca** uh deez•koo•teh•kuh |

## *Business Travel*

| | |
|---|---|
| I'm here on business. | **Estou aqui em negócios.** ee•stawoo uh•kee eng neh•gaw•see•oosz |
| Here's my business card. | **Tome o meu cartão.** taw•meh oo meeoo kuhr•tohm |
| Can I have your card? | **Posso ter o seu cartão?** paw•soo tehr oo sehoo kuhr•tohm |
| I have a meeting with... | **Tenho um apontamento com...** tay•nyoo oong uh•paun•tuh•mehn•too kaum... |
| Where's...? | **Onde é...** aund eh... |
| – the business center | **– o centro de negócios** oo sehn•troo deh neh•gaw•see•oosz |
| – the convention hall | **– o centro de convenção** oo sehn•troo deh kaun•vehn•sohmz |
| – the meeting room | **– o centro de reuniões** oo sehn•troo deh rree•oo•nee•ohmz |

## *Travel with Children*

| | |
|---|---|
| Is there a discount for children? | **Há desconto para crianças?** ah dehs•caun•too puh•ruh kree•uhn•suhs |
| Can you recommend a babysitter? | **Pode recomendar-me uma babysitter qualificada?** pawd reh•koo•mehn•dahr•meh oo•muh bay•bee•sit•tur kwahl•ee•fee•kah•duh |
| Do you have a child's seat? | **Pode trazer uma cadeirinha de criança?** pawd truh•zehr oo•muh kuh•day•ree•nyuh deh kree•uhn•suh |
| Where can I change the baby? | **Onde posso mudar o bebé?** aund paw•soo moo•dahr oo beh•beh |

## For the Disabled

| | |
|---|---|
| Is there...? | **Há...?** ah... |
| – access for the disabled | **– acesso para deficientes físicos** uh•seh•soo puh•ruh deh•fee•see•ehntz fee•see•kooz |
| – a wheelchair ramp | **– uma rampa de cadeira de rodas** oo•muh ruhm•puh deh kuh•day•ruh deh raw•thuhz |
| – a handicapped- [disabled-] accessible toilet | **– uma casa de banho acessível para deficientes** oo•muh kah•zuh deh buh•nyoo uh•seh•see•vehl puh•ruh deh•fee•see•ehntz |
| I need... | **Preciso de...** preh•see•zoo deh... |
| – assistance | **– assistência** uh•see•stehn•see•uh |
| – an elevator [lift] | **– um elevador** oong eh•leh•vuh•daur |

## Emergencies

| | |
|---|---|
| Help! | **Socorro!** soo•kau•rroo |
| Go away! | **Vá-se embora!** vah•seh ehng•baw•ruh |
| Call the police! | **Chame a polícia!** shuh•meh uh poo•lee•see•uh |
| Stop thief! | **Pára ladrão!** pah•ruh luh•drohm |
| Get a doctor! | **Chame um médico!** shuh•meh oong meh•dee•koo |
| Fire! | **Fogo!** fau•goo |
| I'm lost. | **Estou perdido♂/perdida♀.** ee•stawoo pehr•dee•thoo♂/pehr•dee•thuh♀ |
| Can you help me? | **Pode ajudar-me?** pawd uh•zsoo•dahr•meh |

## Health

| | |
|---|---|
| I'm sick [ill]. | **Estou doente.** ee•stawoo doo•ehnt |
| I need an English-speaking doctor. | **Preciso de um médico que fale inglês.** preh•see•zoo deh oong meh•dee•koo keh fah•leh eeng•lehz |
| It hurts here. | **Dói-me aqui.** doy•meh uh•kee |

# Reference

## Numbers

| | | | |
|---|---|---|---|
| 0 | **zero** zeh·roo | 19 | **dezanove** deh·zuh·nawv |
| 1 | **um**♂/**uma**♀ oong♂/oo·muh♀ | 20 | **vinte** veent |
| 2 | **dois**♂/**duas**♀ doyz♂/thoo·uhz♀ | 21 | **vinte e um**♂/**uma**♀ veent ee oong♂/oo·muh♀ |
| 3 | **três** trehz | 22 | **vinte e dois**♂/**duas**♀ veent ee doyz♂/thoo·uhz♀ |
| 4 | **quatro** kwah·troo | 30 | **trinta** treeng·tuh |
| 5 | **cinco** seeng·koo | 31 | **trinta e um**♂/**uma**♀ treeng·tuh ee oong♂/oo·muh♀ |
| 6 | **seis** sayz | 40 | **quarenta** kwuh·rehn·tuh |
| 7 | **sete** seht | 50 | **cinquenta** seeng·kwehn·tuh |
| 8 | **oito** oy·too | 60 | **sessenta** seh·sehn·tuh |
| 9 | **nove** nawv | 70 | **setenta** seh·tehn·tuh |
| 10 | **dez** dehz | 80 | **oitenta** oy·tehn·tuh |
| 11 | **onze** aunz | 90 | **noventa** noo·vehn·tuh |
| 12 | **doze** dauz | 100 | **cem** sehn |
| 13 | **treze** trehz | 101 | **cento e um**♂/**uma**♀ sehn·too ee oong♂/oo·muh♀ |
| 14 | **catorze** kuh·taurz | 200 | **duzentos**♂/**duzentas**♀ doo·zehn·tooz♂/doo·zehn·tuhz♀ |
| 15 | **quinze** keengz | 500 | **quinhentos**♂/**quinhentas**♀ kee·nyehn·tooz♂/kee·nyehn·tuhz♀ |
| 16 | **dezasseis** dehz·eh·sayz | 1,000 | **mil** meel |
| 17 | **dezassete** dehz·eh·seht | 10,000 | **dez mil** dehz meel |
| 18 | **dezoito** dehz·oy·too | 1,000,000 | **um milhão** oong mee·lyohm |

## Time

| | |
|---|---|
| What time is it? | **As horas, por favor?** uhz aw•ruhz poor fuh•vaur |
| From nine o'clock to five o'clock. | **Das nove às cinco horas.** duhz nawv ahz seeng•koo aw•ruhz |
| 5:30 *a.m./p.m.* | **Cinco e meia *de manhã/da tarde.*** seeng•koo ee may•uh *deh muh•nyuh/duh tahrd* |

## Days

| | |
|---|---|
| Monday | **segunda-feira** seh•goon•duh fay•ruh |
| Tuesday | **terça-feira** tehr•suh fay•ruh |
| Wednesday | **quarta-feira** kwahr•tuh fay•ruh |
| Thursday | **quinta-feira** keen•tuh fay•ruh |
| Friday | **sexta-feira** say•stuh fay•ruh |
| Saturday | **sábado** sah•buh•thoo |
| Sunday | **domingo** doo•meeng•goo |

## Dates

| | |
|---|---|
| yesterday | **ontem** awn•teng |
| today | **hoje** auzseh |
| tomorrow | **amanhã** uh•muh•nuh |

## Months

| | | | |
|---|---|---|---|
| January | **Janeiro** zher•nay•roo | July | **Julho** zsoo•lyoo |
| February | **Fevereiro** feh•vray•roo | August | **Agosto** uh•gaus•too |
| March | **Março** mahr•soo | September | **Setembro** seh•tehm•broo |
| April | **Abril** uh•breel | October | **Outubro** aw•too•broo |
| May | **Maio** meye•oo | November | **Novembro** noo•vehm•broo |
| June | **Junho** zsoo•nyoo | December | **Dezembro** deh•zehm•broo |

# Spanish

## Pronunciation

Underlined letters indicate that that syllable should be stressed. The acute accent ´ indicates stress, e.g. **río**, ree-oh. Some Spanish words have more than one meaning. In these instances, the accent mark is also used to distinguish between them, e.g.: **él** (he) and **el** (the); **sí** (yes) and **si** (if).

There are some differences in vocabulary and pronunciation between the Spanish spoken in Spain and that in the Americas—although each is easily understood by the other. This section is specifically geared to travelers in Spain.

### Consonants

| Letter | Approximate Pronunciation | Symbol | Example | Pronunciation |
|---|---|---|---|---|
| b | 1. as in English | b | **bueno** | bweh•noh |
| | 2. between vowels as in English, but softer | b | **bebida** | beh•bee•dah |
| c | 1. before e and i like th in thin | th | **centro** | thehn•troh |
| | 2. otherwise like k in kit | k | **como** | koh•moh |
| ch | as in English | ch | **mucho** | moo•choh |
| d | 1. as in English | d | **donde** | dohn•deh |
| | 2. between vowels and especially at the end of a word, like th in thin, but softer | th | **usted** | oos•teth |
| g | 1. before e and i, like ch in Scottish loch | kh | **urgente** | oor•khehn•teh |

| Letter | Approximate Pronunciation | Symbol | Example | Pronunciation |
|---|---|---|---|---|
| | 2. otherwise, like g in get | g | **ninguno** | neen•goo•noh |
| h | always silent | | **hombre** | ohm•breh |
| j | like ch in Scottish loch | kh | **bajo** | bah•khoh |
| ll | like y in yellow | y | **lleno** | yeh•noh |
| ñ | like ni in onion | ny | **señor** | seh•nyohr |
| q | like k in kick | k | **quince** | keen•theh |
| r | trilled, especially at the beginning of a word | r | **río** | ree•oh |
| rr | strongly trilled | rr | **arriba** | ah•rree•bah |
| s | 1. like s in same | s | **sus** | soos |
| | 2. before b, d, g, l, m, n, like s in rose | z | **mismo** | meez•moh |
| v | like b in bad, but softer | b | **viejo** | beeyeh•khoh |
| z | like th in thin | th | **brazo** | brah•thoh |

Letters f, k, l, m, n, p, t, w, x and y are pronounced as in English.

## Vowels

| Letter | Approximate Pronunciation | Symbol | Example | Pronunciation |
|---|---|---|---|---|
| a | like the a in father | ah | **gracias** | grah•theeyahs |
| e | like e in get | eh | **esta** | ehs•tah |
| i | like ee in meet | ee | **sí** | see |
| o | like o in rope | oh | **dos** | dohs |
| u | 1. like oo in food | oo | **uno** | oo•noh |

| Letter | Approximate Pronunciation | Symbol | Example | Pronunciation |
|---|---|---|---|---|
| | 2. silent after g and q | | **que** | keh |
| | 3. when marked ü, like we in well | w | **antigüedad** | ahn•tee•gweh•dahd |
| y | 1. like y in yellow | y | **hoy** | oy |
| | 2. when alone, like ee in meet | ee | **y** | ee |
| | 3. when preceded by an a, sounds like y + ee, with ee faintly pronounced | aye | **hay** | aye |

## Basic Expressions

| | |
|---|---|
| Hello. | **Hola.** oh•lah |
| Goodbye. | **Adiós.** ah•deeyohs |
| Yes. | **Sí.** see |
| No. | **No.** noh |
| OK. | **De acuerdo.** deh ah•kwehr•doh |
| Excuse me! (to get attention) | **¡Disculpe!** dees•kool•peh |
| Excuse me. (to get past) | **Perdón.** pehr•dohn |
| I'm sorry. | **Lo siento.** loh seeyehn•toh |
| Please. | **Por favor.** pohr fah•bohr |
| Thank you. | **Gracias.** grah•theeyahs |
| You're welcome. | **De nada.** deh nah•dah |
| Where's the restroom [toilet]? | **¿Dónde están los servicios?** dohn•deh ehs•tahn lohs sehr•bee•theeyohs |

# Arrival and Departure

| | |
|---|---|
| I'm on *vacation [holiday]/business.* | **Estoy aquí *de vacaciones/en viaje de negocios.*** ehs•toy ah•kee *deh bah•kah•theeyoh•nehs/ehn beeyah•kheh deh neh•goh•theeyohs* |
| I'm going to... | **Voy a...** boy ah... |
| I'm staying at the... Hotel. | **Me alojo en el Hotel...** meh ah•loh•khoh ehn ehl oh•tehl... |

## Passport Control and Customs

| | |
|---|---|
| I'm just passing through. | **Estoy de paso.** ehs•toy deh pah•soh |
| I'd like to declare... | **Quiero declarar...** keeyeh•roh deh•klah•rahr... |
| I have nothing to declare. | **No tengo nada que declarar.** noh tehn•goh nah•dah keh deh•klah•rahr |

# Money and Banking

| | |
|---|---|
| Where's...? | **¿Dónde está...?** dohn•deh ehs•tah... |
| – the ATM | **– el cajero automático** ehl kah•kheh•roh aw•toh•mah•tee•koh |
| – the bank | **– el banco** ehl bahn•koh |
| – the currency exchange office | **– la casa de cambio** lah kah•sah deh kahm•beeyoh |
| When does the bank *open/close*? | **¿A qué hora *abre/cierra* el banco?** ah keh oh•rah *ah•breh/theeyeh•rrah* ehl bahn•koh |
| I'd like to change *dollars/pounds* into euros. | **Quiero cambiar *dólares/libras* a euros.** keeyeh•roh kahm•beeyahr *doh•lah•rehs/lee•brahs* ah ew•rohs |
| I'd like to cash traveler's checks [cheques]. | **Quiero cobrar cheques de viaje.** keeyeh•roh koh•brahr cheh•kehs deh beeyah•kheh |

## *Transportation*

| | |
|---|---|
| How do I get to town? | **¿Cómo se llega a la ciudad?** koh·moh seh yeh·gah ah lah theew·dahd |
| Where's...? | **¿Dónde está...?** dohn·deh ehs·tah... |
| – the airport | **– el aeropuerto** ehl ah·eh·roh·pwehr·toh |
| – the train [railway] station | **– la estación de tren** lah ehs·tah·theeyohn deh trehn |
| – the bus station | **– la estación de autobuses** lah ehs·tah·theeyohn deh aw·toh·boo·sehs |
| – the subway [underground] station | **– la estación de metro** lah ehs·tah·theeyohn deh meh·troh |
| How far is it? | **¿A qué distancia está?** ah keh dees·tahn·theeyah ehs·tah |
| Where do I buy a ticket? | **¿Dónde se compra el billete?** dohn·deh seh kohm·prah ehl bee·yeh·teh |
| A *one-way/round-trip [return]* ticket to... | **Un billete de *ida/ida y vuelta* a...** oon bee·yeh·teh deh *ee·dah/ee·dah ee bwehl·tah* ah... |
| How much? | **¿Cuánto es?** kwahn·toh ehs |
| Is there a discount? | **¿Hacen descuento?** ah·then dehs·kwehn·toh |
| Which...? | **¿De qué...?** deh keh... |
| – gate | **– puerta de embarque** pwehr·tah deh ehm·bahr·keh |
| – line | **– línea** lee·neh·ah |
| – platform | **– andén** ahn·dehn |
| Where can I get a taxi? | **¿Dónde puedo coger un taxi?** dohn·deh pweh·doh koh·khehr oon tah·xee |

### Asking Directions

| | |
|---|---|
| How far is it to...? | **¿A qué distancia está...?** ah keh dees·tahn·theeyah ehs·tah... |

| | |
|---|---|
| Where's…? | **¿Dónde está…?** dohn•deh ehs•tah… |
| – …Street | **– la calle…** lah kah•yeh… |
| – this address | **– ésta dirección** ehs•tah dee•rek•theeyohn |
| Can you show me on the map? | **¿Me lo puede indicar en el mapa?** meh loh pweh•deh een•dee•kahr ehn ehl mah•pah |
| I'm lost. | **Me he perdido.** meh eh pehr•dee•doh |

### You May Hear…

| | |
|---|---|
| **todo recto** toh•doh rehk•toh | straight ahead |
| **a la izquierda** ah lah eeth•keeyehr•dah | left |
| **a la derecha** ah lah deh•reh•chah | right |
| ***en/doblando*** **la esquina** *ehn/doh•blahn•doh* lah ehs•kee•nah | *on/around* the corner |
| **al lado de** ahl lah•doh deh | next to |
| **después de** dehs•pwehs deh | after |
| **al** ***norte/sur*** ahl *nohr•teh/soor* | north/south |
| **al** ***este/oeste*** ahl *ehs•teh/oh•ehs•teh* | east/west |
| **en el semáforo** en ehl seh•mah•foh•roh | at the traffic light |
| **en el cruce** en ehl kroo•theh | at the intersection |

## Accommodations

| | |
|---|---|
| I have a reservation. | **Tengo una reserva.** tehn•goh oo•nah reh• sehr•bah |
| My name is… | **Me llamo…** meh yah•moh… |
| When's check-out? | **¿A qué hora hay que desocupar la habitación?** ah keh oh•rah aye keh deh•soh•koo•pahr lah ah•bee•tah•theeyohn |
| Can I leave this in the safe? | **¿Puedo dejar esto en la caja fuerte?** pweh•doh deh•khahr ehs•toh ehn lah kah•khah fwehr•teh |

| | |
|---|---|
| Can I leave my bags? | **¿Podría dejar mi equipaje?** poh•dree•ah deh• khahr mee eh•kee•pah•kheh |
| Can I have *the bill/ a receipt*? | **¿Me da *la factura/un recibo*?** meh dah *lah fahk•too•rah/oon reh•thee•boh* |

## *Internet and Communications*

| | |
|---|---|
| Where's an internet cafe? | **¿Dónde hay un cibercafé?** dohn•deh aye oon thee•behr•kah•feh |
| Can I *access the internet/check e-mail*? | **¿Puedo *acceder a Internet/revisar el correo electrónico*?** pweh•doh *ahk•theh•dehr ah een•tehr•neht/reh•bee•sahr ehl koh•rreh•oh eh•lehk•troh•nee•koh* |
| Can I have your phone number? | **¿Me puede dar su número de teléfono?** meh pweh•deh dahr soo noo•meh•roh deh teh•leh•foh•noh |
| Here's my *number/ e-mail address*. | **Aquí tiene mi *número/dirección de correo electrónico*.** ah•kee teeyeh•neh mee *noo•meh•roh/dee•rehk•theeyohn deh koh•rreh•oh eh•lehk•troh•nee•koh* |
| Call me. | **Llámeme.** yah•meh•meh |
| E-mail me. | **Envíeme un correo.** ehn•bee•eh•meh oon koh•rreh•oh |
| Hello. This is… | **Hola. Soy…** oh•lah soy… |
| Can I speak to…? | **¿Puedo hablar con…?** pweh•doh ah•blahr kohn… |
| Can you repeat that? | **¿Puede repetir eso?** pweh•deh reh•peh•teer eh•soh |
| I'll call back later. | **Llamaré más tarde.** yah•mah•reh mahs tahr•deh |
| Bye. | **Adiós.** ah•deeyohs |
| Where's the post office? | **¿Dónde está la oficina de correos?** dohn•deh ehs•tah lah oh•fee•thee•nah deh koh•rreh•ohs |

I'd like to send this to… **Quiero mandar esto a…** keeyeh•roh mahn•dahr ehs•toh ah…

## *Eating Out*

Can you recommend a good *restaurant/bar*? **¿Puede recomendarme un buen *restaurante/bar*?** pweh•deh reh•koh•mehn•dahr•meh oon bwehn *rehs•taw•rahn•teh/bahr*

Is there *a traditional Spanish/an inexpensive* restaurant nearby? **¿Hay un restaurante *típico español/barato* cerca de aquí?** aye oon rehs•taw•rahn•teh *tee•pee•koh ehs•pah•nyohl/bah•rah•toh* thehr•kah deh ah•kee

A table for…, please. **Una mesa para…, por favor.** oo•nah meh•sah pah•rah…pohr fah•bohr

A menu, please. **Una carta, por favor.** oo•nah kahr•tah pohr fah•bohr

What do you recommend? **¿Qué me recomienda?** keh meh reh•koh•meeyehn•dah

I'd like… **Quiero…** keeyeh•roh…

Some more…, please. **Quiero más…, por favor.** keeyeh•roh mahs… pohr fah•bohr

Enjoy your meal! **¡Que aproveche!** keh ah•proh•beh•cheh

The check [bill], please. **La cuenta, por favor.** lah kwen•tah pohr fah•bohr

Is service included? **¿Está incluido el servicio?** ehs•tah een•kloo•ee•doh ehl sehr•bee•theeyoh

Can I have a receipt? **¿Podría darme un recibo?** poh•dree•ah dahr•meh oon reh•thee•boh

### Breakfast

**los cereales (calientes/fríos)** lohs theh•reh•ah•lehs (kah•leeyehn•tehs/free•ohs) (cold/hot) cereal

**la mantequilla** lah mahn•teh•kee•yah butter

**la mermelada/la jalea** lah mehr•meh•lah•dah/khah•leh•ah jam/jelly

| | |
|---|---|
| **el pan** ehl pahn | bread |
| **la tortilla** lah tohr•tee•yah | omelet |
| **la tostada** lah tohs•tah•dah | toast |

## Appetizers [Starters]/Tapas

| | |
|---|---|
| **las aceitunas (rellenas)** lahs ah•theyee•too•nahs (reh•yeh•nahs) | (stuffed) olives |
| **los boquerones en vinagre** lohs boh•keh•roh•nehs ehn bee•nah•greh | anchovies marinated in garlic and olive oil |
| **el pan con tomate** ehl pahn kohn toh•mah•teh | toasted bread with garlic, tomato and olive oil |

## Soup

| | |
|---|---|
| **el consomé al jerez** ehl kohn•soh•meh ahl kheh•rehth | chicken broth with sherry |
| **el gazpacho** ehl gahth•pah•choh | cold tomato soup |
| **la sopa…** lah soh•pah… | …soup |
| **– de tomate** deh toh•mah•teh | – tomato |
| **– de verduras** deh behr•doo•rahs | – vegetable |

## Fish and Seafood

| | |
|---|---|
| **el bacalao** ehl bah•kah•laoh | cod |
| **el lenguado** ehl lehn•gwah•doh | sole |
| **el pulpo** ehl pool•poh | octopus |
| **la trucha** lah troo•chah | trout |
| **la zarzuela de pescado** lah thahr•thweh•lah deh pehs•kah•doh | mixed fish and seafood cooked in broth, served over bread |

## Meat and Poultry

| | |
|---|---|
| **la butifarra** lah boo•tee•fah•rrah | spiced pork sausage, popular in Cataluña and Valencia |
| **la carne de cerdo** lah kahr•neh deh thehr•doh | pork |
| **la carne de vaca** lah kahr•neh deh bah•kah | beef |

**el conejo** ehl koh•neh•khoh — rabbit

**la codorniz** lah koh•dohr•neeth — quail

**el jamón serrano** ehl khah•mohn seh•rrah•noh — dry-cured serrano ham

**el pato** ehl pah•toh — duck

**el pollo** ehl poh•yoh — chicken

**la ternera** lah tehr•neh•rah — veal

| | |
|---|---|
| rare | **muy poco hecho ♂ /hecha ♀** mooy poh•koh eh•choh ♂ /eh•chah ♀ |
| medium | **medio hecho ♂ /hecha ♀** meh•deeyoh eh•choh ♂ /eh•chah ♀ |
| well-done | **bien hecho ♂ /hecha ♀** beeyehn eh•choh ♂ / eh•chah ♀ |

## Paella

**la paella…** lah pah•eh•yah… — paella…

**– de marisco** deh mah•rees•koh — – with shellfish

**– de verduras** deh behr•doo•rahs — – with vegetables

**– valenciana** bah•lehn•theeyah•nah — – with rice, saffron, vegetables, rabbit, and chicken, from the Valencia region

**– zamorana** thah•moh•rah•nah — – with ham, pork loin, pig's feet; popular in the Zamora region

## Vegetables

**la acelga** lah ah•thehl•gah — chard

**el ajo** ehl ah•khoh — garlic

**la alcachofa (salteada)** lah ahl•kah•choh•fah (sahl•teh•ah•dah) — (sauteed) artichoke

**el calabacín** ehl kah•lah•bah•theen — zucchini [courgette]

**la judía verde** lah khoo•dee•ah behr•deh — green bean

**la lechuga** lah leh•choo•gah — lettuce

**el pimiento relleno** ehl pee•meeyehn•toh reh•yeh•noh — stuffed pepper

## Fruit

**el albaricoque** ehl ahl•bah•ree•koh•keh — apricot

**la fresa** lah freh•sah — strawberry

**la mandarina** lah mahn•dah•ree•nah — tangerine

**la manzana** lah mahn•thah•nah — apple

**el melocotón** ehl meh•loh•koh•tohn — peach

**el plátano** ehl plah•tah•noh — banana

**la sandía** lah sahn•dee•ah — watermelon

## Dessert

**el brazo de gitano** ehl brah•thoh deh khee•tah•noh — sponge cake roll with cream filling

**el flan** ehl flahn — caramel custard

**el helado** ehl eh•lah•doh — ice cream

**la manzana asada** lah mahn•thah•nah ah•sah•dah — baked apple

**el pastel de queso** ehl pahs•tehl deh keh•soh — cheesecake

# *Drinks*

| | |
|---|---|
| The *wine list/drink menu*, please. | **La carta de *vinos/bebidas*, por favor.** lah kahr·tah deh *bee·nohs/beh·bee·dahs* pohr fah·bohr |
| I'd like a *bottle/glass* of *red/white* wine. | **Quiero *una botella/un vaso* de vino *tinto/blanco.*** keeyeh·roh *oo·nah boh·teh·yah/oon bah·soh* deh bee·noh *teen·toh/blahn·koh* |
| Another *bottle/glass*, please. | ***Otra botella/Otro vaso*, por favor.** *oh·trah boh·teh·yah/oh·troh bah·soh* pohr fah·bohr |
| I'd like a local beer. | **Quiero una cerveza española.** keeyeh·roh oo·nah thehr·beh·thah ehs·pah·nyoh·lah |
| Cheers! | **¡Salud!** sah·looth |
| A *coffee/tea*, please. | **Un *café/té*, por favor.** oon *kah·feh/teh* pohr fah·bohr |
| Black. | **Solo.** soh·loh |
| With… | **Con…** kohn… |
| – milk | **– leche** leh·cheh |
| – sugar | **– azúcar** ah·thoo·kahr |
| – artificial sweetener | **– edulcorante artificial** eh·dool·khoh·rahn·teh ahr·tee·fee·theeyahl |
| A…, please. | **Un…, por favor.** oon…pohr fah·bohr |
| – juice | **– zumo** thoo·moh |
| – soda | **– refresco** reh·frehs·koh |
| – (sparkling/still) water | **– agua (*con/sin* gas)** ah·gwah (*kohn/seen* gahs) |

## Aperitifs, Cocktails and Liqueurs

| | |
|---|---|
| **el coñac** ehl koh·nyahk | brandy |
| **el jerez fino** ehl kheh·rehth fee·noh | pale, dry sherry |
| **el oporto** ehl oh·pohr·toh | port |
| **la sangría** lah sahn·gree·ah | wine punch |
| **el tequila** ehl teh·kee·lah | tequila |

## *Talking*

| | |
|---|---|
| Hello! | **¡Hola!** oh·lah |
| Good morning. | **Buenos días.** bweh·nohs dee·ahs |
| Good afternoon. | **Buenas tardes.** bweh·nahs tahr·dehs |
| Good evening. | **Buenas noches.** bweh·nahs noh·chehs |
| How are you? | **¿Cómo está?** koh·moh ehs·tah |
| Fine, thanks. | **Bien, gracias.** beeyehn grah·theeyahs |
| Excuse me! (to get attention) | **¡Perdón!** pehr·dohn |
| What's your name? | **¿Cómo se llama?** koh·moh seh yah·mah |
| My name is… | **Me llamo…** meh yah·moh… |
| Nice to meet you. | **Encantado♂/Encantada♀.** ehn·kahn·tah·doh♂/ehn·kahn·tah·dah♀ |
| Where are you from? | **¿De dónde es usted?** deh dohn·deh ehs oos·teth |
| I'm from the *U.S./U.K.* | **Soy *de Estados Unidos/del Reino Unido.*** soy *deh ehs·tah·dohs oo·nee·dohs/dehl reyee·noh oo·nee·doh* |
| Goodbye. | **Adiós.** ah·deeyohs |
| See you later. | **Hasta luego.** ah·stah lweh·goh |

When addressing strangers, always use the more formal **usted** (singular) or **ustedes** (plural), as opposed to the more familiar **tú** (singular) or **vosotros** (plural), until told otherwise. If you know someone's title, it's polite to use it, e.g., **doctor** (male doctor), **doctora** (female doctor). You can also simply say **Señor** (Mr.), **Señora** (Mrs.) or **Señorita** (Miss).

## Communication Difficulties

| | |
|---|---|
| Do you speak English? | **¿Habla inglés?** ah·blah een·glehs |
| I don't speak (much) Spanish. | **No hablo (mucho) español.** noh ah·bloh (moo·choh) ehs·pah·nyol |

| | |
|---|---|
| Can you speak more slowly? | **¿Puede hablar más despacio?** pweh•deh ah•blahr mahs dehs•pah•theeyoh |
| I (don't) understand. | **(No) entiendo.** (noh) ehn•teeyehn•doh |

## *Sightseeing*

| | |
|---|---|
| Where's the tourist information office? | **¿Dónde está la oficina de turismo?** dohn•deh ehs•tah lah oh•fee•thee•nah deh too•rees•moh |
| Do you have tours in English? | **¿Hay visitas en inglés?** aye bee•see•tahs ehn een•glehs |
| Can I have a *map/guide*? | **¿Puede darme *un mapa/una guía*?** pweh•deh dahr•meh *oon mah•pah/oo•nah gee•ah* |

### Sights

| | |
|---|---|
| Where is...? | **¿Dónde está...?** dohn•deh ehs•tah... |
| – the castle | **– el castillo** ehl kahs•tee•yoh |
| – the downtown area | **– el centro** ehl thehn•troh |
| – the museum | **– el museo** ehl moo•seh•oh |
| – the shopping area | **– la zona comercial** lahs thoh•nah koh•mehr•theeyahl |

## Shopping

| | |
|---|---|
| Where's the *market/ mall [shopping centre]*? | **¿Dónde está el *mercado/centro comercial*?** dohn•deh ehs•tah ehl *mehr•kah•doh/then•troh koh•mehr•theeyahl* |
| I'm just looking. | **Sólo estoy mirando.** soh•loh ehs•toy mee•rahn•doh |
| Can you help me? | **¿Puede ayudarme?** pweh•deh ah•yoo•dahr•meh |
| I'm being helped. | **Ya me atienden.** yah meh ah•teeyehn•dehn |
| How much? | **¿Cuánto es?** kwahn•toh ehs |
| That one, please. | **Ése♂/Ésa♀, por favor.** eh•seh♂/eh•sah♀ pohr fah•bohr |
| That's all. | **Eso es todo.** eh•soh ehs toh•doh |
| Where can I pay? | **¿Dónde se paga?** dohn•deh seh pah•gah |
| I'll pay *in cash/by credit card.* | **Voy a pagar *en efectivo/con tarjeta de crédito.*** boy ah pah•gahr *ehn eh•fehk•tee•boh/kohn tahr•kheh•tah deh kreh•dee•toh* |
| A receipt, please. | **Un recibo, por favor.** oon reh•thee•boh pohr fah•bohr |

### Stores

| | |
|---|---|
| Where *is/are*...? | **¿Dónde *está/están*...?** dohn•deh *ehs•tah/ ehs•tahn*... |
| – the bakery | **– la panadería** lah pah•nah•deh•ree•ah |
| – the bookstore | **– la librería** lah lee•breh•ree•ah |
| – the department stores | **– los grandes almacenes** lohs grahn•dehs ahl•mah•theh•nehs |
| – the pastry shop | **– la pastelería** lah pahs•teh•leh•ree•ah |
| – the supermarket | **– el supermercado** ehl soo•pehr•mehr•kah•doh |

### Clothing

| | |
|---|---|
| I'd like... | **Quiero...** keeyeh•roh... |

| | |
|---|---|
| Can I try this on? | **¿Puedo probarme esto?** pweh•doh proh•bahr•meh ehs•toh |
| It doesn't fit. | **No me queda bien.** noh meh keh•dah beeyehn |
| Do you have this in a *bigger/ smaller* size? | **¿Tiene esto en una talla más *grande/ pequeña*?** teeyeh•neh ehs•toh ehn oo•nah tah•yah mahs *grahn•deh/peh•keh•nyah* |

### Color

| | |
|---|---|
| I'd like something... | **Busco algo...** boos•koh ahl•goh... |
| – black | **– negro** neh•groh |
| – blue | **– azul** ah•thool |
| – brown | **– marrón** mah•rrohn |
| – green | **– verde** behr•deh |
| – gray | **– gris** grees |
| – orange | **– naranja** nah•rahn•khah |
| – red | **– rojo** roh•khoh |
| – white | **– blanco** blahn•koh |
| – yellow | **– amarillo** ah•mah•ree•yoh |

## *Sports and Leisure*

| | |
|---|---|
| Where's...? | **¿Dónde está...?** dohn•deh ehs•tah... |
| – the beach | **– la playa** lah plah•yah |
| – the park | **– el parque** ehl pahr•keh |
| – the pool | **– la piscina** lah pees•thee•nah |
| Can I rent [hire] golf clubs? | **¿Puedo alquilar palos de golf?** pweh•doh ahl•kee•lahr pah•lohs deh golf |

## *Culture and Nightlife*

| | |
|---|---|
| Do you have a program of events? | **¿Tiene un programa de espectáculos?** teeyeh•neh oon proh•grah•mah deh ehs•pehk•tah•koo•lohs |

| | |
|---|---|
| Where's...? | **¿Dónde está...?** dohn•deh ehs•tah... |
| – the downtown area | – **el centro** ehl thehn•troh |
| – the bar | – **el bar** ehl bahr |
| – the dance club | – **la discoteca** lah dees•koh•teh•kah |

## *Business Travel*

| | |
|---|---|
| I'm here on business. | **Estoy aquí en viaje de negocios.** ehs•toy ah•kee ehn beeyah•kheh deh neh•goh•theeyohs |
| Here's my business card. | **Aquí tiene mi tarjeta.** ah•kee teeyeh•neh mee tahr•kheh•tah |
| Can I have your card? | **¿Puede darme su tarjeta?** pweh•deh dahr•meh soo tahr•kheh•tah |
| I have a meeting with... | **Tengo una reunión con...** tehn•goh oo•nah reh•oo•neeyon kohn... |
| Where's...? | **¿Dónde está...?** dohn•deh ehs•tah... |
| – the business center | – **el centro de negocios** ehl thehn•troh deh neh•goh•theeyohs |
| – the convention hall | – **el salón de congresos** ehl sah•lohn deh kohn•greh•sohs |
| – the meeting room | – **la sala de reuniones** lah sah•lah deh reh•oo•neeyo•nehs |

## *Travel with Children*

| | |
|---|---|
| Is there a discount for kids? | **¿Hacen descuento a niños?** ah•then dehs•kwehn•toh ah nee•nyohs |
| Can you recommend a babysitter? | **¿Puede recomendarme una canguro?** pweh•deh reh•koh•mehn•dahr•meh oo•nah kahn•goo•roh |
| Do you have a *child's seat/ highchair*? | **¿Tienen una *silla para niños/trona*?** teeyeh•nehn oo•nah *see•yah pah•rah nee•nyohs/troh•nah* |
| Where can I change the baby? | **¿Dónde puedo cambiar al bebé?** dohn•deh pweh•doh kahm•beeyahr ahl beh•beh |

## For the Disabled

| | |
|---|---|
| Is there…? | **¿Hay…?** aye… |
| – access for the disabled | **– acceso para los discapacitados** ahk•theh•soh pah•rah lohs dees•kah•pah•thee•tah•dohs |
| – a wheelchair ramp | **– una rampa para sillas de ruedas** oo•nah rahm•pah pah•rah see•yahs deh rweh•dahs |
| – a handicapped- [disabled-] accessible toilet | **– un baño con acceso para discapacitados** oon bah•nyoh kohn ahk•theh•soh pah•rah dees•kah•pah•thee•tah•dohs |
| I need… | **Necesito…** neh•theh•see•toh… |
| – assistance | **– ayuda** ah•yoo•dah |
| – an elevator [a lift] | **– un ascensor** oon ahs•thehn•sohr |

## Emergencies

| | |
|---|---|
| Help! | **¡Socorro!** soh•koh•rroh |
| Go away! | **¡Lárguese!** lahr•geh•seh |
| Stop, thief! | **¡Deténgase, ladrón!** deh•tehn•gah•seh lah•drohn |
| Get a doctor! | **¡Llame a un médico!** yah•meh ah oon meh•dee•koh |
| Fire! | **¡Fuego!** fweh•goh |
| I'm lost. | **Me he perdido.** meh eh pehr•dee•doh |
| Can you help me? | **¿Puede ayudarme?** pweh•deh ah•yoo•dahr•meh |
| Call the police! | **¡Llame a la policía!** yah•meh ah lah poh•lee•thee•ah |

## Health

| | |
|---|---|
| I'm sick [ill]. | **Me encuentro mal.** meh ehn•kwehn•troh mahl |
| I need an English-speaking doctor. | **Necesito un médico que hable inglés.** neh•theh•see•toh oon meh•dee•koh keh ah•bleh een•glehs |
| It hurts here. | **Me duele aquí.** meh dweh•leh ah•kee |

# Reference

## Numbers

0 **cero** theh·roh

1 **uno** oo·noh

2 **dos** dohs

3 **tres** trehs

4 **cuatro** kwah·troh

5 **cinco** theen·koh

6 **seis** seyees

7 **siete** seeyeh·teh

8 **ocho** oh·choh

9 **nueve** nweh·beh

10 **diez** deeyehth

11 **once** ohn·theh

12 **doce** doh·theh

13 **trece** treh·theh

14 **catorce** kah·tohr·theh

15 **quince** keen·theh

16 **dieciséis** deeyeh·thee·seyees

17 **diecisiete** deeyeh·thee·seeyeh·teh

18 **dieciocho** deeyeh·thee·oh·choh

19 **diecinueve** deeyeh·thee·nweh·beh

20 **veinte** beyeen·teh

21 **veintiuno** beyeen·tee·oo·noh

22 **veintidós** beyeen·tee·dohs

30 **treinta** treyeen·tah

31 **treinta y uno** treyeen·tah ee oo·noh

40 **cuarenta** kwah·rehn·tah

50 **cincuenta** theen·kwehn·tah

60 **sesenta** seh·sehn·tah

70 **setenta** seh·tehn·tah

80 **ochenta** oh·chehn·tah

90 **noventa** noh·behn·tah

100 **cien** theeyehn

101 **ciento uno** theeyehn·toh oo·noh

200 **doscientos** dohs·theeyehn·tohs

500 **quinientos** kee·neeyehn·tohs

1,000 **mil** meel

10,000 **diez mil** deeyehth meel

1,000,000 **un millón** oon mee·yohn

## Time

What time is it? — **¿Qué hora es?** keh oh·rah ehs

From one o'clock to two o'clock. — **De una a dos en punto.** deh oo·nah ah dohs ehn poon·toh

5:30 *a.m./p.m.* — **Las cinco y media de la *mañana/tarde.*** lahs theen·koh ee meh·deeyah deh lah *mah·nyah·nah/tahr·deh*

## Days

Monday — **lunes** loo·nehs

Tuesday — **martes** mahr·tehs

Wednesday — **miércoles** meeyehr·koh·lehs

Thursday — **jueves** khweh·behs

Friday — **viernes** beeyehr·nehs

Saturday — **sábado** sah·bah·doh

Sunday — **domingo** doh·meen·goh

## Dates

yesterday — **ayer** ah·yehr

today — **hoy** oy

tomorrow — **mañana** mah·nyah·nah

## Months

January — **enero** eh·neh·roh

February — **febrero** feh·breh·roh

March — **marzo** mahr·thoh

April — **abril** ah·breel

May — **mayo** mah·yoh

June — **junio** khoo·neeyoh

July — **julio** khoo·leeyoh

August — **agosto** ah·gohs·toh

September — **septiembre** sehp·teeyehm·breh

October — **octubre** ohk·too·breh

November — **noviembre** noh·beeyehm·breh

December — **diciembre** dee·theeyehm·breh

# Swedish

## Pronunciation

Swedish has very consistent rules with respect to the sounding of individual letters, i.e. all the letters should be pronounced distinctly, even vowels and consonants at the ends of words. The Swedish language is often referred to as a "musical" language due to the fact that the intonation and rhythm moves up and down, giving the language a musical quality. Despite this stress, like pronunciation, is quite consistent. Most words with two or more syllables have primary stress on the first syllable of the word, and this can be followed by a secondary stress on the second syllable. There are also a number of words with two or more syllables which do not have stress on the first syllable, but often on the last. Stress has been noted in the phonetic transcription with underlining.

### Consonants

| Letter | Approximate Pronunciation | Symbol | Example | Pronunciation |
|---|---|---|---|---|
| c | like s in sit | s | **cykel** | s**ew**·kerl* |
| g | 1. before o, å, a and u, like g in get | g | **gata** | gah·ta |
| | 2. before i, e, ö and ä, like y in yet | y | **get** | yet |
| | 3. after r and l, like y in yet | y | **borg** | bohry |
| j | 1. soft, like y in yet | y | **jag** | yahg |
| | 2. after r and l, like y in yet | y | **familj** | fah·mihly |

*Bold indicates a lengthening of the sound, an extra emphasis on the vowel sound.

| Letter | Approximate Pronunciation | Symbol | Example | Pronunciation |
|---|---|---|---|---|
| k | 1. before o, å, a and u, like k in keep | k | **katt** | kat |
| | 2. before i, e, ö and ä, like ch in chew | | **köpa** | chur·pa |
| q | like k in keep | k | **Blomquist** | bloom·kvihst |
| r | strong, almost trilled, r | | **röd** | rurd |
| s | like s in see | s | **sitta** | siht·a |
| w | like v in very | v | **wennergren** | vehn·eh·grehn |
| z | like s in suit | s | **zebra** | see·bra |

Letters b, d, f, h, m, n, p, t, v and x are generally pronounced as in English.

## Consonant Clusters

| Letter | Approximate Pronunciation | Symbol | Example | Pronunciation |
|---|---|---|---|---|
| ch | like sh in ship | sh | **check** | shehk |
| ck | like ck in tick | k | **flicka** | flih·ka |
| dj, gj, hj, lj | like y in yet | y | **djur** | yeur |
| sj, skj, stj, sch, ch | like sh in shop | sh | **sjal** | shahl |
| sk | 1. before o, å, a and u, like sk in skip | sk | **skala** | skah·la |
| | 2. before i, e, ö and ä, like sh in ship | sh | **skära** | shai·ra |
| tj | like sh followed by ch | shch | **tjock** | shchohk |

## Vowels

| Letter | Approximate Pronunciation | Symbol | Example | Pronunciation |
|---|---|---|---|---|
| a | 1. when long, like a in father | ah | **dag** | dahg |
| | 2. when short, like a in cat | a | **katt** | kat |
| e | 1. when long, like ee in beer | ee | **veta** | vee·ta |
| | 2. when short, like e in fell | eh | **ett** | eht |
| i | 1. when long, like ee in see | ee | **bil** | beel |
| | 2. when short, like i in bit | ih | **mitt** | miht |
| o | 1. when long, like oa in coat | oa | **sko** | sk**oa** |
| | 2. like the exclamation oh | oh | **font** | fohnt |
| u | 1. when long, eu in feud | eu | **ruta** | r**eu**·ta |
| | 2. when short, like u in up | uh | **uppe** | uh·per |
| y | like ew in new | ew | **byta** | b**ew**·ta |
| å | 1. when long, like oa in oar | oa | **gå** | g**oa** |
| | 2. when short, like o in hot | oh | **åtta** | oh·ta |
| ä | 1. when long, like ai in air | ai | **här** | hair |
| | 2. when short, like e in set | eh | **säng** | sehng |

| Letter(s) | Approximate Pronunciation | Symbol | Example | Pronunciation |
|---|---|---|---|---|
| ö | 1. when long, like u in cure | ur | **smör** | sm**ur** |
| | 2. when short, like u in nut | uh | **rött** | ruhrt |

Swedish vowels are divided into two groups: hard and soft. **A**, **o**, **u** and **å** are hard vowels; **e**, **i**, **y**, **ä** and **ö** are soft vowels. Vowels can also be pronounced either long or short. When a vowel is pronounced "long" the sound is longer, but also more open and rounder. The "short" vowel sounds are more closed, literally a "shorter" sound than a long vowel. An easy rule to remember is that if the vowel is followed by a single consonant, as in **stad** (city), it is long. If the vowel is followed by a double consonant, as in **katt** (cat), the vowel is short. The exception to this rule is with the consonants **m** and **n**.

## Basic Expressions

| | |
|---|---|
| Hello! | **Hej!** hay |
| Goodbye. | **Hej då.** hay·d**oa** |
| Yes. | **Ja.** yah |
| No. | **Nej.** nay |
| Okay. | **Okej.** oa·kay |
| Excuse me! (to get attention) | **Ursäkta!** eur·shehk·ta |
| Excuse me. (to get past) | **Ursäkta mig.** eur·shehk·ta may |
| Please. (invitation) | **Varsågod.** vahr·s**oa**·goad |
| Please… (request) | **Snälla…** sneh·la… |
| Thank you. | **Tack.** tak |
| You're welcome. | **För all del.** f**ur**r ahl deel |
| Where is the restroom [toilet]? | **Var är toaletten?** vahr **ai**r t**oa**·ah·leh·tehn |

## *Arrival and Departure*

| | |
|---|---|
| I'm here on *vacation [holiday]/business.* | **Jag är här på *semester/affärsresa.*** yahg air hair p**oa** *seh•mehs•ter/a•fairs•ree•sa* |
| I'm going to... | **Jag ska resa till...** yahg skah ree•sa tihl... |
| I'm staying at a *hotel/youth hostel.* | **Jag bor på *hotell/vandrarhem.*** yahg b**oa**r p**oa** *hoh•tehl/vahnd•rar•hehm* |

### Passport Control and Customs

| | |
|---|---|
| I'm just passing through. | **Jag är bara på genomresa.** yahg air bah•ra p**oa** ye•nohm•ree•sa |
| I would like to declare... | **Jag skulle vilja förtulla...** yahg skuh•ler vihl•ya furr•tuh•la... |
| I have nothing to declare. | **Jag har inget att förtulla.** yahg hahr ihng•eht at furr•tuh•la |

## *Money and Banking*

| | |
|---|---|
| Where's...? | **Var ligger...?** vahr lih•gehr... |
| – the ATM | – **bankomaten** bank•oa•mah•tehn |
| – the bank | – **banken** bank•ehn |
| – the currency exchange office | – **växelkontoret** vehx•ehl•kohn•t**oa**r•eht |
| What time does the bank *open/close*? | **När *öppnar/stänger* banken?** nair *urp•nahr/stehng•ehr* bank•ehn |
| I'd like to change *dollars/pounds* into kronor. | **Jag skulle vilja växla *dollar/pund* till kronor.** yahg skuh•ler vihl•ya vehx•la *doh•lar/pund* tihl kroa•nohr |
| I want to cash some traveler's checks [cheques]. | **Jag skulle vilja lösa in några resecheckar.** yahg skuh•ler vihl•ya l**ur**•sa ihn n**oa**•gra ree•seh•sheh•kar |

## *Transportation*

| | |
|---|---|
| How do I get to town? | **Hur kommer jag till staden?** heur koh•mehr yahg tihl stahd•ehn |

Where is…? **Var ligger…?** vahr lih·gehr…

– the airport **– flygplatsen** flewg·plats·ehn

– the train [railway] station **– järnvägsstationen** yairn·vehgs·sta·shoa·nehn

– the bus station **– bussterminalen** bus·tehr·mee·nah·lehn

– the subway [underground] station **– tunnelbanestationen** teu·nehl·bah·neh·sta·shoan·ehn

How far is it? **Hur långt är det?** heur loangt air dee

Where can I buy tickets? **Var kan jag köpa biljetter?** vahr kan yahg chur·pa bil·yeht·tehr

A *one-way [single]/ round-trip [return]* ticket. **Enkel./Retur.** ehng·kehl/reh·teur

How much does it cost? **Hur mycket kostar det?** heur mew·ker kos·tar dee

Are there any discounts? **Finns det några rabatter?** fihns dee noa·gra ra·bat·ehr

Which gate? **Vid vilken gate?** veed vihl·kehn gayt

Which line? **Vilken kö?** vihl·kehn kur

Which platform? **Vilken plattform?** vihl·kehn plat·fohrm

Where can I get a taxi? **Var kan jag få tag på en taxi?** vahr kan yahg foa tahg poa ehn tax·ee

Please take me to this address. **Var snäll och kör mig till denna address.** vahr snehl ohk churr may tihl deh·na ad·rehs

Where can I rent a car? **Var kan jag hyra en bil?** vahr kan yahg hew·ra ehn beel

I'd like a map. **Jag skulle vilja ha en karta.** yahg skuh·ler vihl·ya hah ehn kahr·ta

## Asking Directions

How far is it to…? **Hur långt är det till…?** heur loangt air dee tihl…

Where's…? **Var ligger…?** vahr lih·gehr…

| | |
|---|---|
| – ...Street | **– ...gata** ...gah·ta |
| – this address | **– denna adress** deh·na ad·rehs |
| Can you show me on the map? | **Kan du visa mig på kartan?** kan deu vee·sa may p**oa** kahr·tan |
| I'm lost. | **Jag har kommit vilse.** yahg hahr koh·miht vihl·ser |

## You May Hear...

| | |
|---|---|
| **rakt fram** rahkt fram | straight ahead |
| **till vänster** tihl vehn·stehr | *on/to* the left |
| **till höger** tihl h**ur**·gehr | *on/to* the right |
| ***i/runt* hörnan** *ee/ruhnt* h**ur**·nan | *on/around* the corner |
| **bredvid** breh·veed | next to |
| **efter** ehf·tehr | after |
| **norr/söder** nohr/s**ur**·dehr | north/south |
| **öster/väster** urs·tehr/vehs·tehr | east/west |

# Accommodations

| | |
|---|---|
| I have a reservation. | **Jag har bokat rum.** yahg hahr boa·kat ruhm |
| My name is... | **Jag heter...** yahg hee·tehr... |
| When's check-out? | **När måste vi checka ut?** nair mos·ter vee sheh·ka eut |
| Can I leave this in the safe? | **Kan jag lämna detta i kassaskåpet?** kan yahg lehm·na deh·ta ee ka·sah·sk**oa**·peht |
| Could we leave our baggage here until...? | **Kan vi lämna vårt bagage här till klockan...?** kan vee lehm·na voart ba·goash hair tihl kloh·kan... |
| Could I have the *bill/receipt*, please? | **Kan jag få *räkningen/kvittot*, tack?** kan yahg f**oa** *rairk·nihng·en/kvih·toht* tak |

## Internet and Communications

| | |
|---|---|
| Where's an internet cafe? | **Var finns det ett internetkafé?** vahr fihns d**ee** eht ihn•tehr•neht•ka•feh |
| Can I access *the internet/check e-mail* here? | **Kan jag *komma ut på internet/kolla e-post* här?** kan yahg *koh•ma eut p***oa** *ihn•tehr•neht /koa•la ee•pohst* hair |
| Can I have your phone number? | **Kan jag få ditt telefonnummer?** kan yahg foa diht teh•leh•**foa**n•nuhm•ehr |
| Here's my *number/ e-mail address.* | **Här är *mitt nummer/min e-postadress.*** hair air miht *nuhm•ehr/mihn ee•pohst•ad•rehs* |
| Call me. | **Var snäll och ring mig.** vahr snehl ohk ring may |
| E-mail me. | **Skicka en e-post till mig.** shih•ka ehn ee•pohst tihl may |
| Hello. This is... | **Hej. Det här är...** hay d**ee** hair air... |
| I'd like to speak to... | **Jag skulle vilja tala med...** yahg skuh•ler vihl•ya tah•la meed... |
| Repeat that, please. | **Kan du upprepa det, tack.** kan deu uhp•ree•pa dee tak |
| I'll be in touch. | **Jag hör av mig snart.** yahg h**ur** afv may snahrt |
| Goodbye. | **Hej då.** hay doa |
| Where is the post office? | **Var ligger posten?** vahr lih•gehr pohs•tehn |

## Eating Out

| | |
|---|---|
| Can you recommend a good *restaurant/ bar*? | **Kan du rekommendera en bra *restaurang/ pub?*** kan deu reh•koh•mehn•**dee**•ra ehn brah *rehs•teu•rang/peub* |
| Is there *a traditional Swedish/an inexpensive* restaurant nearby? | **Finns det *något värdshus/någon billigare restaurang* i närheten?** fihns d**ee** *noa•goht vairds•heus/noa•gohn bihl•ih•ga•rer rehs•teu•rang* ee nair•h**ee**•tehn |
| A table for..., please. | **Ett bord för..., tack.** eht bohrd f**ur**r...tak |

| | |
|---|---|
| A menu, please. | **En meny, tack.** ehn meh·neu tak |
| What do you recommend? | **Vad rekommenderar du?** vahd reh·koh·mehn·dee·rar deu |
| I'd like… | **Jag skulle vilja ha…** yahg skuh·ler vihl·ya hah… |
| Some more…, please. | **Lite mer…, tack.** lee·ter meer…tak |
| Enjoy your meal. | **Smaklig måltid.** smahk·lihg moal·teed |
| The check [bill], please. | **Kan jag få räkningen, tack.** kan yahg foa rairk·nihng·ehn tak |
| Is service included? | **Är serveringsavgiften inräknad?** air ser·veeh·rihngs·afv·yihf·tehn ihn·rairk·nad |
| Can I have the receipt, please? | **Kan jag få kvittot, tack?** kan yahg foa kvih·toht tak |

## Breakfast

| | |
|---|---|
| **bröd** brurd | bread |
| **filmjölk** feel·myurlk | thick yogurt |
| **gröt** grurt | (hot) cereal |
| **müsli** mews·lee | granola [muesli] |
| **smör** smur | butter |

## Appetizers [Starters]

| | |
|---|---|
| **gravlax** grafv·lax | marinated salmon |
| **löjrom** lurj·rohm | bleak roe, served with chopped, raw onions and sour cream and eaten on toast |
| **sill** sihl | marinated herring [whitebait] |
| **viltpastej** vihlt·pa·stay | game pâté |

## Soup

| | |
|---|---|
| **fisksoppa** fihsk·sohp·a | fish soup |
| **grönsakssoppa** grurn·sahks·sohp·a | vegetable soup |

| | |
|---|---|
| **oxsvanssoppa** oax·svans·sohp·a | oxtail soup |
| **ärtsoppa** airt·sohp·a | green or yellow pea soup |

## Fish and Seafood

| | |
|---|---|
| **lax** lax | salmon |
| **räkor** rair·kohr | shrimp [prawns] |
| **skaldjur** skahl·yeur | shellfish |
| **torsk** tohrshk | cod |

## Meat and Poultry

| | |
|---|---|
| **anka** ang·ka | duck |
| **biffkött** bihf·churt | beef |
| **falukorv** fah·leu·kohrv | lightly spiced sausage |
| **fläsk** flehsk | pork |
| **kalvkött** kalv·churt | veal |
| **kyckling** chewk·lihng | chicken |
| **kåldomar med gräddsås och lingon** koal·dohl·mar meed grehd·soas ohk lihng·ohn | chopped [minced] meat and rice stuffed in cabbage leaves |
| **köttbulle** churt·buh·ler | meatball |
| **lamm** lamm | lamb |

| | |
|---|---|
| rare | **blodig** bloa·dihg |
| medium | **medium** mee·dee·uhm |
| well done | **genomstekt** ye·nom·steekt |

## Vegetables

| | |
|---|---|
| **champinjon** sham·pihn·yoan | mushroom |
| **kål** koal | cabbage |
| **potatis** poa·tah·tihs | potato |
| **rädisa** raid·dih·sa | radish |

| | |
|---|---|
| **tomat** toa·maht | tomato |
| **vitlök** veet·lurk | garlic |

## Fruit

| | |
|---|---|
| **apelsin** a·pehl·seen | orange |
| **banan** ba·nahn | banana |
| **blåbär** bloa·bair | blueberry |
| **citron** see·troan | lemon |
| **hjortron** yoahr·tron | cloudberry |
| **smultron** smeul·trohn | wild strawberry |
| **äpple** ehp·leh | apple |

## Dessert

| | |
|---|---|
| **jordgubbar med grädde** yoard·guhb·ar meed greh·deh | strawberries and cream |
| **marängsviss** mah·rehng·svis | meringue with whipped cream and chocolate sauce |
| **ostkaka** oast·kah·ka | traditional southern Sweden curd cake |
| **våffla (med sylt och grädde)** vohf·la meed sewlt ohk greh·der | waffle (with jam and whipped cream) |

# Drinks

| | |
|---|---|
| May I see the *wine list/drink menu*? | **Kan jag få se *vinlistan/drinklistan*?** kan yahg f**oa** see *veen·lihs·tan/drihnk·lihs·tan* |
| I'd like a *bottle/glass* of *red/white* wine. | **Jag skulle vilja ha *en flaska/ett glas rött/vitt* vin.** yahg skuh·ler vihl·ya hah *ehn flas·ka/eht glahs ruhrt/viht* veen |
| The house wine, please. | **Husets vin, tack.** heu·sehts veen tak |
| Another *bottle/glass*, please. | ***En flaska/Ett glas* till, tack.** *ehn flas·ka/eht glahs* tihl tak |
| I'd like a local beer. | **Jag skulle vilja ha en öl från trakten.** yahg skuh·ler vihl·ya hah ehn **ur**l fron trak·tehn |
| Cheers! | **Skål!** sk**oa**l |
| A *coffee/tea*, please. | **En kopp *kaffe/te*, tack.** ehn kohp *ka·fer/tee* tak |
| Black. | **Svart.** svart |
| With… | **Med…** meed… |
| – milk | **– mjölk** myuhlk |
| – sugar | **– socker** soh·kehr |
| – artificial sweetener | **– sötningsmedel** surt·nihngs·mee·dehl |
| – decaf | **– utan koffein** eu·tan koh·feen |
| …, please. | **…, tack.** …tak |
| – Juice | **– Juice** y**oa**s |
| – Soda | **– sodavatten** s**oa**·da·va·tehrn |
| – (*Sparkling/Still*) Water | **– Vatten (*med/utan* kolsyra)** va·tehrn (*meed/eu·tan* koal·s**ew**·ra) |
| Is the tap water safe to drink? | **Kan man dricka kranvattnet?** kan man drih·ka krahn·vat·neht |

## Aperitifs, Cocktails and Liqueurs

| | |
|---|---|
| **akvavit** a•kva•veet | aquavit, the famous Swedish grain- or potato-based spirit |
| **glögg** glurg | mulled wine with port and spices, served hot |
| **punsch** peunsh | sweet liqueur |
| **sprit** spreet | spirits |

# *Talking*

| | |
|---|---|
| Hello! | **Hej!** hay |
| Good morning. | **God morgon.** goad mor•on |
| Good afternoon. | **God middag.** goad mi•dahg |
| Good evening. | **God afton.** goad af•tohn |
| How are you? | **Hur står det till?** heur stoar dee tihl |
| Fine, thanks. And you? | **Bra, tack. Och du?** brah tak ohk deu |
| Excuse me! | **Ursäkta!** eur•shehk•ta |
| What's your name? | **Vad heter du?** vahd hee•tehr deu |
| My name is... | **Jag heter...** yahg hee•tehr... |
| Nice to meet you. | **Trevligt att träffas.** treev•lihgt at trehf•as |
| Where are you from? | **Var kommer du ifrån?** vahr ko•mehr deu ee•froan |
| I'm from the *U.S./U.K.* | **Jag kommer från *USA/Storbritannien.*** yahg koh•mehr froan *eu ehs ah/stoar•bree•tan•yehn* |
| Goodbye. | **Hej då.** hay•doa |
| See you later. | **Vi ses.** vee sees |

## Communication Difficulties

| | |
|---|---|
| Do you speak English? | **Talar du engelska?** tah•lar deu ehng•ehl•ska |
| I don't speak Swedish. | **Jag talar inte svenska.** yahg tah•lar ihn•ter svehn•ska |

| | |
|---|---|
| Could you speak more slowly? | **Kan du tala lite långsammare?** kan deu tah•la lee•ter loang•sam•a•rer |
| I (don't) understand. | **Jag förstår (inte).** yahg furr•stoar (ihn•ter) |

## *Sightseeing*

| | |
|---|---|
| Where's the tourist information office? | **Var ligger turistinformationen?** vahr lih•gehr teu•rihst•ihn•fohr•ma•shoan•ehn |
| Do you have tours in English? | **Finns det några turer på engelska?** fihns dee noa•gra teu•rehr poa ehng•ehl•ska |
| Can I have a *map/guide*, please? | **Kan jag få en *karta/guide*, tack?** kan yahg foa ehn *kahr•ta/gujd* tak |

### Sights

| | |
|---|---|
| Where is...? | **Var ligger...?** vahr lih•gehr... |
| – the castle | – **slottet** sloht•eht |
| – the downtown area | – **centrum** sehn•truhm |
| – the museum | – **museet** muh•see•eht |
| – the shopping area | – **Et affärscentrumet** eht a•ffairs•sehn•truhm•eht |

## *Shopping*

| | |
|---|---|
| Where is the *market/ mall [shopping centre]*? | **Var ligger *torget/affärscentrumet*?** vahr lih·gehr *tohr·yeht/a·ffairs·sehn·truhm·eht* |
| I'm just looking. | **Jag tittar bara.** yahg tih·tar bah·ra |
| Can you help me? | **Kan du hjälpa mig?** kan deu yehlp·a may |
| I'm being helped. | **Jag får hjälp, tack.** yahg f**oa**r yehlp tak |
| How much does it cost? | **Hur mycket kostar det?** heur mew·ker kos·tar d**et** |
| *This/That* one, thanks. | **Den *här/där*, tack.** dehn *hair/dair* tak |
| That's all, thanks. | **Det var allt, tack.** d**ee** vahr alt tak |
| Where do I pay? | **Var kan jag betala?** vahr kan yahg beh·tah·la |
| I'll pay *in cash/by credit card*. | **Jag vill betala *kontant/med kreditkort*.** yahg vihl beh·tah·la *kohn·tant/meed kreh·deet·koart* |
| A receipt, please. | **Kvittot, tack.** kvih·tot tak |

### Stores

| | |
|---|---|
| Where is...? | **Var finns...?** vahr fihns... |
| – the bakery | – **bageriet** bahg·eh·ree·eht |
| – the bookstore | – **bokhandeln** boak·han·dehln |
| – the department store | – **varuhuset** vahr·**eu**·h**eu**s·eht |
| – the pastry shop | – **konditoriet** kohn·deh·toh·ree·eht |
| – the pharmacy [chemist] | – **apoteket** a·poa·tee·keht |
| – the supermarket | – **snabbköpet** snab·ch**ur**·peht |

### Clothing

| | |
|---|---|
| Can I try this on? | **Kan jag prova den här?** kan yahg proa·va dehn hair |
| It doesn't fit. | **Den passar inte.** dehn pas·ar ihn·ter |

| | |
|---|---|
| Do you have this in a *bigger/smaller* size? | **Har ni den här i *en större/en mindre* storlek?** hahr nee dehn hair ee *ehn stur·re/ehn mihn·drer* stoar·leek |

### Color

| | |
|---|---|
| I'm looking for something in... | **Jag söker något i...** yahg sur·ker noa·goht ee... |
| – black | **– svart** svart |
| – blue | **– blått** bloat |
| – brown | **– brunt** breunt |
| – green | **– grönt** grurnt |
| – orange | **– orange** oa·ransh |
| – red | **– rött** ruhrt |
| – white | **– vitt** vit |
| – yellow | **– gult** geult |

## Sports and Leisure

| | |
|---|---|
| Where's...? | **Var ligger...?** vahr lih·gehr... |
| – the beach | **– stranden** stran·dehn |
| – the park | **– parken** park·ehn |
| – the pool | **– simbassängen** sihm·ba·sehng·ehn |
| Can I rent [hire] golf clubs? | **Kan man hyra golfklubbor?** kan man hew·ra gohlf·kluh·bohr |

## Culture and Nightlife

| | |
|---|---|
| Do you have a program of events? | **Har ni ett evenemangsprogram?** hahr nee eht eh·vehn·eh·mangs·proa·gram |
| Where's...? | **Var ligger...?** vahr lih·gehr... |
| – the downtown area | **– centrum** sehn·truhm |
| – the bar | **– baren** bah·rehn |
| – the dance club | **– diskoteket** dis·koh·tee·keht |

## Business Travel

| | |
|---|---|
| I'm here on business. | **Jag är här på affärsresa.** yahg air hair p**oa** a•fairs•ree•sa |
| Here's my business card. | **Här är mitt kort.** hair air miht koart |
| Can I have your card? | **Kan jag få ditt kort?** kan yahg f**oa** diht koart |
| I have a meeting with... | **Jag har ett möte med...** yahg hahr eht m**ur**•ter meed... |
| Where's...? | **Var ligger...?** vahr lih•gehr... |
| – the business center | **– businesscentret** bihs•nihs•sehn•treht |
| – the convention hall | **– kongresshallen** kohn•grehs•ha•lehn |
| – the meeting room | **– konferensrummet** kohn•feh•rans•ruhm•eht |

## Travel with Children

| | |
|---|---|
| Is there a discount for kids? | **Har ni barnrabatt?** hahr nee bahrn•rah•bat |
| Can you recommend a babysitter? | **Kan du rekommendera en barnvakt?** kan deu reh•koh•mehn•dee•ra ehn bahrn•vakt |
| Could I have a highchair? | **Kan jag få en barnstol, tack?** kan yahg f**oa** ehn bahrn•st**oa**l tak |
| Where can I change the baby? | **Var kan jag byta på babyn?** vahr kan yahg b**ew**•ta p**oa** bai•been |

## For the Disabled

| | |
|---|---|
| Is there...? | **Finns det...?** fihns d**e**t... |
| – access for the disabled | **– ingång för rörelsehindrade** in•g**oa**ng furr rur•rehl•seh•hihn•dra•der |
| – a wheelchair ramp | **– en rullstolsramp** ehn reul•st**oa**ls•ramp |
| – a handicapped-[disabled-] accessible toilet | **– en handikappanpassad toalett** ehn hand•ee•kap•an•pas•ad toa•ah•leht |

I need... **Jag behöver...** yahg beh•hur•ver...
– assistance **– hjälp** yehlp
– an elevator [lift] **– en hiss** ehn hihs

## Emergencies

Help! **Hjälp!** yelp
Go away! **Ge er iväg!** yeh ehr ee•vairg
Stop thief! **Stoppa tjuven!** stop•a shcheu•vehn
Get a doctor! **Hämta en läkare!** hehm•ta ehn lair•ka•rer
Fire! **Det brinner!** dee brihn•ehr
I'm lost. **Jag har gått vilse.** yahg hahr goat vihl•ser
Can you help me? **Kan du hjälpa mig?** kan deu yehl•pa may
Call the police! **Ring polisen!** rihng poa•lee•sehn

## Health

I'm sick [ill]. **Jag är sjuk.** yahg air sheuk
I need an English-speaking doctor. **Jag behöver en engelsktalande läkare.** yahg beh•hur•vehr ehn ehng•ehlsk•tahl•an•der lair•ka•rer
It hurts here. **Det gör ont här.** dee yurr oant hair

## Reference

### Numbers

0 **noll** nohl
1 **ett** eht
2 **två** tvoa
3 **tre** tree
4 **fyra** few•ra
5 **fem** fehm
6 **sex** sehx
7 **sju** sheu
8 **åtta** oh•ta
9 **nio** nee•oa
10 **tio** tee•oa
11 **elva** ehl•va
12 **tolv** tohlv
13 **tretton** treh•tohn

14 **fjorton** fyeur·tohn
15 **femton** fehm·tohn
16 **sexton** sehx·tohn
17 **sjutton** sheu·tohn
18 **arton** ar·tohn
19 **nitton** nih·tohn
20 **tjugo** shcheu·goa
21 **tjugoett** shcheu·goa·eht
22 **tjugotvå** shcheu·goa·tvoa
30 **trettio** treh·tee·oa
31 **trettioett** treh·tee·oa·eht
40 **fyrtio** fuhr·tee·oa
50 **femtio** fehm·tee·oa
60 **sextio** sehx·tee·oa
70 **sjuttio** sheu·tee·oa
80 **åttio** oh·tee·oa
90 **nittio** nih·tee·oa
100 **hundra** huhn·dra
101 **hundraett** huhn·dra·eht
200 **två hundra** tvoa huhn·dra
500 **fem hundra** fehm huhn·dra
1,000 **ett tusen** eht teu·sehn
10,000 **tio tusen** tee·oa teu·sehn
1,000,000 **en miljon** ehn mihl·yoan

## Time

What time is it? **Hur mycket är klockan?** heur mew·ker air kloh·kan

From 9 o'clock to 5 o'clock. **Från nio till sjutton.** froan nee·oa tihl sheu·tohn

5:30 a.m. **Halv sex på morgonen.** halv sehx poa mor·oh·nehn

5:30 p.m. **Halv sex på kvällen.** halv sehx poa kveh·lehn

## Days

Monday **måndag** moan·dahg
Tuesday **tisdag** tees·dahg
Wednesday **onsdag** oans·dahg
Thursday **torsdag** toash·dahg
Friday **fredag** free·dahg
Saturday **lördag** lurr·dahg
Sunday **söndag** surn·dahg

## Dates

| | |
|---|---|
| yesterday | **igår** ee·goar |
| today | **idag** ee·dahg |
| tomorrow | **imorgon** ee·mo·ron |

## Months

| | | | |
|---|---|---|---|
| January | **januari** ya·neu·ah·ree | July | **juli** yeu·lee |
| February | **februari** fehb·reu·ah·ree | August | **augusti** a·guhss·tee |
| March | **mars** mash | September | **september** sehp·tehm·behr |
| April | **april** ap·rihl | October | **oktober** ohk·toa·behr |
| May | **maj** maiy | November | **november** noh·vehm·behr |
| June | **juni** yeu·nee | December | **december** dee·sehm·behr |

# Turkish

## Pronunciation

Letters underlined in the transcriptions should be read with slightly more stress than the others, but don't overdo this as Turkish is not a heavily stressed language.

### Consonants

| Letter | Approximate Pronunciation | Symbol | Example | Pronunciation |
|---|---|---|---|---|
| c | like j in jam | j | **ceket** | jeh•<u>keht</u> |
| ç | like ch in church | ch | **kaç** | kahch |
| g | like g in ground | g | **gitmek** | geet•<u>mehk</u> |
| ğ | 1. at the end of a word, it lengthens the preceding vowel | | **dağ** | d**ah***|
| | 2. a silent letter between vowels | | **kağıt** | kah•<u>iht</u> |
| | 3. after e, like y in yawn | y | **değer** | deh•<u>yehr</u> |
| h | like h in hit | h | **mahkeme** | mah•keh•<u>meh</u> |
| j | like s in pleasure | zh | **bagaj** | bah•<u>gahzh</u> |
| r | trilled r | r | **tren** | trehn |
| s | like s in sit | s | **siyah** | see•<u>yahh</u> |
| ş | like sh in shut | sh | **şişe** | shee•<u>sheh</u> |

Letters b, d, f, k, l, m, n, p, t, v, y and z are pronounced as in English.

*Bold indicates a lengthening of the sound, an extra emphasis on the vowel sound.

Turkish consonants are typically shorter and harder-sounding than English consonants. When reading Turkish words, be sure to pronounce all the letters.

## Vowels

| Letter | Approximate Pronunciation | Symbol | Example | Pronunciation |
|---|---|---|---|---|
| **a** | like a in father | ah | **kara** | kah•<u>rah</u> |
| **e** | like e in net | eh | **sene** | seh•<u>neh</u> |
| **ı** | similar to i in ill | ih | **tatlı** | taht•<u>lih</u> |
| **i** | like ee in see | ee | **sim** | seem |
| **o** | like o in spot | oh | **otel** | oh•<u>tehl</u> |
| **ö** | similar to ur in fur | ur | **börek** | bur•<u>rehk</u> |
| **u** | like oo in cool | oo | **uzak** | oo•<u>zahk</u> |
| **ü** | like ew in few | yu | **üç** | yuch |

Turkish vowels are quite different from English vowels. As with consonants, they are generally shorter and harder than English vowels. In the pronunciation guide, certain vowels are followed by an "h" to emphasize the shortness of the sound.

## Diphthongs

| Letters | Approximate Pronunciation | Symbol | Example | Pronunciation |
|---|---|---|---|---|
| **ay** | like ie in tie | ie | bay | bie |
| **ey** | like ay in day | ay | bey | bay |
| **oy** | like oy in boy | oy | koy | koy |

# Basic Expressions

| | |
|---|---|
| Hello. | **Merhaba.** mehr•hah•bah |
| Goodbye. (said by departing party) | **Hoşçakalın.** hohsh•chah•kah•lihn |
| Goodbye. (said by party staying behind) | **Güle güle.** gyu•leh gyu•leh |
| Yes. | **Evet.** eh•vet |
| No. | **Hayır.** hah•yihr |
| OK. | **Tamam.** tah•mahm |
| Excuse me! (to get past, to get attention) | **Afedersiniz!** ahf•eh•dehr•see•neez |
| Sorry! | **Özür dilerim!** ur•zyur dee•leh•reem |
| Please. | **Lütfen.** lyut•fehn |
| Thank you. | **Teşekkür ederim.** teh•sheh•kyur eh•deh•reem |
| You're welcome. | **Bir şey değil.** beer shay deh•yeel |
| Where is the restroom [toilet]? | **Tuvalet nerede?** too•vah•let neh•reh•deh |

# Arrival and Departure

| | |
|---|---|
| I'm here on *vacation [holiday]*/*business*. | ***Tatil*/*İş* için buradayım.** *tah•teel*/*eesh* ee•cheen boo•rah•dah•yihm |
| I'm going to... | **...gidiyorum.** ...gee•dee•yoh•room |
| I'm staying at the...Hotel. | **...otelinde kalıyorum.** ...oh•teh•leen•deh kah•lih•yoh•room |

## Passport Control and Customs

| | |
|---|---|
| I'm just passing through. | **Sadece geçiyorum.** sah•deh•jeh geh•chee•yoh•room |
| I would like to declare... | **...beyan etmek istiyorum.** ...beh•yahn eht•mehk ees•tee•yoh•room |

| | |
|---|---|
| I have nothing to declare. | **Beyan edeceğim birşey yok.** beh•yahn eh•deh•jeh•yeem beer shay yohk |

## *Money and Banking*

| | |
|---|---|
| Where's...? | **...nerede?** ...neh•reh•deh |
| –the ATM | - **Paramatik** pah•rah•mah•teek |
| –the bank | - **Banka** bahn•kah |
| –the currency exchange office | - **Döviz bürosu** dur•veez byu•roh•soo |
| What time does the bank *open/close*? | **Banka saat kaçta *açılıyor/kapanıyor*?** bahn•kah sah•aht kach•tah *ah•chih•lih•yohr/ kah•pah•nih•yohr* |
| I'd like to change *dollars/pounds* into lira. | ***Dolar/İngiliz Sterlini* bozdurmak istiyorum.** *doh•lahr/een•gee•leez stehr•lee•nee* bohz•door•mahk ees•tee•yoh•room |
| I want to cash some traveler's checks [cheques]. | **Seyahat çeki bozdurmak istiyorum.** seh•yah•haht chek•ee bohz•door•mahk ees•tee•yoh•room |

## *Transportation*

| | |
|---|---|
| How do I get to town? | **Şehire nasıl gidebilirim?** sheh•hee•reh nah•sıhl gee•deh•bee•lee•reem |
| Where's...? | **...nerede?** ...neh•reh•deh |
| –the airport | - **Havaalanı** hah•vah•ah•lah•nıh |
| –the train [railway] station | - **Tren garı** trehn gah•rih |
| –the bus station | - **Otobüs garajı** oh•toh•byus gah•rah•jih |
| –the subway [underground] station | - **Metro istasyonu** meht•roh ees•tahs•yoh•noo |
| How far is it? | **Ne kadar uzakta?** neh kah•dahr oo•zahk•tah |

| | |
|---|---|
| Where can I buy tickets? | **Nereden bilet alabilirim?** neh•reh•dehn bee•leht ah•lah•bee•lee•reem |
| A *one-way [single]/ round-trip [return]* ticket. | **Sadece *gidiş/ gidiş-dönüş* bileti.** sah•deh•jeh *gee•deesh/ gee•deesh•dur•nyush* bee•leh•tee |
| How much? | **Ne kadar?** neh kah•dahr |
| Are there any discounts? | **İndirim var mı?** een•dee•reem vahr mih |
| Which...? | **Hangi...?** hahn•gee... |
| –gate? | **– kapı?** kah•pih |
| –lane? | **– hat?** haht |
| –platform? | **– peron?** peh•rohn |
| Where can I get a taxi? | **Nerede taksi bulabilirim?** neh•reh•deh tahk•see boo•lah•bee•lee•reem |
| Please take me to this address. | **Lütfen beni bu adrese götürün.** lyut•fehn beh•nee boo ahd•reh•seh gur•tyu•ryun |
| Where can I rent a car? | **Nereden bir araba kiralayabilirim?** neh•reh•dehn beer ah•rah•bah kee•rah•lah•yah•bee•lee•reem |
| Can I have a map? | **Bir harita alabilir miyim?** beer hah•reeh•tah ah•lah•bee•leer•mee•yeem |

## Asking Directions

| | |
|---|---|
| How far is it to...? | **...buradan ne kadar uzakta?** ...boo•rah•dahn neh kah•dahr oo•zahk•tah |
| Where's...? | **...nerede?** ...neh•reh•deh |
| –...Street | **– ...Caddesi** ...jahd•deh•see |
| –this address | **– Bu adres** boo ahd•rehs |

Can you show me on the map? **Bana haritada gösterebilir misiniz?** bah•nah hah•ree•tah•dah gurs•teh•reh•bee•leer mee•see•neez

I'm lost. **Kayboldum.** kie•bohl•doom

## You May Hear...

| | |
|---|---|
| **doğru ilerde** doh•roo ee•lehr•deh | straight ahead |
| **solda** sohl•dah | on the left |
| **sağda** sah•dah | on the right |
| **köşede/köşeyi dönünce** kur•sheh•deh/ kur•sheh•yee dur•nyun•jeh | *on/around* the corner |
| **yanında** yah•nihn•dah | next to |
| **...sonra** ...sohn•rah | after... |
| **kuzey/güney** koo•zay/gyu•nay | north/south |
| **doğu/batı** doh•oo/bah•tih | east/west |

# Accommodations

I have a reservation. **Yer ayırtmıştım.** yehr ah•yihrt•mihsh•tihm

My name is... **İsmim...** ees•meem...

When's check-out? **Saat kaçta otelden ayrılmamız gerekiyor?** sah•aht kahch•tah oh•tehl•dehn ie•rihl•mah•mihz geh•reh•kee•yohr

Can I leave this in the safe? **Bunu kasaya koyabilir miyim?** boo•noo kah•sah•yah koh•yah•bee•leer mee•yeem

Can I leave my bags? **Eşyalarımı bırakabilir miyim?** ehsh•yah•lah•rih•mih bih•rah•kah•bee•leer mee•yeem

Can I have *the bill/ a receipt*? ***Hesap/Fiş* alabilir miyim?** *heh•sahp/feesh* ah•lah•bee•leer mee•yeem

# Internet and Communications

| | |
|---|---|
| Where's an internet cafe? | **İnternet kafe nerede?** een•tehr•neht kah•feh neh•reh•deh |
| Can I *access the internet/check e-mail* here? | **Burada *internete girebilir/ postalarımı kontrol edebilir* miyim?** boo•rah•dah *een•tehr•neh•teh gee•reh•bee•leer/ pohs•tah•lah•rih•mih kohn•trohl eh•deh•bee•leer* mee•yeem |
| Can I have your phone number? | **Telefon numaranızı öğrenebilir miyim?** teh•leh•fohn noo•mah•rah•nih•zih ur•reh•neh•bee•leer mee•yeem |
| Here's my *number/ e-mail address.* | **İşte *numaram/ e-posta adresim.*** eesh•teh *noo•mah•rahm/eh•pohs•tah ahd•reh•seem* |
| Call me. | **Beni arayın.** beh•nee ah•rah•yihn |
| E-mail me. | **Bana yazın.** bah•nah yah•zihn |
| Hello, this is... | **Merhaba, ben...** mehr•hah•bah behn... |
| I'd like to speak to... | **...ile konuşmak istiyorum.** ...ee•leh koh•noosh•mahk ees•tee•yoh•room |
| Can you repeat that, please? | **Tekrar eder misiniz lütfen?** tehk•rahr eh•dehr mee•see•neez lyut•fehn |
| I'll call back later. | **Daha sonra arayacağım.** dah•hah sohn•rah ah•rah•yah•jah•ihm |
| Where is the post office? | **Postane nerede?** pohs•tah•neh neh•reh•deh |

# Eating Out

| | |
|---|---|
| Can you recommend a good *restaurant/ bar*? | **İyi bir *lokanta/ bar* önerebilir misiniz?** ee•yee beer *loh•kahn•tah/bahr* ur•neh•reh•bee•leer mee•see•neez |

| | |
|---|---|
| Is there *a traditional Turkish/ an inexpensive* restaurant near here? | **Yakınlarda *geleneksel Türk yemekleri/ ucuz yemek* sunan bir lokanta var mı?** yah•kihn•lahr•dah *geh•leh•nehk•sehl tyurk yeh•mehk•leh•ree/ oo•jooz yeh•mehk* soo•nahn beer loh•kahn•tah vahr mih |
| A table for..., please. | **...kişi için bir masa lütfen.** ...kee•shee ee•cheen beer mah•sah lyut•fehn |
| A menu, please. | **Menü lütfen.** meh•nyu lyut•fehn |
| What do you recommend? | **Ne önerirsiniz?** neh ur•neh•reer•see•neez |
| I'd like... | **...istiyorum.** ...ees•tee•yoh•room |
| Some more..., please. | **Biraz daha...istiyorum lütfen.** bee•rahz dah•hah...ees•tee•yoh•room lyut•fehn |
| Enjoy your meal. | **Afiyet olsun.** ah•fee•yeht ohl•soon |
| The check [bill], please. | **Hesap lütfen.** heh•sahp lyut•fehn |
| Is service included? | **Servis dahil mi?** sehr•vees dah•heel mee |
| Can I have a receipt, please? | **Lütfen fiş alabilir miyim?** lyut•fehn feesh ah•lah•bee•leer mee•yeem |

## Breakfast

| | |
|---|---|
| **bal** bahl | honey |
| **ekmek** ehk•mehk | bread |
| **reçel** reh•chehl | jam |
| **süt** syut | milk |
| **yumurta** yoo•moor•tah | eggs |

## Appetizers [Starters]

| | |
|---|---|
| **arnavut ciğeri** ahr•nah•voot jee•yeh•ree | fried liver morsels |
| **börek** bur•rehk | hot filo pastries |

| | |
|---|---|
| **dolma** dohl•mah | stuffed bell peppers |
| **patlıcan salatası** paht•lih•jahn sah•lah•tah•sih | eggplant [aubergine] salad |
| **pilaki** pee•lah•kee | beans in olive oil |

## Soup

| | |
|---|---|
| **et suyuna çorba** eht soo•yoo•nah chohr•bah | consommé |
| **kremalı çorba** kreh•mah•lih chohr•bah | cream soup |
| **sebze çorbası** sehb•zeh chohr•bah•sih | vegetable soup |
| **tavuk çorbası** tah•vook chohr•bah•sih | chicken soup |

## Fish and Seafood

| | |
|---|---|
| **alabalık** ah•lah•bah•lihk | trout |
| **lüfer** lyu•fehr | bluefish |
| **midye** meed•yeh | mussels |
| **kılıç şiş** kih•lihch sheesh | swordfish kebabs grilled with bay leaves, tomatoes and green peppers |
| **uskumru pilakisi** oos•koom•roo pee•lah•kee•see | mackerel fried in olive oil, with potatoes, celery, carrots and garlic; served cold |

## Meat and Poultry

| | |
|---|---|
| **Çerkez tavuğu** chehr•kehz tah•voo•oo | Circassian chicken: boiled chicken with rice and nut sauce |
| **dana** dah•nah | veal |
| **kuzu** koo•zoo | lamb |

| | |
|---|---|
| **ördek** ur•rdehk | duck |
| **pirzola** peer•zoh•lah | chops |
| **sığır eti** sih•**ih**r eh•tee | beef |
| **tavuk** tah•vook | chicken |
| **yoğurtlu kebab** yoh•oort•loo keh•bahb | kebab on toasted bread with pureed tomatoes and seasoned yogurt |

| | |
|---|---|
| rare | **az pişmiş** ahz peesh•meesh |
| medium | **orta ateşte** ohr•tah ah•tehsh•teh |
| well-done | **iyi pişmiş** ee•yee peesh•meesh |

## Vegetables

| | |
|---|---|
| **biber** bee•behr | peppers |
| **domates** doh•mah•tehs | tomatoes |
| **kabak** kah•bahk | zucchini [courgette] |
| **mantar** mahn•tahr | mushrooms |
| **marul** mah•rool | lettuce |
| **patates** pah•tah•tehs | potatoes |
| **pirinç** pee•reench | rice |
| **taze fasulye** tah•zeh fah•sool•yeh | green beans |

## Fruit

| | |
|---|---|
| **elma** ehl•mah | apples |
| **erik** eh•reek | plums |
| **karpuz** kahr•pooz | watermelon |
| **muz** mooz | bananas |
| **nar** nahr | pomegranates |

| | |
|---|---|
| **portakal** pohr•tah•kahl | orange |
| **üzüm** yu•zyum | grapes |

## Dessert

| | |
|---|---|
| **baklava** bahk•lah•vah | filo pastry filled with honey and pistachio nuts |
| **kadayıf** kah•dah•yihf | shredded wheat dessert, similar to baklava |
| **kazandibi** kah•zahn•dee•bee | oven-browned milk pudding |
| **sütlaç** syut•lahch | rice pudding |

## Drinks

| | |
|---|---|
| May I see the *wine list/drink menu*, please? | ***Şarap listesini/ İçecek menüsünü*** **görebilir miyim lütfen?** *shah•rahp lees•teh•see•nee/ee•cheh•jehk meh•nyu•syu•nyu* gur•reh•bee•leer mee•yeem lyut•fehn |
| I'd like a *bottle/ glass* of *red/white* wine. | **Bir *şişe/ bardak kırmızı/ beyaz* şarap istiyorum.** beer *shee•sheh/bahr•dahk kihr•mih•zih/beh•yahz* shah•rahp ees•tee•yoh•room |
| Another *bottle/ glass*, please. | **Bir *şişe/ bardak* daha lütfen.** beer *shee•sheh/bahr•dahk* dah•hah lyut•fehn |
| May I have a local beer? | **Yerel bir bira alabilir miyim?** yeh•rehl beer bee•rah ah•lah•bee•leer mee•yeem |
| Cheers! | **Şerefe!** sheh•reh•feh |
| A *coffee/tea*, please. | ***Kahve/ Çay*** **lütfen.** *kah•hveh/chie* lyut•fehn |
| Black. | **Sütsüz.** syut•syuz |
| With milk. | **Sütlü.** syut•lyu |

| | |
|---|---|
| With sugar. | **Şekerli.** sheh•kehr•lee |
| With artificial sweetener. | **Yapay tatlandırıcılı.** yah•pie taht•lahn•dih•rih•jih•lih |
| ..., please. | **...lütfen.** ...lyut•fehn |
| –Fruit juice | – **Meyve suyu** may•veh soo•yoo |
| –Soda | – **Soda** soh•dah |
| –(*Sparkling/Still*) Water | – (***Maden/ Sade***) **Su** (*mah•dehn/sah•deh*) soo |

## Apéritifs, Cocktails and Liqueurs

| | |
|---|---|
| **bira** bee•rah | beer |
| **cin** jeen | gin |
| **rakı** rah•kih | spirit made from distilled grapes and aniseed, similar to French pastis or Lebanese arak |
| **viski** vees•kee | whisky |
| **votka** voht•kah | vodka |

# *Talking*

| | |
|---|---|
| Hello. | **Merhaba.** mehr•hah•bah |
| Good morning. | **Günaydın.** gyu•nie•dihn |
| Good afternoon. | **İyi günler.** ee•yee gyun•lehr |
| Good evening. | **İyi akşamlar.** ee•yee ahk•shahm•lahr |
| Hi! | **Selam!** seh•lahm |
| How are you? | **Nasılsınız?** nah•sihl•sih•nihz |
| Fine, thanks. | **İyiyim, teşekkürler.** ee•yee•yeem teh•shehk•kyur•lehr |
| Excuse me! | **Afedersiniz!** ahf•eh•dehr•see•neez |

What's your name? **İsminiz nedir?** ees•mee•neez neh•deer

My name is... **İsmim...** ees•meem...

Pleased to meet you. **Tanıştığımıza memnun oldum.** tah•nihsh•tih•ih•mih•zah mehm•noon ohl•doom

Where are you from? **Nerelisiniz?** neh•reh•lee•see•neez

I'm from the *U.S./U.K.* **Amerikalıyım/Ingiltereliyim.** ah•meh•ree•kah•lih•yihm/een•gihl•teh•reh•lih•yihm

Goodbye. (said by departing persons) **Hoşçakalın.** hosh•chah kah•lihn

Goodbye. (said by persons staying behind) **Güle güle.** gyu•leh gyu•leh

See you later. **Tekrar görüşmek üzere.** tehk•rahr gur•ryush•mehk yu•zeh•reh

## Communication Difficulties

Do you speak English? **İngilizce biliyor musunuz?** een•gee•leez•jeh bee•lee•yohr moo•soo•nooz

I don't speak Turkish. **Türkçe bilmiyorum.** tyurk•cheh beel•mee•yoh•room

Can you speak more slowly? **Daha yavaş konuşabilir misiniz lütfen?** dah•hah yah•vahsh koh•noo•shah•bee•leer•mee•see•neez lyut•fehn

I understand. **Anladım.** ahn•lah•dihm

I don't understand. **Anlamadım.** ahn•lah•mah•dihm

# *Sightseeing*

Where's the tourist office? **Turist danışma bürosu nerede?** too•reest dah•nihsh•mah byu•roh•soo neh•reh•deh

| | |
|---|---|
| Do you have tours in English? | **İngilizce turlarınız var mı?** een•geh•leez•jeh toor•lah•rih•nihz vahr mih |
| Can I have a *map/guide*? | ***Harita/Rehber* alabilir miyim?** *hah•ree•tah/reh•ber* ah•lah•bee•leer mee•yeem |

## Sights

| | |
|---|---|
| Where is...? | **...nerede?** ...neh•reh•deh |
| – the castle | – **Kale** kah•leh |
| – the downtown area | – **Şehir merkezi** sheh•heer mehr•keh•zee |
| – the mosque | – **Caml** jah•mee |
| – the museum | – **Müze** myu•zeh |
| – the shopping area | – **Alış veriş merkezi** ah•lihsh veh•reesh mehr•keh•zee |

Turkish

## *Shopping*

| | |
|---|---|
| Where is the *market/mall [shopping centre]*? | ***Market/ Alış veriş merkezi* nerede?** *mahr-keht/ah-lihsh veh-reesh mehr-keh-zee* neh-reh-deh |
| I'm just looking. | **Sadece bakıyorum.** sah-deh-jeh bah-kih-yoh-room |
| Can you help me? | **Bana yardım edebilir misiniz?** bah-nah yahr-dihm eh-deh-bee-leer mee-see-neez |
| I'm being helped. | **Yardım alıyorum.** yahr-dihm ah-lih-yoh-room |
| How much? | **Ne kadar?** neh kah-dahr |
| That one. | **unu.** shoo-noo |
| That's all, thanks. | **Hepsi bu, teşekkürler.** hehp-see boo teh-shehk-kyur-lehr |
| Where do I pay? | **Nereye ödeyeceğim?** neh-reh-yeh ur-deh-yeh-jeh-yeem |
| I'll pay in *cash/by credit card.* | ***Nakit/ Kredi kartı* ile ödeyeceğim.** *nah-keet/ kreh-dee kahr-tih* ee-leh ur-deh-yeh-jeh-yeem |
| A receipt, please. | **Fatura lütfen.** fah-too-rah lyut-fehn |

## Stores

| | |
|---|---|
| Where is...? | **...nerede?** ...neh-reh-deh |
| –the bakery | – **Fırın** fih-rihn |
| –the bookstore | – **Kitapçı** kee-tahp-chih |
| –the department store | – **Mağaza** mah-ah-zah |
| –the pastry shop | – **Pastane** pahs-tah-neh |
| –the pharmacy [chemist] | – **Eczane** ehj-zah-neh |
| –the supermarket | – **Süpermarket** syu-pehr-mahr-keht |

## Clothing

| | |
|---|---|
| Can I try this on? | **Bunu deneyebilir miyim?** boo•noo deh•neh•yeh•bee•leer mee•yeem |
| It doesn't fit. | **Olmadı.** ohl•mah•dih |
| Do you have this in a *bigger/smaller* size? | **Bunun daha *büyük/ küçük* bedeni var mı?** boo•noon dah•hah *byu•yyuk/kyu•chyuk* beh•deh•nee vahr mih |

## Color

| | |
|---|---|
| I'm looking for something in... | **...bir şeyler arıyorum.** ...beer shay•lehr ah•rih•yoh•room |
| –black | - **Siyah** see•yah |
| –blue | - **Mavi** mah•vee |
| –brown | - **Kahverengi** kah•veh•rehn•gee |
| –green | - **Yeşil** yeh•sheel |
| –orange | - **Portakal rengi** pohr•tah•kahl rehn•gee |
| –red | - **Kırmızı** kihr•mih•zih |
| –white | - **Beyaz** beh•yahz |
| –yellow | - **Sarı** sah•rih |

# *Sports and Leisure*

| | |
|---|---|
| Where's...? | **...nerede?** ...neh•reh•deh |
| –the beach | - **Plaj** plahj |
| –the park | - **Park** pahrk |
| –the pool | - **Yüzme havuzu** yyuz•meh hah•voo•zoo |
| Can I rent [hire] golf clubs? | **Golf sopası kiralayabilir miyim?** gohlf soh•pah•sih•kee•rah•lah•yah•bee•leer mee•yeem |

## Culture and Nightlife

| | |
|---|---|
| Do you have a program of events? | **Bir rehberiniz var mı?** beer reh•beh•ree•neez vahr mih |
| Where's...? | **...nerede?** ...neh•reh•deh |
| –the downtown area | – **Şehir merkezi** sheh•heer mehr•keh•zee |
| –the bar | – **Bar** bahr |
| –the dance club | – **Diskotek** dees•koh•tehk |
| Is there a cover charge? | **Giriş ücretli mi?** gee•reesh yuj•reht•lee mee |
| I'm here on business. | **İş için burdayım.** eesh ee•cheen boor•dah•yihm |
| Here's my business card. | **Buyrun kartvizitim.** booy•roon kahrt•vee•zee•teem |
| Can I have your card? | **Kartınızı alabilirmiyim?** kahr•tih•nih•zih ah•lah•bee•leer mee•yeem |
| I have a meeting with... | **...ile bir randevum var.** ...ee•leh beer rahn•deh•voom vahr |
| Where's...? | **...nerede?** ...neh•reh•deh |
| –the business center | – **İş merkezi** eesh mehr•keh•zee |
| –the convention hall | – **Kongre salonu** kohng•reh sah•loh•noo |
| –the meeting room | – **Toplantı odası** tohp•lahn•tih oh•dah•sih |

## Travel with Children

| | |
|---|---|
| Is there a discount for children? | **Çocuklar için indirim var mı?** choh•jook•lahr ee•cheen een•dee•reem vahr mih |
| Can you recommend a babysitter? | **Bir çocuk bakıcısı önerebilir misiniz?** beer choh•jook bah•kih•jih•sih ur•neh•reh•bee•leer mee•see•neez |

| | |
|---|---|
| Could we have a *child's seat/ highchair*? | ***Çocuk sandalyesi/Yüksek sandalye*** **alabilir miyiz?** *choh-jook sahn-dahl-yeh-see/yyuk-sehk sahn-dahl-yeh* ah-lah-bee-leer mee-yeez |
| Where can I change the baby? | **Bebeğin altını nerede değiştirebilirim?** beh-beh-yeen ahl-tih-nih neh-reh-deh deh-yeesh-tee-reh-bee-lee-reem |

## For the Disabled

| | |
|---|---|
| Is there...? | **...var mı?** ...vahr mih |
| – access for the disabled | – **Engelli girişi** ehn-gehl-lee gee-ree-shee |
| – a wheelchair ramp | – **Tekerlekli sandalye rampası** teh-kehr-lehk-lee sahn-dahl-yeh rahm-pah-sih |
| – a handicapped-[disabled-] accessible restroom [toilet] | – **Özürlü tuvaleti** ur-zyur-lyu too-vah-leh-tee |
| I need... | **...ihtiyacım var.** ...eeh-tee-yah-jihm vahr |
| – assistance | – **Yardıma** yahr-dihm-ah |
| – an elevator [lift] | – **Asansöre** ah-sahn-sur-reh |

## Emergencies

| | |
|---|---|
| Help! | **İmdat!** eem-daht |
| Go away! | **Çekil git!** cheh-keel geet |
| Stop thief! | **Durdurun, hırsız!** door-doo-roon hihr-sihz |
| Get a doctor! | **Bir doktor bulun!** beer dohk-tohr boo-loon |
| Fire! | **Yangın!** yahn-gihn |
| I'm lost. | **Kayboldum.** kie-bohl-doom |
| Can you help me? | **Bana yardım edebilir misiniz?** bah-nah yahr-dihm eh-deh-bee-leer mee-see-neez |
| Call the police! | **Polis çağırın!** poh-lees chah-ih-rihn |

# Health

| | |
|---|---|
| I'm sick [ill]. | **Hastayım.** hahs·tah·yihm |
| I need an English-speaking doctor. | **İngilizce konuşan bir doktora ihtiyacım var.** een·gee·leez·jeh koh·noo·shahn beer dohk·toh·rah eeh·tee·yah·jihm vahr |
| It hurts here. | **Burası acıyor.** boo·rah·sih ah·jih·yohr |

# Reference

## Numbers

0 **sıfır** sih·fihr
1 **bir** beer
2 **iki** ee·kee
3 **üç** yuch
4 **dört** durrt
5 **beş** behsh
6 **altı** ahl·tih
7 **yedi** yeh·dee
8 **sekiz** seh·keez
9 **dokuz** doh·kooz
10 **on** ohn
11 **on bir** ohn beer
12 **on iki** ohn ee·kee
13 **on üç** ohn yuch
14 **on dört** ohn durrt
15 **on beş** ohn besh
16 **on altı** ohn ahl·tih
17 **on yedi** ohn yeh·dee
18 **on sekiz** ohn seh·keez
19 **on dokuz** ohn doh·kooz
20 **yirmi** yeer·mee
21 **yirmi bir** yeer·mee beer
22 **yirmi iki** yeer·mee ee·kee
30 **otuz** oh·tooz
31 **otuz bir** oh.tooz beer
40 **kırk** kihrk
50 **elli** ehl.lee
60 **altmış** ahlt.mihsh
70 **yetmiş** yeht.meesh
80 **seksen** sehk.sehn
90 **doksan** dohk.sahn
100 **yüz** yyuz
101 **yüz bir** yyuz beer
200 **ikiyüz** ee.kee yyuz
500 **beşyüz** behsh yyuz
1,000 **bin** been
10,000 **on bin** ohn been
1,000,000 **bir milyon** beer meel.yohn

## Time

| | |
|---|---|
| What time is it? | **Saat kaç?** sah•aht kahch |
| From nine o'clock to 5 o'clock. | **Saat dokuzdan beşe.** sah•aht doh•kooz•dahn beh•sheh |
| 5:30 *a.m./p.m.* | **Öğleden *önce/sonra* beş buçuk.** ur•leh•dehn *urn•jeh/sohn•rah* behsh boo•chook |

## Days

| | |
|---|---|
| Monday | **Pazartesi** pah•zahr•teh•see |
| Tuesday | **Salı** sah•lih |
| Wednesday | **Çarşamba** chahr•shahm•bah |
| Thursday | **Perşembe** pehr•shehm•beh |
| Friday | **Cuma** joo•mah |
| Saturday | **Cumartesi** joo•mahr•teh•see |
| Sunday | **Pazar** pa•zar |

## Dates

| | |
|---|---|
| yesterday | **dün** dyun |
| today | **bugün** boo•gyun |
| tomorrow | **yarın** yah•rihn |

## Months

| | | | |
|---|---|---|---|
| January | **Ocak** oh•jahk | July | **Temmuz** tehm•mooz |
| February | **Şubat** shoo•baht | August | **Ağustos ah**•oos•tohs |
| March | **Mart** mahrt | September | **Eylül** ay•lyul |
| April | **Nisan** nee•sahn | October | **Ekim** eh•keem |
| May | **Mayıs** mah•yihs | November | **Kasım** kah•sihm |
| June | **Haziran** hah•zee•rahn | December | **Aralık** ah•rah•lihk |